WINNING THE SOCIAL MEDIA WAR

HOW CONSERVATIVES CAN FIGHT BACK, RECLAIM THE NARRATIVE, AND TURN THE TIDES AGAINST THE LEFT

By Alex Bruesewitz

BOMBARDIER BOOKS

Published by Bombardier Books
An Imprint of Post Hill Press
ISBN: 978-1-64293-910-1
ISBN (eBook): 978-1-64293-911-8

Winning the Social Media War:
How Conservatives Can Fight Back, Reclaim the Narrative, and Turn the Tides Against the Left

Cover Design by Philip Chalk
Interior Design by Yoni Limor

Post Hill Press
New York • Nashville
posthillpress.com

Published in the United States of America
1 2 3 4 5 6 7 8 9 10

To my mom for her love and giving me a passion for politics; my business partner, Derek Utley, for believing in me; and my siblings, Kyle, Lindsay, and Nick, for always supporting me.

And to the patriots whose devotion to this country knows no bounds. Keep believing and fighting for what you believe: the best is yet to come.

Table of Contents

Foreword

By Charlie Kirk

IN THE FALL OF 2014, our two-year-young organization, Turning Point USA, launched a ten-week college campus campaign entitled "Big Government Sucks." The name was edgy and creative (hold that thought). And the content for activities and learning in each of the ten weeks focused on different elements of big government's interference in our free-market economy. The campaign was a huge success and drew national press coverage.

It even led to my being known not just by my name but by people saying, "Charlie Kirk? Oh, he's the big government sucks guy." The phrase itself found its way into the American political lexicon, even being heard used on stage in the 2016 Republican presidential primary campaign.

Move the clock forward to the fall of 2019, five short but very event-filled years later, and the "big government sucks" guy was on a college campus speaking tour and becoming known as the "culture warrior." While the virtues and principles of free-market capitalism remained very near to my heart, the country had found itself in the early, but rapidly advancing, stages of a cultural revolution reminiscent of Mao's China.

In five years, the debate had moved from issues like government-run health care and the complexity of the tax code to topics of race, class, and gender. It felt like, overnight, we had experienced a sort of political "climate change." The "man-made" cause of that change? Marxist-socialist political activists joined and supported by Big Tech, especially through their various social media platforms.

As I sit here writing this foreword in early 2021, we have now witnessed the true power of a fully operational Big Tech, social media death star. During the cataclysmic year that was 2020, we saw the power of Big Tech and social media used to distort and hide information from the public relating to the Chinese coronavirus, we saw it used to fuel a narrative of pervasive racism and police violence that stoked the fires of racial tension and led to riots, and we saw it used to silence political speech both before and after an election. Big Tech's power has reached an almost unimaginable height.

But in flexing their muscle so boldly and blatantly in 2020, that power of Big Tech has also become obvious. Hopefully this will lead to their ultimate undoing. Any time a tyrant in any form starts to exercise ruthless and absolute power before having it fully consolidated, they run the risk of overthrow. It remains to be seen if Big Tech has reached the point of invincibility. Every American is now aware of how much of our communication they control, and even staunch free-market advocates like Mark Levin are calling for the government to intervene. Governors like Florida's Ron DeSantis are taking steps at the state level to try to take a bite out of Big Tech's power.

Such positions and moves by conservatives would have been almost unthinkable only a few years ago. If I had been asked to write this foreword by Alex back in 2016, back in the "big government sucks" heyday, I would have written a very different piece. I would have focused on the sort of "wild west" nature of social media and how it was providing this essentially unfiltered way to share thoughts and ideas. It was, in a real sense, a microcosm of what American free enterprise was like prior to the government stepping in to overregulate, before big government sucked.

All that has changed. The strong Marxist-socialist movement that has taken hold inside the Democrat Party recognized that any sort of free and uncensored exchange of ideas on a large scale ultimately benefits the very kinds of ideals that were embraced by our Founding Fathers (imagine if Thomas Paine had access to a Twitter account). If there is one thing that Marxist-socialists cannot tolerate it is the free and open exchange of ideas. Like the soon-to-be-banned Grinch of Dr. Seuss's imagination who needed to stop Christmas from coming, they had to find a way to stop conservatives from communicating.

They found their "way" in the ideologically receptive minds of Mark Zuckerberg, Jack Dorsey, and other tech giant CEOs who share their globalist and Marxist-socialist vision of America. By setting their "sites" against what they would define as offensive and hurtful language about race, class, and gender they found a "compassionate" excuse for censoring speech. The Silicon Valley masters of the universe were now only going to allow the "truth" to be shared and discussed across their platforms.

The "truth," as they and their Marxist-socialist allies see it.

As a result, today the entire landscape of social media has changed. It can easily be likened to a high-tech digital version of modern-day China or Eastern Europe during its decades behind the Iron Curtain. Facebook, Twitter, Instagram, Snapchat, each of these platforms holds unilateral and almost unrestricted power to silence any voice or chloroform any idea they find inconsistent with their political and social ideals. Contrary to a common misconception, these Big Tech giants have the Constitution on their side. It is the government that is prohibited from controlling our speech, not a private company. If the government orders a website taken down for content, the owner can go to court and will likely win. When Big Tech takes down a site or a post, there is virtually no recourse.

Wanting to survive, I now practice the art of self-censorship. I sometimes hear people tell me that I'm acting cowardly by giving in, by backing down to Big Tech's speech code. I believe I am simply not acting foolishly. My job is to reach as many people as I can with the necessary facts and messages. I can either carefully craft my words to get them to over 1.5 million Twitter followers and expand their reach exponentially through their friends, or I can say something to trigger Big Tech and have my messages reach zero followers.

One of the greatest dissident leaders in history was Poland's Solidarnosc (Solidarity) leader Lech Walesa. The once-imprisoned, Nobel Peace Prize-winning labor union member helped to lift up Poland's side of the Iron Curtain by leading an unyielding, steady form of protest that pushed the edges of the system without triggering widespread arrests and imprisonments. As Walesa would point out later in his autobiography, Poland had already produced enough martyrs. It was time to try a different approach.

It is that spirit, Walesa's spirit, that conservatives who wish to use social media platforms need to embrace. We need to work within the system to generate enough awareness, energy, and courage to change the system. We do not need to make lengthy lists of digital martyrs who have been de-platformed by Big Tech. We need to keep track of them, but we do not need to mass-produce them.

There are theatrical comedy and tragedy elements to my relationship with Big Tech and social media. I am grateful for the opportunity that social media gave me going back into the early part of the last decade to reach millions of people with my messages. I don't know what might have happened if I had turned eighteen thirty years earlier and decided to start a campus-based organization built around free-market and constitutional principles. I suppose there would have been a way to do it, but I can't imagine it taking off as quickly and having had as much impact as has TPUSA.

Today, however, a key element of my stump speech is to warn against the power of the same Big Tech companies whose platforms have helped me take the stage. The power they have accumulated is simply too great. Even the man who first discovered the virtues of free-market capitalism (a term he never used), Adam Smith, warned us about the damage to the public interest that could be done when any one or more companies become so large as to accumulate too much power. More than the railroads of Teddy Roosevelt's time, more than Standard Oil, more than Ma Bell, Big Tech has now crossed into the territory about which Smith warned.

I do believe that Big Tech has overplayed its hand. It is beyond ironic that a young conservative like Alex Bruesewitz is writing a book attacking their power and that a person like myself who started an organization promoting free markets is writing the foreword. People like us should be the natural defenders of private enterprise, business success, and limited regulation. Yet, here we are, both of us joined together with other conservative leaders to say "enough!" In censoring our speech, Big Tech, which is a big business, shunned a natural ally (conservatives) and replaced them with an uncomfortable ally (Democrat Marxist-socialists). The long-term consequences of such a strategic decision remain to be seen.

In the meantime, this book is a valuable read. It will help you understand the lay of the land in the world of Big Tech social media and what people like "us" can do to be more successful. One thing for certain is that we need to be more creative, and we need to learn how to have fun. There is much to be said for embracing the title of the "happy digital warrior." While fighting for our freedom, we must not forget to enjoy this great gift given freely to us by God. That gift is what we call life.

Chapter 1:

INTRODUCTION - THE SHIFT

Narrative Is Everything

ANDREW BREITBART, FORMER JOURNALIST and founder of *HuffPost* and *Breitbart*, once famously said, "Politics is downstream from culture,"[1] and perhaps upstream from culture are the influencers and those who craft the narrative which routes the river. Since the inception of the internet, access to politicians and the interconnectivity of the political masses have made trends more difficult to navigate, required quicker reaction times, and caused more drastic national impacts and effects.

This connectivity is not going away. Social media companies report even greater numbers joining their platforms on a monthly basis, and most companies and nearly all political staffs have a full-time position devoted to social media. Furthermore, social media companies have created Washington-based lobbying

1 Dan McLaughlin, "Politics Is Still Downstream of Culture," *RedState* (May 4, 2016), https://redstate.com/dan_mclaughlin/2016/05/04/politics-still-downstream-culture-n58816.

teams to preserve their economic might and security from a Congress wholly unable to manage or understand the enhanced impact social media companies have on speech, growth, and messaging of individuals, politicians, organizations, and companies—which is to say that these types of platforms and their efficacy will only become more relevant and necessary in the future.

Therefore, as its importance and attention have increased dramatically, possessing proficiency in building a voice and generating a following on social media is required to curate a national or international following and spread messages to further personal, professional, or political agendas. A single tweet or hashtag can lead to entire movements that shift our culture and alter our way of life. And since a touch of a button can become a societal reckoning or paradigm-shifting moment, it's crucial to understand how and why the landscape shifts the way it does and the machinations behind these shifts.

Social media has made accessing people easier, garnering eyeballs. But claiming a narrative and augmenting it with facts and compelling information is how effective policy is crafted, implemented, and retains staying power.

In many ways, conservatives have failed to effectively create and curate strong voices that both hurdle the barriers imposed by centralized, progressive social media companies and resonate with the American people. It's a failing from a utility perspective: conservatives lack power in several arenas that draw attention, from Hollywood to professional sports to national media to Big Tech and Wall Street. But it's also a failing from a storytelling perspective. Perhaps it's not just that a utopia is more appealing (albeit unrealistic) but also that conservatives have failed to cultivate a compelling and sound bite-friendly/down-to-earth narrative as to why those values, norms, and political mechanics matter and are worthy of preserving. Often, conservatives have to get into the weeds of issues in order to make their arguments. They're much more esoteric than some of the arguments made by their liberal counterparts—which tend to tug on people's heartstrings more.

I fear that if conservatives don't adapt, we very well may fall victim to those who preach progress without the gumption or facts to back up their promises as the institutions that have held up our civil order crumble beneath us.

That's where my concern lies, and that is why I am writing this book for you.

Since I was very young, I have known the importance of politics and the political process and what being the guy at the helm means for steering this country in the right and wrong direction—which is why I jumped into conservative politics early.

As a first order of business, let me introduce myself. I was raised in Ripon, Wisconsin. And from an early age, I found myself drawn to conservatism and Republican politics. (It's a funny coincidence that my hometown was the birthplace of the GOP.) I have my mother to thank for a lot of my political aspirations and interest as I grew up sitting with her in the living room watching prime-time Fox News.

I was galvanized by watching the news and concerned about what the world could look like if young people like me didn't get involved early and often. By watching the campaign by Scott Walker for governor of Wisconsin, I realized I was adamant about fighting the regulations and economic oppression that the Obama administration had and would level against small businesses and companies to stifle our nation's growth and make us weaker abroad. During this time, my teachers were so adamantly opposed to Scott Walker that I did what most teenagers did, I rebelled. I remember once all my teachers went down to Madison, Wisconsin, to protest, and I realized that I wanted to be the opposite of what they were doing at all costs. And so, I became a conservative. I realized that every election carried significant consequences, with our very way of life being tested, evaluated, and voted on with each election.

I decided that I wanted to become more involved in politics. While voicing my conservatism online, I became friends with other conservative voices like Charlie Kirk.

It wasn't long afterward that I began to express support for Donald Trump, even before he announced his candidacy for president of the United States. I knew that our nation needed a strong leader with the convictions of putting this nation first and rejecting the status quo of a corrupt Washington, DC, to which he would later correctly attribute the name, "The Swamp."

I knew in April 2015 that Donald Trump would win because of his grasp of what works on social media and how to use it effectively to direct the conversation and voice his opinions. The president used social media to advance his agenda in the White House, and his strategies are modeled and used to this day by candidates and other politicians alike.

In the past several years, I have made electing "America First" conservatives my life's focus, drawing on my knowledge of social media and learning from those who have gone ahead of me. I started X Strategies LLC in May 2017 with this mission in mind. Since starting the company, we have advised dozens of conservative candidates and politicians with a staggeringly high success rate.

I wanted to write this book for you in the hope that you can gain the knowledge you need to see how important social media is for crafting narratives that can affect public policy changes and draw on mine and others' experiences to make our nation great. Social media is one of many tools for telling stories and spreading information.

And as I was writing this book, people would ask me *why* I wanted to write this book, and the answer has been that, frankly, I'd been thinking about it for quite a while. While this project has certainly evolved from what I had originally in my mind, the main goal has stayed the same: social media has become, in my view, the battleground of the political landscape. President Trump certainly changed the game, but then came along people like Alexandria Ocasio-Cortez, and she really got it. And then everybody just seemed to want to be online. And I've been doing it at a high level for almost ten years now, solely focused on conservative politics. We built a very successful company around our knowledge and leveraging politics and social media for conservative wins. And so, I figured, why hold all those secrets? Why not just write this book and let the American public really understand how the political game works online and what they're saying.

I titled this book *Winning the Social Media War* because there is a distinction between truth and the things the Left and Big Tech allows people to see, believe, and share online with their friends. It's like the Mandela effect but daily, hourly, at the touch of fingertips on Twitter and Facebook. Most Americans spend precious few minutes reading the news because they have commitments, jobs, families, other interests that consume their time and focus. Reaching them might require multiple types of media over a prolonged period. We used to rely on solid reporting, and as Adolph S. Ochs, former owner of the *New York Times*, used to say "all the news that's fit to print"[2] within our papers delivered to our doors. But you'd be woefully misinformed and manipulated to rely on what certain outlets will tell you to your face on TV and in print journalism. It seems like not a day goes by without the Fake News Media propelling a story out into the media with reckless abandon only to later retract the story in whole or in part with a tiny parenthetical or italicized caveat at the bottom of the article online or deep within the paper for those who still read the old gray lady.

2 Professor W. Joseph Campbell, "Story of the Most Famous Seven Words in US Journalism," *BBC* (February 10, 2012), https://www.bbc.com/news/world-us-canada-16918787.

Therein lies the rub.

Most Americans are fed a narrative rather than news. They say to you, "Well, maybe Trump didn't say this exact thing, but the gist is there—orange man bad—so what came across was justified in some ways and likely happened just off camera." Facts be damned. And the examples are numerous and grow by the day.

I wrote in *Human Events* about how Trump for four years was called every variant of "racist" the Left could think of. They wanted to attach that label to avoid addressing the real gains that Trump put in place for African American voters, including funding for historically Black colleges, criminal justice reform, and record low Black unemployment. It's a sleight of hand because the media and the Left wanted to distract the American people from the actual fact that Joe Biden, in 1994, wrote and helped get to President Clinton's desk the Violent Crime Control and Law Enforcement Act (the "Crime Bill"). The legislation, a "tough on crime" posture, is considered by experts as a key cause of mass incarceration in the 1990s, a policy that disproportionately impacted Black men, incentivizing states to build more prisons and pass truth-in-sentencing laws.[3] If we are to hold our leaders accountable during their tenure in office, it's difficult not to see that Joe Biden incentivized the prison-industrial complex through his crime bill, capturing countless Black men for low-level crimes. And how he sat in the vice-presidential seat while cops gunned down unarmed Black men—with little to no real reform to show for it. But the prevailing media narrative never got around to critically analyzing these facts because their ultimate aim was to undermine President Trump.[4]

---

3 Alex Bruesewitz, "Expect Little Change in Police Reform with a Biden Presidency," *Human* Events (June 4, 2020), https://humanevents.com/2020/06/04/expect-little-change-in-police-reform-with-a-biden-presidency/.

4 Alex Bruesewitz, "Expect Little Change in Police Reform with a Biden Presidency," *Human* Events (June 4, 2020), https://humanevents.com/2020/06/04/expect-little-change-in-police-reform-with-a-biden-presidency/.

Just think about the entire Justice Brett Kavanaugh confirmation process. If you tuned into the hearing the day that Senator Feinstein released to the news[5] that someone had accused Justice Kavanaugh of rape in high school and never tuned in again, you'd know only a fraction of what actually happened. Decorum and due process seemingly don't have a place in the halls of the US Senate. (We know they never really were a characteristic of certain facets of our media giants.)

In the days that followed, if you only got a snippet of the news, you perhaps might think Justice Kavanaugh is a gang rapist and formerly part of some sex cult in suburban Washington, DC. Later, you might think he lacked the "judicial restraint"[6] to be a Supreme Court justice. Or failed to have the proper "temperament," as NPR put it.[7] Lest we forget we are supposed to be polite and judicious when the media and Senate Democrats accuse us in front of the country and world of gang rape.

They ran a narrative that was constantly evolving with the sole focus of preventing Justice Kavanaugh from his rightful seat on the Supreme Court.

Facts be damned and wholly outcome determinative.

But then conservatives hit back. Republican senators one after another presented alternative facts and explanations and elicited other testimony. The conservative media fought back and pooled facts with a stronger, more believable narrative. And won.

But think about areas where we aren't as effective.

If you only subscribed to the Fake News Media, you'd believe things that would run contrary, in large part, to facts.

---

5 Manu Raju, "Why Dianne Feinstein Waited to Take the Brett Kavanaugh Allegations to the FBI," *CNN* (September 18, 2018), https://www.cnn.com/2018/09/17/politics/dianne-feinstein-brett-kavanaugh-allegations/index.html.

6 Susan Svrluga, "'Unfathomable': More than 2,400 Law Professors Sign Letter Opposing Kavanaugh's Confirmation," *Washington Post* (Oct. 4, 2018), https://www.washingtonpost.com/education/2018/10/04/unprecedented-unfathomable-more-than-law-professors-sign-letter-after-kavanaugh-hearing/.

7 Lulu Garcia-Navarro and Susan Hennessey, "Kavanaugh's Temperament," September 30, 2018, in *Weekend Edition Sunday*, https://www.npr.org/2018/09/30/653086714/kavanaughs-temperament.

On climate change, in 2019, Greta Thunberg sailed across the Atlantic Ocean from England as a media spectacle to draw attention to climate change. Lauded as a champion of reducing her carbon footprint, what the elite don't want you to focus on is the fact that the stunt alone by its carbon emissions undermined the very premise of the trip itself.[8] And while tending to our environment and conserving our precious natural resources is ultimately very important, the Left balks when criticizing the actual aggressors against the environment like China or India. But a child sails and furthers a narrative, wins votes, and businesses and, by extension, Americans suffer.

And the Left has little restraint when using children to further their aims.

After the tragic school shooting at Parkland, Florida, the Left propped up an assortment of children on the national stage under the March for Our Lives movement to further the aim of gun-grabbing by the government. Never mind the facts of a county sheriff, local government, and FBI that failed the students of Stoneman Douglas High School; a gun was involved, and that was enough to curtail the Second Amendment rights enshrined in our Constitution. Any time these teenagers were criticized for their views or perhaps lack of knowledge of the issues, the media and leftist organizations shielded them from scrutiny and criticism.

But that's just for kids who spread the right messages. Nick Sandmann and his buddies were in Washington, DC, for the annual March for Life when a Native American protestor walked through the group banging a traditional drum. As Sandmann notes (and published by CNN), "because we were being loudly attacked and taunted in public, a student in our group asked one of our teacher chaperones for permission to begin our school spirit chants to counter the hateful

---

8 Jack Elsom and Darren Boyle, "Greta Thunberg's Two-Week Trip across Atlantic in 'Zero-Carbon Yacht' May Generate More Emissions than It Saves as Two of the Crew Have to FLY to New York to Bring the Boat Back to Europe," *Daily Mail* (Aug. 17, 2019), https://www.dailymail.co.uk/news/article-7365909/Greta-Thunbergs-Atlantic-trip-zero-carbon-yacht-generate-emissions-saves.html.

things that were being shouted at our group. The chants are commonly used at sporting events. They are all positive in nature and sound like what you would hear at any high school. Our chaperone gave us permission to use our school chants. We would not have done that without obtaining permission from the adults in charge of our group."[9] The activist found his way to banging his drum in Sandmann's face. Sandmann, smiling awkwardly, stood his ground. But he committed the grave mortal sin in this day and age—he was wearing a MAGA hat. The media tore him to pieces along with his classmates. Lies were spread by the media and leftist organizations that have since been proven false and litigated to undisclosed settlements to some of the schoolboys for defamation.

Conservatives were slow to defend the boys, with even some outlets running alongside the leftist media to reprimand them. We lost in the short game because the Left had crafted a very particular (incorrect) narrative that all people wearing MAGA hats are bigoted, racist Trump supporters. And therefore, since some of the boys were wearing these hats, then the allegations they were chanting "build the wall" and racial epithets at the Native American protestors must be true. And we let it happen, at least in the short term.

We have to fight back and reclaim the narrative.

Unfortunately, in the past four years, there are dozens of examples where conservatives lost, failing to effectively curate a narrative that one, convinced the American people even when facts were on our side and two, reached the American people due to the constraints imposed on a liberal media apparatus hell-bent on subduing conservatism. Big Tech machinated to stifle real dialogue and diffusion of conservative voices.

This book offers a manual on how to fight back.

---

9 "Statement of Nick Sandmann, Covington Catholic High School Junior, Regarding Incident at the Lincoln Memorial," *CNN* (January 23, 2019), https://www.cnn.com/2019/01/20/us/covington-kentucky-student-statement/index.html.

I am a young man and, God willing, have a lot of life experience ahead of me. As such, I don't pretend to have all the answers to every social media movement or political cause or politician. Knowing so, I have aggregated my thoughts with those of many political leaders, social media influencers, and those individuals whom I believe have led in creating a following.

To be clear, and to avoid any confusion or conflation, I am not saying that every individual I have interviewed for this book shares my beliefs, either completely or in part, or I theirs as well. Rather, I have reached out to countless politicians, leaders, influencers, and causes, hoping to generate for you a book that has meaning and can address and coalesce themes from which you, the reader, can glean certain value. That is also to say that any mention of an individual or quote from an interviewee isn't a referendum on their character but a standalone piece of advice or an opinion that I have deemed worthy of inclusion. Unlike the leftist media that requires individuals to be perfect manifestations of progressivism to be worthy of providing sage advice, I have viewed individuals who have been willing to talk to me for this book as individuals who have measured success and, therefore, are worthy of delivering counsel. Please read into their inclusion as such.

This book is built upon my personal experience and interviews with influencers, policymakers, politicians, candidates for office, and professionals in the business of growth and influence online. My insights in this book come from years of trial and error and early success. The solutions, suggestions, and tactics described in this book come from lessons I have learned over the years and certainly are not answers for every individual or every cause or mission. In my business, we strive to learn and roll with the times much as technology is constantly evolving and requires growth and on-the-job learning.

Interviews were conducted with questions produced by me or my employees and assistants. To produce accurate quotes and for my own recollection for this book, all interviews were recorded with the consent of the interviewees, and those quotes have been reproduced here where necessary and appropriate with minor editing (with the approval of the interviewees) for clarity and context.

Many of the individuals I interviewed for this book are "controversial" figures, and all bring different perspectives to this movement. It goes without saying that their views are their own and that I am bringing these ideas together to enable my readers to have a full, deep understanding of what is effective on the right and take a big-tent approach to how to reclaim the narrative.

The structure of this book traces the multifaceted approach I believe is necessary to winning back the narrative. First, I will give my approach to craft and disseminating messages and narratives. In Chapter 3, we spoke with a number of public officials, politicians, and their aides and staffers behind the scenes who curate their images and messages. In Chapter 4, I examine several political movements and how conservatives succeeded in combating particular movements or created their own. In Chapter 5, I write about organizations that are on the front line of implementing policy and how they work with policymakers and influencers to achieve their goals. In Chapter 6, I write about my conversations with conservative influencers and what the environment is like in an evolving influencer space from Twitter to Facebook to Parler. In Chapter 7, I examine the role of the media. In Chapter 8, I write about the relationship with simplifying messages with memes and internet culture. In Chapter 9, I detail the evil of cancel culture. In Chapter 10, I write about censorship and what this means for conservatives when trying to reach audiences with our messages. And lastly, I discuss what all this means for conservatism going forward into the future.

For years, conservatives wrongly believed that the only way to win was with facts and logic. While important, the American people are also heavily influenced by narratives. The cultural outcomes over the past decade have borne that out. Storytelling and effective storytelling on social media are required tools if conservatives hope to reclaim relevance and be impactful for generations to come.

Bridging this learning gap is where this book fits in and furthers the conversation and conservatism. I hope you find this tool kit useful as we work together to win hearts and minds and reclaim the narrative. The future of our country depends on it.

As Andrew Breitbart said, "Narrative is everything."[10]

What's at Stake?

Politics ebbs and flows with the tides, and if it seems the narratives repeat themselves, it's because they do. The allegations by Democrats of Republicans stealing the election in 2016 echo those made in 2000 when Gore lost to President Bush. The liberal patty-cake with violent rioters is nothing novel and has been repeated throughout our country's history—a perpetual willingness to flirt with political violence so long as it enables them to win elections or further "righteous causes."

And so far as the pendulum doesn't swing too far one way or the other, Washington, DC, remains unchanged and unchallenged. The K Street lobbyists and campaign strategists pocket what they can, the contractors in northern Virginia get their government contracts, everyone gets reelected, and the Swamp remains as putrid and shallow as it ever was.

But something broke these people when Donald Trump was elected.

---

10 Larry Solov, "Andrew: One Year Later," *Breitbart* (February 28, 2013), https://www.breitbart.com/the-media/2013/02/28/andrew-one-year-later/.

A businessman and TV celebrity, Donald Trump exposed that deviation from the status quo; that is, undermining Washington's conventional wisdom threatened the existing power structures in a way that had never been exposed before. Though every politician would like to pretend they are the protagonist of their very own *Mr. Smith Goes To Washington*, in reality, most become a cypress knee in the Swamp rather quickly. Those who don't are often primaried, propagated by the media as "crazy" or "radical," and sent on their way. That paradigm, however, was shaken by a man who was rich enough to not need to pander to the Establishment and either shameless or dull to criticism from years of being in the spotlight.

And what Trump exposed was truly remarkable. For you can't always tell how fast the current is moving till you start swimming upstream. And the Trump administration swam upstream. On China, on ending foreign wars, on trade, on school choice, on criminal justice reform, President Trump bucked the conventional wisdom of Washington. And at every moment, they hated him for it. And, while he had a voice on his Twitter account, he was able to mock them for it. But that was while he had a voice.

We've now entered a dark age for conservatism, one in which the Democrats control the House, the Senate, and the White House. But also, the Democrats control the media and social media. The riot that occurred on January 6, 2021, at the Capitol gave the pretext for social media companies to crack down on speech, even going so far as banning the president of the United States—all under the guise of protecting America from "white supremacy domestic terrorism." And while I will cover this more extensively in my chapter on the media, it's telling that as of this writing, the media has essentially set up lawn chairs outside of the press office of the White House and feels comfortable regurgitating Biden administration talking points. (There are no book deals for reporters in a friendly administration.)

But this just means that for patriots, the stakes are that much larger. The Establishment has struck back. The media has become their useful puppets once again. And Big Tech is the mouth box, judge, and executioner of all speech and thought in this country.

It's a perilous road ahead.

It's a cultural battle. It's a spiritual battle. It's really a battle for the heart and soul of our nation. And it's one trending topic on Twitter at a time. If you look throughout history, every fifteen years, every twenty years, there was a historical moment. There was a march. There was an event that captured the whole world's attention. And now it's every other day that something happens. And politicians use these huge moments as political points to try to sway the public opinion. And so, people like AOC jump out in front of every single trending topic and drive deeper a political movement into seemingly innocuous events. It breaks, and it breaks, and social media moves the national conversation sometimes immeasurably further, whereby we look back even days, and I am almost shocked with how far we've deviated from the country that I know.

Fox News contributor Tomi Lahren spelled a dire future if we lose this social media war and cultural battle. I asked her what we will become. She was candid with her response:

> *"Venezuela. That's what's at stake. We become like every other great nation that is opposed to socialism and then falls into communism. That's what we'll become. And it's not radical to say that. It's not a conspiracy theory to say that. It's quite obvious what's ahead. We are at a crossroads in our country, not only with the election, but with the censorship and the stifling of conservative voices, cancel culture, what's going on in our college campuses and even younger*

> *with our middle school and our elementary school classrooms. Couple that with a pandemic and the fear mongering that has come along with it and the violence and amplify everything that we were already seeing in the last four plus years. So what's at stake is the very heart of our country, our freedoms, what makes this nation great, and what has kept it great for generations. And that cannot be overstated. That is the battle that we are fighting for. Failure is not an option."*[11]

Newsmax host, Carl Higbie, echoed this point when I sat down with him to discuss what's ahead for our great nation:

> *"If conservatives roll over, and we lose this social media, cultural, and narrative war, everything is at stake. And it doesn't stop here. This is difficult for me to say: the Left is going to change this country forever unless people take a stand. They're already on their way to creating a parallel economy for conservatives, and that's fine in the short term: conservatives are better at economics than liberals. But eventually that will cause the liberal economy to crash. However, in the meantime, we're getting booted off free-speech platforms. And I guarantee you Joe Biden is going to pass some sweeping gun legislation that is unconstitutional, but before it even gets to the Supreme Court, people are just going to say no. And at that point, the liberal agenda doesn't realize this possibly because they are stuck in the notion that says, 'I can do this because I said so.' I use the analogy, punched in the face. There are two types of people in the world, and this can be literally or figuratively. There are the people who have been punched in the face*

11 Interview with Tomi Lahren, December 29, 2020, via phone.

> *and there are the people who have not. And people who haven't been punched in the face cannot begin to lecture people who have known what it's like. And I use that phrase as a metaphor, as a hardship. But this is a good example because the liberals are going to say, 'We're going to go take the guns.' 'Guns are now illegal.' 'Go take them all.' OK, and then what is Chuck Schumer going to do? Come knock on my door to take my guns? Of course not. He's going to make a law that then some sheriffs are going to say no. And then what? They don't have any power to enforce in a civilized society, and the liberals will have removed the notion of civilized society because they will have ordered people to do things that they don't believe are lawful orders and therefore they say no. And now you have the fractured beginning."*[12]

And much in the same vein of faithfulness to the basic human right to self-preservation and protection, I explore the Parkland shooting with survivors and parents of the shooting and discover that what Carl fears isn't happening as overtly as many realize. Underpinning each policy point of the Left is a massive, coherent narrative that slowly disseminates like oil in the ocean, killing off our freedoms with the tides. Yet, as I will show through my interviews in this book, the Democrats' policy spread isn't as clearly seen as an oil spill—which is why social media and fighting the culture war online has become so vital. It forces the conversation into the daylight.

And never forget how important narratives are, especially when the Left and media will just lie to you.

Trump coined the phrase the "Fake News Media" early on in his campaign after repeated lies and misdirection and narrative falsehoods from our "revered" media institutions. Never mind the fact that these institutions are stocked with

12 Interview with Carl Higbie, January 12, 2021, via phone.

adolescents LARPing as professionals. By being "mean" to the press or daring to question their ever so carefully chosen words and reporting, somehow the American people were told that Trump was "dangerous"[13] and a threat to democracy and freedom of the press. And the "beleaguered press"[14] never missed an opportunity to discuss how much they were like our fighting troops in the trenches of the First Amendment battling mean names! As if the elementary school playground somehow compared to the actual shedding of blood defending freedom. But hey, maybe prep school playgrounds are more rough-and-tumble than I realize, though I imagine that would be debunked entirely just by shaking Jon Ossoff's and Former Interior Secretary Ryan Zinke's hands back-to-back for an empirical study. Just a thought.

And if you were to believe the insanity of the Left, that Trump and Republicans were actually some sort of diabolical, destructive force against a free and impartial (ha!) press, you might have missed the fact that an Associated Press Fact Check in 2018 found that "Trump may use extraordinary rhetoric to undermine trust in the press, but Obama arguably went farther—using extraordinary actions to block the flow of information to the public."[15] The report goes on to say that:

> ***"In 2013 the Obama administration obtained the records of 20 Associated Press office phone lines and reporters' home and cell phones, seizing them without notice, as part of an investigation into the disclosure of information about a foiled al-Qaida terrorist plot. AP was not the target of the investigation. But it called the seizure a 'massive and unprecedented intrusion'***

13 Savannah Behrmann, "Report: Trump's Attacks on the Press 'Dangerously Undermined Truth and Consensus,'" *USA TODAY* (April 16, 2020), https://www.usatoday.com/story/news/politics/2020/04/16/report-trumps-attacks-press-dangerously-undermined-truth/5150134002/.

14 Olivia Nuzzi, "The Beleaguered Chroniclers of the Trump White House Four Years of History, Day after Day after Day" (January 5, 2021), https://nymag.com/intelligencer/2021/01/trump-white-house-press-corps.html.

15 Calvin Woodward and Christopher Rugaber, "AP FACT CHECK: Obama doesn't always tell the straight story," *AP News* (Sept. 11, 2018), https://apnews.com/article/ffc60235c26c470c9047e0da6ff19f95.

> *into its news-gathering activities, betraying information about its operations 'that the government has no conceivable right to know.' Obama's Justice Department also secretly dogged Fox News journalist James Rosen, getting his phone records, tracking his arrivals and departures at the State Department through his security-badge use, obtaining a search warrant to see his personal emails and naming him as a possible criminal conspirator in the investigation of a news leak. 'The Obama administration,' The New York Times editorial board wrote at the time, 'has moved beyond protecting government secrets to threatening fundamental freedoms of the press to gather news.'"*[16]

But let's not let facts get in the way of a good narrative, shall we?

Over the course of writing this book, I conducted dozens of exclusive interviews with politicians, candidates, media personalities, influencers, directors, organization presidents, leaders, and even a guy who runs a meme account on Instagram to deliver to you a coherent message that our country is headed the wrong direction, and unless we push back against very powerful forces, this country will have merely been an experiment. We cannot let it be so. Listen to the words of all of us, help us, learn from this book, and let's reclaim the inheritance our Founders left for us.

---

16 Calvin Woodward and Christopher Rugaber, "AP FACT CHECK: Obama doesn't always tell the straight story," *AP News* (Sept. 11, 2018), https://apnews.com/article/ffc60235c26c470c9047e0da6ff19f95.

Chapter 2:
THE PLAYBOOK

"Reasonable people aren't on social media."

- Chris Harrison, former host of *The Bachelor*[17]

I PROMISED YOU A PLAYBOOK. A guide to beating back on a political Left who seemingly is willing to undermine each and every one of our political institutions and isn't opposed to winning at all costs. To a large extent, I have found that the rules have evolved and continue to evolve, and as such, this book serves as a building block and comment on the here and now: the America that changed after Trump was elected and the radical Left who sought to undermine his successes and alter our culture at all costs. And make no mistake, this playbook will serve you into the future as the themes and motivations remain largely indifferent to any one political wave or presidency. So let's grow together.

This chapter lays out the method for gaining followers and being a more effective communicator with your audience, whether you're an individual looking to grow a "brand" on

17 Rachel Lindsay, "Chris Harrison & Rachel Lindsay Talk 'Bachelor' Contestant Rachael Kirkconnell," *extratv*, Feb. 9, 2021, https://www.youtube.com/watch?v=9hmY1gSAuRk.

social media or build an online following, an organization looking to learn from other successful conservative organizations, or a candidate seeking political office. I am giving you my tools and tricks that I have learned from firsthand experience on the campaign trail, building my own brand, and navigating shifting political movements. I want you to learn how to generate momentum on social media, gain followings, and translate those followings into greater influence, either on social media or in politics that furthers the agenda that makes this country great.

I started building my Twitter account when I was sixteen years old. I was sitting in study hall in Wisconsin.

I was naïve at first with just generating tons of follows. I would follow up to a thousand people and get a few hundred followers in return. And I would do that every single day. And at the beginning of Twitter, that was how many people grew. If you look at Barack Obama, for example, President Obama, as of this writing, "follows" nearly six hundred thousand accounts. And in large part, he did that because he was early on. He was mass following accounts to grow his own account. And that was an interesting tactic that Twitter just got rid of. At first, I was focused on Twitter.

A couple of years later, I met my business partner, Derek. Both at that time and now, Derek possesses a strong understanding of how to grow Facebook pages and is efficient with ad spend. We were assessing each other's strengths and our platform capabilities, and we thought aloud together that we could probably create a company out of this. And we did.

We started our company in 2017, shortly after Trump was inaugurated. But my business partner and I were both very digitally active long before that, advising on other endeavors. And I realized quickly that my interests, our skill set, and the moment were prime for what we were trying to do. We were watching how the political landscape was coming online, how these politicians wanted to be online, needed to be online. We knew this meant that politicians and candidates needed outside consulting to more effectively disseminate conservative messaging.

Years later, we have grown a successful business. And but for my desire to actually deliver results rather than merely get paid, I might have sat back and enjoyed the ride. Lots of consultants do. But for me, this is about activism. It's about putting the correct people in the best position to be successful in Washington, and to be truly great and effective in this digital age, that means being a strong communicator online.

So I have outlined some of those techniques I use in my day-to-day work.

What I want you to take away from this chapter are my six points of advice that I always give my clients when they come to me hoping to build their brand, run for office, or grow their organization. Simply put, my method is:

1. Be bold.
2. Study your brand.
3. Be coalition-minded.
4. Be content-focused.
5. Be quick, reactive, and topical.
6. Build out a strong network.

What I tell each of my clients is don't get into the business of politics if you want to be timid and aren't willing to get in the trenches and fight. Politics is a nasty business and requires those willing to set aside meekness for a higher cause. Grinding through attacks and roadblocks is the only way to achieve any degree of success and stature in this business. I am often reminded of that old Latin proverb: "fortune favors the bold." And in this case, politics rewards the mighty and the agile, and it never hurts to have a hint of good fortune.

All of my experience and all of my exclusive interviews have borne out that to be timid is to lose in the game of politics. Each of my interviewees has stepped into politics with both feet, and each of them in some way has taken tremendous heat from the Left and public, suffered personal attacks, death threats, or been canceled. But the reward, their successes have been instrumental for the conservative movement. Each of them has been a puzzle piece in furthering conservative public policy and protecting the greatest country in the world.

And I use puzzle pieces specifically because my second point is that each of my interviewees has studied and self-reflected to assess where they fit in the conservative movement. I know it's a bit ugly to use the word "brand" to describe what you bring to the table, as if you're some corporate product, but to an extent it's necessary because you can't be all things to all people, and in a day and age where information, content, people are ubiquitous, it's all the more important to evaluate what your strengths are and where you can best fit in. Think of it this way: being a mile wide, inch deep is helpful at cocktail parties, but you want the guy who's a mile deep on a particular topic to be the one who goes to battle for you on a specific topic.

I also make my clients aware of how important curating a public-facing image is. The public attention span is quite short. Shorter than you'd like. And even in a twenty-four-hour news cycle, you might only get a few seconds to capture someone's attention. Squandering big moments, especially ones in politics, will not get you or your message very far. That's why image and perception management is necessary to get to the platform to have your voice heard.

So I always tell my clients that holistic self-reflection is important. What I mean by that is politics and public service require self-reflection but also assessment of how you are perceived and what you bring to the table. It's not enough to say this makes me happy, and, therefore, I do that thing. It requires also knowing that if you are a particular expert of X, and you are given an opportunity to champion X, then there is almost a duty to fulfill X. Learning what impact you can have requires not only knowing what you bring to the table, but also asking friends and family what your strengths and weaknesses are. And still further, there is the larger public perception of where you fit into the movement. And that is more difficult to establish good metrics on other than by measuring the reaction to your content.

Content is king. The road to a large following and public policy success is paved with good ideas, many of which are never translated to print, screen, radio, TV, or social media. The armchair pundit doesn't command the following and the policy outcomes that come with it that an individual or organization does that is willing to put in the work making video, writing, tweeting consistently, or working on issues with a public communication platform. As unfortunate as it sounds, and as I wrote about being bold, it's not enough anymore to paddle under the surface of the water or in a back room and hope your ideas get noticed. You need to be consistently delivering your ideas in people's faces, being unafraid and unrelinquishing. Too often, my clients say, "Won't people get sick of this idea or that idea or seeing me on their screen?" I always tell them, "Keep making content, and I will tell you when we need to pull back," because the secret sauce is that for every person out there making content, working tirelessly to protect freedom and promote organizations and individuals serving that aim, there are thousands of people scared to press "send" on an email. Being willing to go out there and actually make a difference is surely and always preferable to self-regulating to the point you restrict your passion and creative flow. Not to mention, in this business, if you're not working, you're dying.

I always tell my clients that it's imperative to be quick, reactive, and topical in their content. In this space, as you grow your following, more and more people are going to look to you for takes on particular issues. And it's a dual axiom approach because when you are growing, people might not necessarily know who you are but will begin seeing consistent, quick reactions to the news of the day or issues that matter to America first. That will resonate over time so that when you grow and establish a set of followers, this noticing of your content will become an expectation of content. After expectation of content comes the willingness of your followers to share or defer to your content as the go-to source. And so, as an overarching principle, when we get enough conservatives across all issues and platforms who have established this type of engagement and reach, we will be more effective in reclaiming the narrative and winning the culture war.

What follows is a series of tips and tricks from experts, pundits, politicians, and thought leaders who have gone before and established themselves. People who have been bold, studied their brand, found their way into conservatism, and decided to produce content to further the cause of freedom. I will filter in my commentary, and I hope that you will find their words useful because this battle is important. It's for the very freedoms we hold dear. It's for a nation that was out of many, one. As Ronald Reagan said in his first inaugural address as governor of California:

"Perhaps you and I have lived with this miracle too long to be properly appreciative. Freedom is a fragile thing and is never more than one generation away from extinction. It is not ours by inheritance, it must be fought for and defended constantly by each generation, for it comes only once to a people. Those who have known freedom and then lost it have never known it again."[18]

Be Bold

No notable or interesting thing has been done without courage. The moon landing, the beach invasion at Normandy during World War II, Nixon going to China, and walking across the bridge in Selma, Alabama, all required sacrifice or a willingness to stand in the breach and go into the unknown, uncertain of life and limb. Note I make reference to feats of courage made decades ago because we live in a time now that outside of our great fighting men and women in our armed forces or our service people in blue across the country, acts of courage, especially political courage, seem to be fewer and further between.

Corporations have become polite vehicles for the whims of the radical Left. Many churches and places of worship hoping to be do-gooders have surrendered the Bible or their religious convictions at the feet of the woke and become inadvertent allies of unhinged progressivism. Much of the political middle cowers at the awesome might that the intersection of Hollywood, the media, and corporate America can exert, afraid to voice political dissidence for fear of social, political, or economic annihilation. We live in times when voicing political disagreement from the Right is called an "act of violence," "hate speech," or considered "dangerous." We

18 Ronald Reagan Presidential Library & Museum Archives, "January 5, 1967: Inaugural Address (Public Ceremony)," https://www.reaganlibrary.gov/archives/speech/january-5-1967-inaugural-address-public-ceremony.

live in a time when activists will take your picture at a Trump rally, find out where you work, and try their hardest in their ample spare time to get you fired for merely showing up.

I tell you this to show you how far we've come and the road we will continue to wind down till the America you and I know is no more. That is, if we do nothing.

And I am telling you, friend, that we cannot do nothing. The stakes are too high, and the reversal at a certain point requires too great a sacrifice. I interviewed Congresswoman Marjorie Taylor Greene of Georgia, and I believe she put it well when she noted what's at stake in the culture war and narrative battle:

> ***"I think the reason why I'm there is because I'm terrified we're about to lose the greatest country in the world and not one of us earned our freedom. An American is born into this wonderful country with an amazing constitution and freedoms and rights that we have."***[19]

She correctly says that if we do nothing, the only way that we earn our freedoms back is through more blood. As someone who values every American life and cherishes American blood, those stakes are too high. We must be on the front lines right now, defending her.

What's scarier is the congresswoman knows that protecting our freedoms and keeping us out of war might be highly unpopular in Congress. "I'm going to boldly continue to do the things I've said I'm going to do, because I'm not there to be friends. I'm not there to get invited to the cocktail parties. It's not about being a member of the club. I'm there to do a job, and it's the job that people voted for me to do."[20]

That is why what I am asking you to get involved, and the tool kit I have prepared for you does require some sacrifice but not the ultimate sacrifice. For our small, humble sacrifices

19 Interview with Congresswoman-elect Marjorie Taylor Greene, December 10, 2020, via phone.

20 Interview with Congresswoman-elect Marjorie Taylor Greene, December 10, 2020, via phone.

now, getting involved in media, running for office, starting an organization, and building a following are small ways that we collectively band together to fight back against a growingly radical branch of the Democratic Party who seeks to damage this nation beyond repair.

And so, it's time—it's time to be bold.

"We have to buckle up, and if you don't want to fight, get out of politics,"[21] Congressional candidate Anna Paulina Luna told me when we spoke following her tremendous race to unseat Congressman Charlie Crist in Florida's Thirteenth Congressional District.[22] Anna, a US Air Force veteran, is one of the many firebrand, bold leaders who sacrificed for our country with her service but didn't stop there, but also suffered character assassination and other attacks by the Left during her campaign to serve our country in Congress. We will hear more from her later in the book.

Will Ricciardella, an editor at the *Washington Examiner*, also urges young conservatives to be bold. He told me, "I think the problem [with conservatives] is fear and the safety that they won't be accepted by the Left. And particularly young conservatives come into media thinking, 'Oooh, I want to get mentioned, or I want to have somebody at *The New York Times* mention my story or get a pat on the head on Twitter.' They try to get validation from liberals who are really propagandists."[23] Will cited examples: "If you look at people like Kaitlan Collins, who came from *The Daily Caller*, Oliver Darcy, who also came from conservative media, they've been co-opted by CNN. The stuff they come out with is total garbage, it's liberal propaganda, it's nonsense. There's no journalistic standards to it anymore. This happens to a lot of conservatives: they have a lot of fear."[24] He depicts this

---

21 Interview with Anna Paulina Luna, December 10, 2020, via phone.

22 Josh Solomon, "Florida 13th District: Charlie Crist Defeats Anna Paulina Luna U.S. House District 13 Covers Pinellas County South of Dunedin," *Tampa Bay Times* (November 3, 2020), https://www.tampabay.com/florida-politics/elections/2020/11/03/florida-13th-district-crist-takes-early-lead-over-luna/.

23 Interview with Will Ricciardella, December 17, 2020, via phone.

24 Interview with Will Ricciardella, December 17, 2020, via phone.

fear through the lens of a moral narrative the Left has insulated itself with. "The Left maintains this moral high ground all the time. And conservatives fear not being perceived as moral. The Left will call us a 'moron,' a 'jerk,' or say, 'You're stupid.'"[25] I can cite countless examples of this over the years from as simple as any congressional race in 2020, or the relentless attacks on our Georgia Senate candidates, to as extreme and nasty as the attacks on Supreme Court Justice Brett Kavanaugh.

It's a cautionary tale more generally for conservatives since cancel culture is a very real thing (much as the Left tries to deny its existence). *Breitbart*'s Alex Marlow told me that "whenever a new voice announces itself on the right, the Left is going to try to cancel you and take you out. And for some people, it makes you stronger because of certain people, because the Right really wants fighters. They feel like they're underrepresented in that regard. The Left has more fighters.... You are going to get targeted if you announce yourself as a powerful conservative voice."[26]

The entry into the space of politics isn't going to be an easy one. Social media has opened an entirely new avenue of vitriol. From my own social media accounts, I can tell you that people can be nasty. The attacks can be baseless and the responses so peculiar, they border on the deranged. And worse, I manage social media accounts for many public figures, and I can tell you that the private messages to these people for their controversial opinions (or failure to express certain opinions) are horrible to receive and read through and not for the faint of heart.

That's just the general meanness of the internet; there are also greater stakes for conservatives. Unless you're a journalist working for a conservative publication, conservatives online are subject to a broader threat online by expressing their polit-

25 Interview with Will Ricciardella, December 17, 2020, via phone.
26 Interview with Alex Marlow, January 27, 2021, via phone.

ical opinions. As I will address in Chapters 9 and 10, if the mob comes for you for a "bad" opinion, your job and livelihood are not safe, nor are those closest around you. Being bold online comes at a real risk and potential cost.

But, to protect our culture, values, and way of life, it is a necessary risk. I have spoken with leading politicians, thinkers, people who have been canceled, and influencers who will provide some guidance for how to brave this environment, especially online.

Maybe the thing to do to be bold is to be indifferent. Have some peace of mind; no matter how recent or far back you look, conservatives have been lambasted, vilified with the nastiest terms you ever saw. So you know you're in good company. The media savaged them. No amount of placating them will satisfy them and their demands. For example, we all saw how much the media ran to the aid of John McCain when Donald Trump was criticizing him and attacking him. It was as if they had been champions of John McCain all along. But we remember when McCain ran against Obama and how often they said, "John McCain is a huge racist and misogynist, sexist, et cetera." We remember that. I don't know that they remember, but we can remember.

Always remember that even in cancellation or being under attack, there is opportunity. Being bold these days is almost counterculture. Saying what's on your mind is almost rare. Some days in the liberal media space, saying the sky is blue feels like it's going to get you reprimanded by blue check Twitter. But facing the mob head-on, there is opportunity in this outrage. A prime example of this was when Camryn Kinsey[27] (you should follow her!) was bold when she added her opinion as a D1 athlete to the very important conversation around transgender athletes at the NCAA level. She saw some backlash and faced some pushback. But ultimately,

27 Camryn Kinsey (@camrynbaylee), Twitter, https://twitter.com/camrynbaylee?ref_src=twsrc%5Egoogle%7Ctwcamp%5Eserp%7Ctwgr%5Eauthor.

she was rewarded greatly. Many people who perhaps weren't in the position to make such bold statements found that her message resonated with them and decided to follow her and will now see her other messages. She gained tens of thousands of followers off of one bold moment.

If you're passionate about a topic: don't hold back.

Study Your Brand

I hate treating people and candidates and politicians as products for consumption. But in the world of social media, tweets and Facebook posts are almost like ads for yourself. And like any good commercial, you have to present the best product and message the correct way or no one will buy.

Self-awareness is one of the most important things in life. I had this conversation recently. I have spent the last four years of my life telling everybody else's story and selling people's stories for them. But I think about my story: If I ran for office right now, what is my story to sell? And the answer is I don't really know. I see this because I get how incredibly hard it is to self-reflect and sell yourself.

But I want to encourage you in this process: it's never too late to start your story or create your brand. Find what you're passionate about or what others have praised you for. Delve into an area of study, whether it's policy, law, music, whatever that you're attracted to and commit to becoming proficient or, better yet, an expert at it. Like I wrote earlier, mile wide, inch deep is great on a first date, but not when people want to rely on your expertise.

Be incredibly self-aware. Or at least have friends who are brutally honest with you. If you come to me and say, "I've never really done something that exciting, I wasn't really that great of a student, and I have no plans to do anything exciting in my life," it's not that inspiring. You're probably like a lot of politicians in Washington, but you're not somebody I personally want to work with, and it is certainly going to be difficult to build an audience without tons and tons of money and pleading. Even then, without curiosity and self-awareness, no amount of money is going to build a lasting audience.

It's also important to surround yourself with people who mirror back to you what your brand is or could be. What do I mean by that? I pride myself on building a friendship network that provides constant feedback both on my content online but also personally. Am I growing? Is the conversation I am participating in one that people are interested in? Am I adding value to that conversation? I thought Amber Athey said it well when she told me, "It's important to always surround yourself with some basic principles of why am I doing this? …I always try to remember that I'm doing this for people like my family or my friends back home who might be Trump supporters or are members of Middle America that feel like they've been left behind. And there's really no outlet or journalist out there who speaks to their concerns. And so, I try to approach my job daily with the goal in mind, giving a voice to people who would otherwise be voiceless. And that way, it's not about me. Obviously, I'm trying to advance my career and do a good job and make money to survive. But there has to be something else underpinning why you're doing this. There has to be some other passion besides I want to be famous, or I want to be on TV, or I want people to syndicate my column on the show, and some other principle grounding you when you're making your way through politics in general, let alone journalism."[28]

And so, it is understanding what you bring to the table, understanding whether you have an emotional connection to a specific topic. When it comes to running for office, crafting a narrative surrounding a brand is especially important. I have worked with veterans who served our country, business folks, people heartbroken about losing a loved one to our

28 Interview with Amber Athey, January 13, 2021, via phone.

senseless illegal immigration policies, candidates who tell the story that their mom wanted to abort them but didn't. It's about crafting a story that people can connect with and through it to you. You go through your whole life and see what the most interesting thing about you is and see if it has a political angle to it, and then you throw it out there. This requires understanding what issues you can capitalize on and how those issues and personal identity fit into modern life and the current political movement.

The abundance of content on social media and the purity of prior campaigns (at least public-facing ones) for a while gave politicians the reputation as inauthentic people, with highly edited and cleansed statements or talking points that were so dumbed down and devoid of any emotion as to be almost robotic. There has been a pushback on that now. Authenticity is rewarded and expected from our leaders. It was one of the reasons that Donald Trump's candidacy was so successful.

I talked to thousands and thousands of Trump voters over the years, and their very first thing is that he sounds like us when I hear him talk. I see him. It sounds like one of my friends is saying that or tweeting that, and it makes people feel like they know him. They think that he was the most transparent president in history. A lot of his avid supporters love how open he was online. I know people who literally would just sit around all day waiting to see what he would tweet. People felt a human connection towards him that they probably didn't feel so much towards other people that they know. And when you have people like the mainstream media saying that he doesn't act presidential, that resonated with the American public because it's a lot easier to talk to a guy who jokes around. There's something to be said for using big words, but sometimes there is such a difference between Harvard scholar Obama who talks unrelatedly as opposed to Trump. People just felt like they knew Trump on a personal level. It was weird. People would make you laugh and smile about things he said like that was a friend of theirs who did it or said it. And so, that was always fascinating for me to see. But he came in really at the height of social media. He is, I still think, the social media president.

How important is authenticity in a movement? We often hear and deep down know how different politicians are when on TV or on stage and behind closed doors. But does that cross into the influencer space on Twitter and Instagram? "Here's the thing. Social media rewards authenticity a lot. You know, for all that being said about how it's a source of misinformation, it's hard to be successful on social media if your voice isn't authentic because people can recognize that it isn't, that you're faking it," says Will Chamberlain, editor in chief and publisher of *Human Events*.[29] I asked Kyle Kashuv, who as of this writing has over 302,000 followers on Twitter, if he found that his internet personality was authentic to his day-to-day, and he responded: "I think I mostly am authentic. I think some people have a persona online that I think is different than offline. But no, I think, for me, my online to offline personality is practically one to one."[30] And Kyle has seen staggering success online by truing up his online and offline persona. Others I work with, some of their most viral moments online are moments you wouldn't expect: expressing a vulnerable sentiment about a loss in the family, posting a selfie without makeup, discussing a failure. Social media has encouraged us to publish our successes. But over time, people have come to realize that everyone's life is not perfect all the time and often reward people for showing a different side uncommon on social media.

Defining your brand early also prevents someone else from defining it for you. In my interview with former Georgia State Representative and now gubernatorial candidate Vernon Jones, he put it well when he said that your opponents will try

29 Interview with Will Chamberlain, November 20, 2020, via phone.
30 Interview with Kyle Kashuv, November 30, 2020, via phone.

to define you because "once you become defined, you become confined to that definition."[31] What he means by that is if the radical Left can make you out to be the laundry list of slurs they like to throw at conservatives (e.g., racist, bigot, homophobe), they can run the narrative on who you are before you can establish your own name. And if they take the holeshot from you, they have a serious advantage on your public perception going forward, because reshaping your public image can be very difficult once the media publishes something that confines you.

Vernon's sentiment echoes communist Saul Alinsky's thirteenth rule in his book *Rules for Radicals*: "Pick the target, freeze it, personalize it, and polarize it. Cut off the support network and isolate the target from sympathy. Go after people and not institutions; people hurt faster than institutions."[32]

When you pick your brand, the image that you want to convey, you have to be hyper-focused at least initially. First, make your Twitter feed very clean. When you scroll through your Twitter feed, people should be able to see a lot of your tweets, not retweets. People need to get a sense immediately about who you are and what your account is like. While it's important to showcase your friends' work and accounts that you agree with, being a voice rather than an echo is hugely important.

There is some disagreement on tweet format. But keep in mind, you only have 280 characters to work with. I find that while it's tempting to use all 280 for words—some people like to jam as much as they can into a tweet—readability is important too. Presentation is key, and this translates when you start posting your messaging to Facebook and Instagram, where aesthetics matter almost as much as the message itself.

---

31 Interview with Georgia General Assembly Representative Vernon Jones (Democrat, GA-91), December 23, 2020, via phone.

32 Saul Alinsky, *Rules for Radicals: A Pragmatic Primer for Realistic Radicals* (United States: Random House, 1972).

I often counsel my clients to keep in mind the type of brand "look" they want and, in the initial phases of their social media use, to emulate "looks" that they hope to grow into. This might mean learning Photoshop or how to best craft a tweet that appears structurally similar to tweets like Charlie Kirk's or others who do well on social media.

To be clear, these are just fluff tips. These come only after you have followed the early steps: assessing what kind of messenger you want to be and the type of content you want to produce and have taken the steps to build out a network for long-term success.

Be Coalition-Minded

Find a group of like-minded people and work together to grow your following.

Coalitions are important. Some are formal coalitions, but many are informal. This is related to networking, which we will cover as well in this book. But finding a group with a similar mission and working in tandem to accomplish those goals is vitally necessary to the success of our long-term mission. "No one can be an island. If you try to stand on your own, you will fall, especially as a conservative," says Jack Posobiec, senior editor for *Human Events*, "and it's probably one of the worst things about conservatives on social media."[33] During my time on social media, I have seen senseless and broad-based attacks against our own, infighting that not only cuts against our cause but gives unneeded ammunition to a rabid Left.

While we might have some policy disagreements as a whole, is there any real doubt that the Heritage Foundation, National Rifle Association, and Americans for Prosperity are

33 Interview with Jack Posobiec, December 10, 2020, via phone.

on the same side? Delineating minor disputes into broad-based attacks on social media only hurts us.

So be someone who wants to bring people together. Sometimes the withheld jab is a more prudent approach, especially if it's really friendly fire.

Chiefly important is also to find these groups and connections. After all, the aim is to build an audience. When you start your social media account, you only have a few followers, who are almost always friends. So, you might be wondering, where can you find a coalition and build a base? I always recommend that it's helpful to be specialized at first; often, the more specific, the better. On Facebook, for example, there are groups where you can find people that solely like the Second Amendment or the Fair Tax or any number of specific policy areas. Becoming known in these groups and bridging several together only takes being willing to request to join and participate in the conversation. Sometimes these groups have thousands of passionate patriots who want to hear what you have to say, and you can leverage these audiences cross-platform. The same goes for Twitter and YouTube. Finding people who are talking about what you are talking about only requires being willing to look.

But coalitions are a great way to build momentum on Twitter when you automatically have all these different allies promoting your content.

The Left knows this. David Spady has spent his life in media, and he notes that the "Left is much more willing to work together as a community than the Right."[34] Buck Sexton echoed David. "The Left sticks together and rewards their ideological warriors. It's obviously a lot easier because they have control of most of the cable news channels, almost all the major newspapers, the major publishers, entertainment platforms, things like Netflix and Amazon Prime. And, there are all these ways that the Left takes care of its own, and the

34 Interview with David Spady, December 7, 2020, via phone.

Right needs to get much better at that. And also needs to view this as a team sport. Conservative media has to be a team sport or else we will lose. There are, unfortunately, a lot of people out there, including some who are quite big, who are just constantly worried about fighting their own little turf battles. They don't really care about what's happening with the movement. They don't really care about what it means for conservatives politically in general.... They need to see who elevates, who brings up the next generation, who tries to build allies and coalitions on the right to be more effective in our messaging. That has to be our attitude and approach. And that's something we can honestly learn from the Left because they're much better at that."[35] I agree with Buck that we need to reward conservatives who focus on building up a coalition and mentorship. "That's always been my desire.... There are a lot of people who would say that I helped get them their start or I had them on regularly on radio and helped build awareness of their writing or whatever their career was in the early days. We need a lot of that. And we also need control of institutions that can give people platforms."[36] And it's not just mentorship. As David Spady puts it, we need to be committed at a grassroots level to building conservatism into the future, "from our donor communities to our grassroots activist groups to things like we do with Win Red, and they do with ActBlue, where they're more collectivist just in their very nature, and we're more entrepreneurial and individualistic. And so that dynamic is something that I think allows them to cross-pollinate and promote their various things where we're much more focused on advancing our own organization, our digital platform or whatever for our own benefit."[37] Viewing social media as a team game is a failing of the Right. "One of the things that concerns me is that we don't back each other

35 Interview with Buck Sexton, June 1, 2021, via phone.

36 Interview with Buck Sexton, June 1, 2021, via phone.

37 Interview with David Spady, December 7, 2020, via phone.

up because so many conservatives look at this as a zero-sum game. Whereas if you look at the Left, they're just in it to beat conservatives.... We need those alliances, those sort of bridges between someone who's new, who is just getting in the game versus someone who becomes a facilitator for building that person up. And I know the people who helped build me up, and they've had their ups and downs."[38]

On a more nationwide level, I observed in 2016 how effective the president was at pooling together various messages to be successful in his election. I asked Matt Whitlock what role President Trump plays in coalition building for conservatives in the future. "It's important to remember when you look at the House victories across the board and even the Senate victories, a coalition that's been built right now really wouldn't be possible without [President Trump]. He sparked an energy in working-class voters and also just sort of a revitalization for our politics to where suddenly we are credibly seen as the party for American workers and the party that's looking out for working families. And that's a really valuable place to be. We look at these incredible gains in the House that continue to come in. I don't think that coalition is built without the work of [President Trump] and his team. There are a lot of people out there that may disagree with a lot of what he has said and things that he's done. But you can't deny the role that he's played in shaping the current makeup of this electorate. Whatever his involvement is, whether his lawsuits are successful and he remains president or, there's a new administration, I think he's going to have a voice going forward because he played such a role in establishing where the party is now. And I think that he has the ability to be an incredible force for good in helping candidates and helping the party continue to move in that direction in the most productive way."[39] Brad Parscale, a man who changed the way candidates

38 Interview with Jack Posobiec, December 10, 2020, via phone.

39 Interview with Matt Whitlock, November 17, 2020, via phone.

will campaign after the 2016 election, notes that "the president generated the greatest grassroots campaign in history. People will be riding his coattails for a generation."[40]

In terms of building a coalition behind particular ideas, Ron Coleman put it well when he said, "It's not a matter of competing narratives. It's a matter of legitimacy and brand equity and that those are very, very hard to come by. But they have to be undertaken."[41] Sometimes it's not easy, but going it together beats going it alone.

Be Content-Focused

"It's very difficult to put forward a message without being propagandistic, and the best way to do that is to tell stories."[42]

- Jordan Peterson

I'm constantly on my phone. I have clients in all phases of their political journey responding to an entire suite of issues on any given day. As I am writing this, since 6:00 a.m.—it's 10:00 a.m. now—I've responded to a text from a gubernatorial candidate, texted a number of our media companies, chiefs of staff of members of Congress in several states, I am texting reporters.... And that's all just messaging about content. This morning alone, we have sent out dozens of tweets, launched a Facebook ad, and have had kick-off calls for several of our messaging campaigns of our candidates. I say all this to tell you that on any given day at any given moment, we are producing content for our clients.

40 Interview with Brad Parscale, January 29, 2021, via phone.

41 Interview with Ron Coleman, December 22, 2020, via phone.

42 Jordan Peterson, "Interview with Matthew McConaughey," *The Jordan B. Peterson Podcast*, January 10, 2021. YouTube video, 1:09:00, https://www.youtube.com/watch?v=y8wBjH8aXw4.

We do so because if people don't hear from us, there is only room to lose members of the audience. For better or worse, social media has propelled the entertainment, short-attention-span aspect of our culture. Especially in politics, if we are not communicating, someone else is holding the attention of our constituents and viewers.

The sweet spot for a lot of clients depends on what the actual goals are. While a candidate might only need to send a few tweets per day, more if responding to an ongoing crisis, a person hoping to become an "influencer" might need to be more active, writing original content and responsive content.

We treat content creation like a job because it is one. We have a daily process where we interact with our clients to provide structured material. If you're not planning content and it's exclusively reactive, you're losing. Anyone can be an echo, but being a leader requires speaking first. We coordinate with campaigns and our internal team to make sure that messaging makes sense and is responsive to the national conversation and the local district. Keep in mind that some content can be information you have created before. Everything doesn't have to be brand new. Topics that will get good interaction regardless of the news cycle include: "We'll always defend the Second Amendment" or "We'll always defend the unborn." This usually serves as a substantive reminder to our audience that we have a voice but also acts as a placeholder for newer content reacting to trends. I always recommend studying some of the biggest accounts and following their lead at first. Content on social media doesn't have to be perfectly original to do well, as everyone recycles content. There is no such thing as copyrighting tweets or memes, so effectively using popular ideas in a circular, well-timed way lends well to visibility.

Secondly, quality is key. "Create content that matters. At the end of the day, it's content, content, content," Tyler Bowyer, chief operating officer of TPUSA, told me.[43] Regur-

---

43 Interview with Tyler Bowyer, December 28, 2020, via phone.

gitating viewpoints or having unattractive or basic messaging isn't going to produce the outcomes you desire. "Something long and wordy is going to lose people, this generation of instant gratification, people can't pay attention to things for a long period of time, so you need to grab people's attention instantly,"[44] counsels Andrea Catsimatidis, chair of the Manhattan Republican Party. "Whether it's a shocking graphic or punchy sentences, short to the point, you need to grab people's attention,"[45] she says, "operating in a liberal city, we also win by framing a message as a logical argument. This difficulty is framing that logical argument as an emotional one, and that's something that I've really tried to do because it hits people more, and it also attracts more people to you, because it's very hard for liberals to argue with an emotional argument."[46] Creating high-quality, in-depth content requires thoughtfulness and effort.

Thirdly, you have to know your audience and at least initially target a specific audience. Will Ricciardella, formerly of the *Washington Examiner* and now *Fox News*, notes, "You have to engage them even if you only have seven thousand followers, you're their dad. Every day, you're testing material. Little by little. You have a following accustomed to certain material, and over time, you adjust this content to reach outside of your following. Sometimes you share things that are completely out of your following. It's knowing content to reach out to different audiences while gauging your own interests. Full-time job."[47] When Congresswomen Greene ran for office, she told me that when she started campaigning, she connected to her audience by posting videos on her Facebook page. "I put every bit of information about myself, about where I would be, pictures of me. I would do my videos and talk about issues, policy, just everything about myself so that people could get to know me. And it worked.

44 Interview with Andrea Catsimatidis, January 12, 2021, via phone.

45 Interview with Andrea Catsimatidis, January 12, 2021, via phone.

46 Interview with Andrea Catsimatidis, January 12, 2021, via phone.

47 Interview with Will Ricciardella, December 17, 2020, via phone.

People want to like the person they're voting for. They want to know what they think. And social media is the best tool to do that. And the best way to do it is to make sure that it's not just pictures or articles. You see a lot of candidates just use memes, but that's kind of boring after a while. Things are different now. And I think voters are more aware, more educated. And so, they want to know more about the candidate that they're going to vote for. And social media is the best tool for that."[48] Managing your audience requires full-time focus and long-term commitment. I know many people who want to start a Twitter following and either don't post with any frequency or don't bother to learn and study what their audience responds to.

Guys like Buck Sexton know how important it is to develop a broad skill set in content. "When I started my career, I knew that with the rapidly changing environment, particularly with what digital is doing to the whole conservative media world, that I had to be able to write, to do audio, to do video, to do everything, and that it was going to require consistency and persistence to get anywhere. And I think increasingly what people are seeing is those two critical ingredients. You not only have to post good things, post things on Facebook that engage your audience, but you have to work, have quips and quick takes on Twitter that are worthwhile, but you have to do it consistently and at a volume that can get you beyond a lot of the noise out there. That's critical in audience building is that people have that expectation. So it's not just once a day you post on Twitter or Facebook or once a week or whatever it may be, but that they know that you're going to be there commenting regularly on issues of critical importance. And then I think that's how you build an audience instead of just getting occasional eyeballs and having a clickbait-based career."[49]

48 Interview with Congresswoman-elect Marjorie Taylor Greene, December 10, 2020, via phone.

49 Interview with Buck Sexton, June 1, 2021, via phone.

Be Quick, Reactive, and Topical

Twitter promotes what people are talking about. When you're starting out, engaging with your followers is supremely important. I engaged all the time, responding to messages, responding to comments. I would do that a lot. People like that. People think you're friendly. It's tempting to fall into the trap of talking about what your friends are talking about, but to grow, you have to follow the conversations and trends. Always be ready to react and flow with the news cycle. It's a truism in the media that very rarely can you create your own news cycle. Becoming "fluent" or conversant on every topic should be paramount to becoming an "expert" on any one topic.

I changed my strategy and went from being a reply guy to talking about larger trends.

Nowadays, our team will get called on a pressing issue, and we will be monitoring the situation, and our team will come up with copy after having a conversation with the candidate, and we'll come out with the statement. We actively watch how social media is talking about the issue and prepare a coherent response. We've been on the front lines on crisis comms for numerous other politicians.

The name of the game of Twitter is assessing where your opinion falls within the news cycle and where it falls within the broader conversation. Because for better or not, over the past decade, social media dictates what's being talked about on the news almost as much as what's actually happening in the world does. That's been one change I've seen over the last four or five years. The producers for all major cable shows look to see what's being talked about on Twitter, and then they'll use those tweets to lead their shows and create segments.

Charlie Kirk is someone who does particularly well at getting messages out quickly. He "kind of hones his message and gets it out there. There are few people on the right who have this sort of impact that he has got."[50] Sometimes it means being irreverent and willing to go into the fray on ongoing issues.

At the end of being quick and reactive, conservatives need to do better at spiking the football. When we get stuff done, we need to keep on talking about it. We're people of action. We're not people of talk. When I get something done, I don't go back the next day and call the guy to tell him I solved his problem. "I solved it, here, let's talk about it. Remember yesterday? I kicked ass. I did this for you." No, I want to go on to the next topic or issue. But, unfortunately, that's not politics. Conservatives need to do a better job of continuing to talk about our successes.

Build Out a Strong Network

Anybody can grow on social media. It's not rocket science. Most people will see an account with tens of thousands of followers and ask, how did they get that? But the reality is it's pretty simple. You just have to know where to look and how to start.

Let's just start with this: Remember when, as a kid, you learned not to talk to strangers? I am telling you to do the opposite—you need to talk to strangers online. My whole life, I've met strangers online, and many of those strangers have become some of my best friends and closest allies and are the most helpful people I've ever met. Unless you're networking, making digital relationships, you will not grow online.

I met Charlie Kirk in 2014 on Twitter. And he became a very important friend in my life. I think my first message to him was something like, "Keep up the good work. We need young political leaders and business leaders like us to take on the fight." I was sixteen and in high school when I sent that message.

50 Interview with Will Chamberlain, November 20, 2020, via phone.

Most of my staff I've met online.

I went from being a relatively unknown guy with a Twitter account to now I probably have programmed into my phone the cell phone numbers of one hundred members of Congress, hundreds of staffers, and dozens of former Trump administration staffers and officials.

All because of networking, and it all began online.

At first, it might seem daunting. You approach someone and build that network for the purpose of adding to your ability to get things done. But the other school of thought is to approach relationships to learn from somebody.

When I first started, I needed a lot more from people; I needed their business. So, when I reached out to these people, running a young company, new to politics, I was trying to gin up business and make connections. It was an early start, and I was hungry, and I took every call, responded to every message, reached out to every single person I wanted to talk to. That's what it takes to start.

Now, having built that network, I can be more discerning with my network and build out a group of people who get things done and add real value. I always stress how crucial it is to surround yourself with loyal, intelligent people.

Making those relationships matters. If you have two thousand Twitter followers, and you meet someone and say they have ten thousand Twitter followers, that's still a lot more than you. You build that friendship. Be genuine. Obviously, don't be a fake person. Find people you connect with and start building out a team. Over time, these real friendships will translate into gradually helping each other out and promoting each other's work. Your base grows.

Chapter 3:

THE POLITICIANS AND CANDIDATES

PEGGY NOONAN, *WALL STREET Journal* columnist and former speechwriter for President Ronald Reagan, was right when she said that "our political leaders will know our priorities only if we tell them, again and again, and if those priorities begin to show up at the polls."[51] You can have the coolest influencers and the best-laid plans, but unless you're the party wielding the instruments of power in our government, it's all for nothing. I have devoted my life to helping conservatives win elections with great success for those who have followed our strategies.

And with this book, I want to give out some of those strategies that we employ at my firm but also hear from candidates and politicians across the country who have taken up the fight, put their name out there, and tried to make America great.

Many of the tricks and tools to winning elections have stayed the same. I won't lie to you—money and the ability to raise money are foundational in American politics. Some of the best candidates are dead in the water without the ability to raise cash or be independently wealthy. Same goes

51 "Time to Vote," *The Salt Lake Tribune* (October 24, 2012), https://archive.sltrib.com/article.php?id=55134192&itype=CMSID.

for the intangibles that make a candidate successful. I won't go into all of them, but when I take on a client, we sit down and go through an exhaustive discussion to make them the most successful candidate we can. This will always be true in American politics.

But now, social media is a new tool that candidates and politicians are using that has helped them gain notoriety, engage with constituents, and improve their candidacy or stature in Congress.

Otherwise unknown candidates have leapt into legitimacy through social media using engagement and developing a following as a premier way of garnering early support and fundraising. Much of Donald Trump's early success in his 2016 run is attributed to his use of social media. There are countless examples nationwide of candidates who followed his example and propelled themselves into the national spotlight through well-timed, clever social media usage. Notable examples include Kim Klacik with her Baltimore video, Lauren Boebert's use of Twitter to gain early primary support and recognition, and Scherie Murray's social media campaign against AOC in New York. Some candidates spent smart money on social media and launched successful bids for Congress, such as Congresswoman Marjorie Taylor Greene of Georgia's Fourteenth Congressional District.

On the conservative side, politicians have also begun using social media in a more authentic manner to combat leftist politics where ideas are more radical, like on social media. During his candidacy, President Donald Trump used social media in a novel way: as an offensive tool to direct media attention and steer the conversation of the day but also as a defensive tool to curb a media apparatus hell-bent on undermining any and every aspect of his presidency. Other politicians have also joined the fray, implementing unique and captivating social media strategies—Senator Ted Cruz and now-retired Senator Orrin Hatch, to name a few.

In all my campaigns, we insist on and swear by an active social media campaign for any higher office and help candidates and politicians, once elected, run and maintain a coherent and intelligent social media strategy pulled from our experience and from the experience of other firms we have worked with in the past.

Our work requires constant check in, and with the twenty-four-hour news cycle, I find myself constantly speaking with my clients, members of Congress, on a daily basis, as well as our political candidates. The members and candidates we work with want to be leaders, and with the speed of new issues arising every single day, these politicians have to react daily and sometimes hourly. And so, they lean on me to do it. It's basically a quasi-constructive role. On a daily basis, I probably talk to two to three politicians or members of their staff and then try to reach out to all of my candidates because the news cycle doesn't sleep. Our company and our staff understand that. Our staff doesn't ask for weekends or time off because we are entrusted with huge responsibilities of being the digital voices for some of the most influential people in America.

And so, when people ask what I do for work, and I say I tweet for a living, people kind of laugh at that. Sure, it's not the most physically demanding job, but it is mentally demanding because you always have to be on; you always have to be alert. And if you miss a second of a news cycle, you can fall behind. We are constantly monitoring the news, watching multiple news channels to see what the Left on CNN is saying and what the last piece on MSNBC says, seeing what our allies are saying. Depending on the cycle, we have to be particularly sensitive because what we tweet often ends up in articles or on one of the major news networks.

As we edge closer to 2022, especially during election years, I travel to a lot of the districts. At first, I was a behind-the-scenes guy. But as our business has expanded, I have learned and seen how important it is for my own branding that politicians build a relationship with me so they can be vocal, and I can be a vocal proponent of the candidates I support and work for as well. This means constantly being online. I'd estimate that for myself I probably send anywhere from five to ten tweets a day. Then for our politicians and clients, we strive to do two to three. And so, our team probably sends out a couple of hundred tweets every day on behalf of politicians and clients. It's a big job for our firm.

But to be clear: working for these candidates and politicians is not a solo effort, and while we are a business, the work we are doing requires a large force. We partner with many larger firms, and we like to be a team player if we think it can help the cause, which is really the difference. I don't have a political science degree. I don't have a political science background. I was never a Hill staffer. I've avoided the standard trajectory of the way DC is run because the way conservatives have to respond in this digital age has to be different.

I'm here for the work. I back up what I say with donations to candidates I believe in. I want to be a steward. I want to make sure my money is going to the right places and is not going merely to line the pockets of any Establishment figure. My team and I want to work to support the conservative agenda because we can do better as a country. We want to promote values and people we align ourselves with. I'm committed to the cause so much that I would do what I do for free but for a little something called FEC laws and in-kind contributions.

I believe in the fight. I believe in the cause. I believe that we have only a few more years to save our country, or we're going to be lost to a point where we can't come back, and I can't let that happen. I started my consulting business when I was nineteen. I wasn't old enough to run for office. And I'm still at this moment not old enough to serve in the United States

Congress. So how I feel I can provide value is by working with candidates and politicians and helping them succeed.

And so, what follows are conversations with candidates and elected officials, some I have worked for and others I have not (yet), who I believe bring a unique perspective to the broader conversation of a social media war. I have bifurcated the chapter between candidates and elected officials. While some of the candidates I highlight were unsuccessful in their bid for higher office, their perspectives are important since, as you will see, they garnered a significant following or financial base and went from virtual unknowns to potential contenders in the future, many in districts where Republicans had no business being competitive or raising money. There's a lesson to be learned there.

I want you to read this chapter and be encouraged by the conservatives who have joined this fight, made public service a priority, and taken to the battlefield politick. Remember, at the end of the day, we can have the best social media strategy in the world with all the influencers conservatism can generate, but if we don't win elections, there is no telling how long freedom can survive.

The Politicians

I like working with politicians who aren't generic Washington politicos. I work with political outsiders, people who go to Washington not to get in the cool kids club but to make a difference. When I meet with a potential client, candidate, or an incumbent, I ask them and myself whether they are in a position to make a difference.

You have to understand: Washington is the ten-thousand-pound stone around the American peoples' necks. It doesn't like to move, it doesn't like being conscientious, it doesn't tolerate radical change, it doesn't even necessarily look out for what's in the best interest of the country. It's intransigent in all the ways that would get someone fired from a corporate job for incompetence. It's unmovable and unchanging in a digital age in which we get a new iPhone every two years.

For politicians who go to Washington, many view themselves as Mr. Smith goes to Washington, but few actually are. Most march in lockstep with party leadership, take hard-working Americans' money, and vote the party line.

I want to break all of that. The difference between the status quo and what the candidates I work with do is their power on social media. They're effective, bold.

You can't be generic. Leadership, whether you're on the right or the left, sends out weekly or daily memos and talking points on issues, and many politicians are happy to just regurgitate those talking points to their social media accounts. The ones who really stand out and make a difference are the ones who think for themselves, who can understand a policy and understand an issue, and craft a narrative around it that they can sell to the American public and to the Republican base. What I do and the advice I give to the politicians I work with is to continue to develop this skill in hopes that the next generation of conservative leaders in Congress, in the Senate, and maybe one day in the White House can be more effective in the digital age with communicating past the DC city limits.

I won't lie to you: after a grueling campaign season, it might seem tempting to take a vacation. But public service is no joke, and when you win, that's when the real work begins. That's when it's time to lead and govern. Part of the work my firm does is keep politicians engaged with their constituents. I tell them that it's important to lead, interact with their constituents, and show them their successes. The time of a passive politician on social media is over.

To prepare this chapter for you, I spoke with a number of politicians across our great country. I asked them their insights on the state of politics, what's at stake in the social media war against a progressive Left, what tips they would offer to candidates, and what they are doing in Washington to protect conservative voices and public policies. Their insights are valuable and unfiltered, and I am happy to share them with you.

Senator Rick Scott

As he was running for governor of the State of Florida, now Senator Rick Scott knew the importance of staying on message with a media apparatus hell-bent on swaying voters and perverting Republican messaging. His "Jobs, jobs, jobs" message resonated with Florida voters, and he became the forty-fifth governor of Florida, serving one of the greatest states (in my unbiased view) for two terms.

Rick Scott might not be someone up to date on the meme or Twitter joke of the day, but where Senator Scott is effective is that he understands the threat that these Big Tech companies pose, and he has shown a willingness to listen to the concerns of the base and the Republican voters who think that their voices will be silenced if they say the wrong thing or do the wrong thing online.

As a leader and politician who has served as an executive and now as a member of the Senate, I asked how his past has shaped his leadership style and effectiveness in delivering sound policy outcomes for the people of Florida and the US more broadly. He told me, "As governor of Florida, I focused on what really mattered to Florida families, which are the same things that matter to all American families: a good job, a great education, safety and the opportunity to live the American Dream. Too often politics becomes an area dominated by career politicians that lose sight of what they were elected to do and the constituents that elected them to do it. I will always fight to help the people of Florida and families across our country to make sure we preserve American values and the qualities that make America great. I want everyone to have the same opportunities I had as a kid, even after starting out in public housing, to live the American Dream."[52]

The Biden administration seeks to virtually undo every triumph of the Trump administration, so I spoke with Senator Scott about how conservatives can push back in messaging for 2022 and outside of elections during the next four years. He told me:

> *"The Biden administration's agenda of more regulation, higher taxes, open borders, socialism, and cancel culture is the exact opposite of what Republicans have achieved for Americans the last four years. And it's the exact opposite of what this country needs. We need to do a better job of explaining the differences. Democrats—with the help of the media—have successfully portrayed their policies as lifting up the little guy, the working-class family, the poor and struggling American. And we've let them get away with it. But it's a lie, and we need to say so. Their policies hurt the very people they claim to be helping. It's all a big lie. They're seriously embracing socialism. Think about that—socialism is the single most discredited idea of the twentieth century, and the Democrats are trying to bring it back! It's responsible for the deaths of tens of millions, primarily the poor, working-class people that Democrats claim to support. Their entire brand is a lie. Their policies are bad for working families. They're bad for minorities in this country. They're bad for the poor and blue-collar workers. We can't cede that ground to the Democrats. We need to make our argument and make it to people that Republicans in DC often ignore. The difference between Democrats and Republicans is simple: Democrats want to control your*

52 Interview with Senator Rick Scott, March 6, 2021, via email.

> *life, and Republicans want to give you a better life. There's no doubt if we focus on the issues that matter to Americans that we will have a successful 2022."*[53]

When Rick Scott ran for governor and the Senate, he was effective in keeping a consistent message of "jobs." I always tell my clients the importance of staying on message no matter how simple and becoming synonymous with that message as a way of defining yourself. I asked Rick Scott how important a clear message was for his campaigns. He said, "Every winning campaign sticks to a winning message. It lets the voters know what you stand for as a leader and what you'll fight for if they elect you. Without a clear message, you're just another face on the screen. My races were never easy, and I haven't won by a landslide. Florida is a 50/50 state. It's hard to win. You have to work every day to be out there and get your message out. Focusing on creating jobs for Florida families was a no-brainer. I grew up in public housing, and I saw how hard my parents worked to support our family. Even as we struggled to make ends meet, my parents were always grateful to have work. My background as a business owner and CEO taught me first-hand how to create those opportunities for others. I wanted to take those exact values into my campaign for governor and into the US Senate."[54]

Going into the future, I asked the senator what his mindset was now that Republicans had lost the Senate, House (with some positive gains), and White House. He told me, "We must draw a clear contrast between a Republican Party that fights for good-paying jobs, for families, and to protect the values that make our country great and a Democrat Party that wants government at the center of our lives, flirts with Socialism, and undermines our fundamental values. If Repub-

53 Interview with Senator Rick Scott, March 6, 2021, via email.

54 Interview with Senator Rick Scott, March 6, 2021, via email.

licans fail to become the party that is trusted to lead America into the future, Democrats will lead America into the past."[55]

Congresswoman Marjorie Taylor Greene

Marjorie Taylor Greene was elected in 2020 to serve as Congresswoman for Georgia's Fourteenth Congressional District.[56, 57] She has already made waves in Washington for her unabashed support of President Trump and his agenda. And while at times her substance and style may be perceived as controversial, her success in winning a seat in Congress is notable and merits consideration and study.

We went to work when we took up the campaign of a new candidate in northwest Georgia, Marjorie Taylor Greene. She had two thousand Twitter followers. When we stopped working with her, she had over three hundred thousand. Marjorie understands the power of social media, and she's successful at it. She obviously posted a really great quarter of fundraising the quarter after she was censored and stripped of committees. She raised millions and millions of dollars from hundreds of thousands of individual contributors. She understands how to use social media. She employs tactics very similar to President Trump's. She's a disruptor, and I think Washington needs that.

I spoke with her, and she gave me particular insights on her success and tactics. For Congresswoman Greene, she approached politics like she approached her CrossFit training and her work at her small business:

> ***"This was my first time running for any type of public office. I've been a business owner for the past two decades. I graduated from UGA with a degree in marketing and sales. So that's my background. That's***

55 Interview with Senator Rick Scott, March 6, 2021, via email.

56 https://www.marjorietaylorgreene.com/.

57 Interview with Congresswoman-elect Marjorie Taylor Greene, December 10, 2020, via phone.

> *my frame of thinking: the sales and marketing and business. And so, when I ran, I was a long shot in the primary. I was running against eight men. There were no other women in my race. And gosh, they were all fantastic candidates, really great resumes, careers, some of them veteran family men. And it was pretty intimidating because I've never run for office before. So, my approach to campaigning and running for office was the same way I would go about getting the customers for the business I own. I own a commercial construction company, and I do CrossFit, and that experience played into campaigning actually in an interesting way, because I learned Facebook when I owned the business and learned that's how to bring in new members. And, you have to tell your demographic about yourself; it's like everything about CrossFit, like the hardest workout that you can ever do. But if you can get people to come and do that, then you're doing really good."*[58]

As a candidate, the media took a keen interest in her. They took an even greater interest in her when she announced her tremendous support for President Trump. I asked her how she handles that criticism and the media attacks. She told me that boldness is what separates her:

> *"Be bold. Take your facts, speak well about it, and then just go forward. And that's what people want. People who want transparency, honesty. They want someone that can tell them the truth and that they're going to vote for you now."*[59]

As someone who's worked in public life and seen the toll that is taken on you and the lengths the media is willing to

58 Interview with Congresswoman-elect Marjorie Taylor Greene, December 10, 2020, via phone.

59 Interview with Congresswoman-elect Marjorie Taylor Greene, December 10, 2020, via phone.

go to discredit and harm a candidate's reputation, I asked Congresswoman Greene how she handles inevitable criticism:

> *"That might be what separates me from other people. I really couldn't care less about criticism; that was just something I made up my mind about. You're going to get a lot of hate and criticism; that's just the nature of politics. And I know who I am. I'm confident in myself. I've got plenty of friends. I'm not out here to try to make new friends. That's not what this is about. If I make some along the way, which I did with [you] and a few other people, that's fantastic. But the key is this is about a job. And politics is a two-edged sword. There are people that are going to love you, and there are people that are going to hate you. So as far as criticisms are concerned, my best advice is to get some really tough skin and do not worry about it, because that's going to be there even if you're perfect. Like if you do everything right, you're still going to get somebody who's going to talk bad about you. And so, I just put that aside. And for me, going into this, if I can't be myself and say what I think and feel, then I personally don't want to do it. That that's who I am. I'll stay home and live my wonderful, great life and make more money doing construction, to be honest with you, than in Congress. But I think for anybody choosing to run for Congress or any other type of public office, I think they have to really know themselves better than their position and just stay with it. And, don't apologize."*[60]

The congresswoman also makes it abundantly clear the stark difference between true America First patriots and those who pretend just to win elections. "Well, one thing that stands out very clear to me, and this has been the case for quite a few

60 Interview with Congresswoman-elect Marjorie Taylor Greene, December 10, 2020, via phone.

years now, is that there are people that call themselves conservative and conservative Republicans. They talk like a conservative Republican. But when it comes to voting, when it comes to the bill's sponsor and co-sponsor, it's a whole other story. And you'll find out they're moderate and that they don't do the thing or follow through on the things that they're telling their constituents or promising on the campaign trail. I don't look at Washington the same way. I don't look at Washington thinking, oh, my gosh, I just want to be there, and I want to be in Congress."[61]

As of this writing, Congresswoman Greene is being viciously targeted by House Democrats and the mainstream media for comments made before she ran for office. And while contrite and offering clarifying and recanting statements of her prior statements, it hasn't diminished the resolve to make her an avatar of a boogey-woman right-winger to score cheap Democrat points. But, for someone like Congresswoman Greene, this hasn't decreased her resolve as well.

Congressman Lance Gooden

I spoke with Congressman Lance Gooden of the great state of Texas about what conservatives can do to win the social media war and take back our country. Congressman Gooden, a proud American and Texan, has already made waves in Congress for his unfiltered style and unapologetic America First perspective.

It's been really fun to work with Congressman Lance and watch his growth over the last year. He spent his first year and a half in Congress learning the ropes, making friends, and learning the game. He has a strong voice, and he crafts messages around important, relevant issues in a way that's clever and gets the attention of not only his voters but the media as well. Most of all, he recognizes that "people are sick

61 Interview with Congresswoman-elect Marjorie Taylor Greene, December 10, 2020, via phone.

and tired of business as usual. The American people know Washington is broken, and Congress is not to be trusted."[62]

Congressman Gooden noted that, in many ways, but for the radicalization of the Left, conservatives would not have to be as on guard against socialism at home and an encroaching China abroad as we are. "There was no one to the left of Maxine Waters until about two years ago. And I have watched this as a member of the Financial Services Committee. I have seen how she and others have helped to shape the narrative. Now, Maxine Waters has become a moderate voice in the Democratic Party,"[63] the congressman told me over the phone. He continued, "The moderates within the Democratic Party are scared. Their party is scared of the Far Left. The Democrats in the middle are terrified by the prospect of Democrats controlling both chambers and the White House."[64] From the campaign trail, I can attest this is true. I have witnessed the Far Left gaining a louder and louder voice in the primaries and those radical voices driving campaign dollars and votes in the general elections.

Congressman Gooden is keenly aware of just how radical the Left has become, in large part due to social media. "Across the board, with a lot of primary challenges from the Left, I think that we're going to see more and more often that candidates are going to start taking their talking points from Twitter to avoid primary challenges. And it's going to move the dialogue and the discourse even further to the left, which is bad for all of us,"[65] he said. And the feedback loop is even more of a multifront battle when you consider that for congressmen like Congressman Gooden, one has to simultaneously combat radicals in Congress and also combat their influences driven by tech companies that have tremendous foreign influences (as we learned from the liberals in 2016).

62 Interview with Congressman Lance Gooden (R-TX), December 30, 2020, via phone.

63 Interview with Congressman Lance Gooden (R-TX), December 30, 2020, via phone.

64 Interview with Congressman Lance Gooden (R-TX), December 30, 2020, via phone.

65 Interview with Congressman Lance Gooden (R-TX), December 30, 2020, via phone.

What's worse is that while our nation combats internal forces seeking to undermine systems and norms and displace us as the leading beacon for the rest of the world, more hostile forces are at work and lie in wait seeking our demise abroad. Congressman Gooden recognized this threat when we spoke of China.

> ***"China has taken a controlling stake on the world stage, all over Africa, and elsewhere. We are so desperate to be liked by all the world, from the Iran deal to our deals in Europe. And then along comes Donald Trump, and he says enough is enough. [For our politicians], America should be put first on the world stage. [Under a Biden administration], we'll go back to the days of America being the security force for the rest of the world."***[66]

Unfortunately, as of this writing, the Biden administration is already hard at work undoing all the progress made in the Trump administration—from kowtowing to the Chinese at the expense of US manufacturing to "resurrecting"[67] the Iran deal (a deal ostensibly designed to give Iran pallets of cash in exchange for not bombing us—how charitable!) and overall making the United States weaker on the global stage.

When it comes to the social media war (as I demonstrate in later chapters), nothing is scarier than Congress's ineptitude in the face of censorship and Big Tech crackdown on conservatives. I discussed with Congressman Gooden the congressional hearings on Twitter, Facebook, and Big Tech. He wondered aloud if this was all a farce, "[The congressional hearings], of course, are a dog and pony show until we actually have the power to do something."[68] Congressman

---

66 Interview with Congressman Lance Gooden (R-TX), December 30, 2020, via phone.

67 Matthew Lee, "Biden Attempt to Resurrect Iran Nuke Deal Off to Bumpy Start," AP (February 23, 2021), https://apnews.com/article/donald-trump-iran-iran-nuclear-diplomacy-middle-east-fe94f33feaa974d-244c0e3cdd6c33dfc.

68 Interview with Congressman Lance Gooden (R-TX), December 30, 2020, via phone.

Gooden has joined forces with Congressman Buck and other GOP members concerned with platform access, going so far as to co-sponsor a number of pieces of legislation targeting Big Tech. Some of his work in 2021 includes co-sponsoring the Ending Platform Monopolies Act, which would promote free and fair competition by reducing tech companies' abilities to "leverage their control across multiple business lines to self-preference and disadvantage competitors."[69] With a potential red wave coming in 2022, there is a real possibility of change coming towards Big Tech and conservatives' access soon.

I think it's important for every member in Texas to be speaking out against the radical leftist climate change agenda, an agenda that, if implemented, would cost billions of dollars and thousands of jobs in Texas alone. It's so critical that if we lose that industry, we lose Texas, we lose those jobs. And not only for the sake of Texas itself, but for the country, we must protect our energy resources. On the climate change fight: "We've got people in the energy sector that need to wake up. Our enemies are always going to work together. China, not so under the radar, is taking advantage of us while we have silly debates on green energy. Their war on the US energy industry continues. And it's very concerning."[70]

Congressman Ken Buck

We spoke to the unapologetic and plainspoken Congressman Ken Buck from Colorado's Fourth District. He understands he doesn't have to have the most followers, but he knows the issues better than anybody. We spoke about what he is doing in Congress about social media companies. Buck is the chairman of our antitrust committee, and he's determined to rein

69 Ken Buck Congressman for Colorado's 4th District, "House Lawmakers Release Series of Bills Aimed at Taking on Big Tech's Monopoly Power," June 11, 2021, https://buck.house.gov/media-center/press-releases/house-lawmakers-release-series-bills-aimed-taking-big-tech-s-monopoly.

70 Interview with Congressman Lance Gooden (R-TX), December 30, 2020, via phone.

in Big Tech. He's going to be at the tip of the spear leading the day of reckoning for Big Tech companies if we take back the House. He's a man of his word, and he understands that these companies have way too much power. "Twitter allowed the President of Iran to launch multiple threats against the United States over the past four years, but they permanently suspend the President of the United States' account. The Big Tech reckoning must come."[71]

I asked him about how odd it is to have to make the case to the American people on social media about the dangers and potential dangers of social media and how that goes shaping a narrative for the American people to digest.

> *"It's ironic, isn't it? We have to use Facebook and Twitter and Google to really get the word out about how corrupt Facebook and Google and Twitter and Apple and Amazon are, but that's the big part of that reality, that they control the information flow in America. They have a monopoly on the information flow. And so, if we're going to move forward, we need to do it partly through those means. I think the interesting thing is that if they try to censor what I'm talking about, they would really have a problem because obviously it doesn't incite anyone to violence and doesn't meet any of their criteria. So it truly would be purely political censorship without any justification. And I think that it would really hurt their cause more not to have a free and open debate about how Big Tech operates. But we are sensitive to the fact that everything we put out there, they are monitoring and will at some point use in a court of law to try to defend themselves."*[72]

71 Ken Buck (@RepKenBuck), Twitter, Jan. 8, 2021, 3:28 p.m., https://twitter.com/RepKenBuck/status/1347686574612475909?s=20.

72 Interview with Congressman Ken Buck, January 27, 2021, via phone.

It's no small feat, though, taking on social media and tech giants. So I asked the congressman what his team has planned:

> *"I think there are a few different strategies. And one is just to make sure that the enforcement agencies, the FTC, the antitrust division, have the resources they need to accomplish their goals. And the second is to deal with these giant corporations, the largest in the history of the world, through antitrust laws and through amendments to the antitrust laws. We have a new economy, and we need to deal with the new technology in new ways. It's really important that we address that through antitrust and has nothing to do with the privacy issues. That has nothing to do with censorship or information flow. It's just strictly any corporation like Google. Having ninety-four percent of the market share of laptop or desktop searches should be subject to antitrust laws. And we need to make sure that those antitrust laws apply, whether it's with these five companies acquiring smaller start-up companies or merging with them or however they're doing it, we need to address the antitrust side of it. And I think there's a privacy issue that's involved. And the European Union has looked at it, and they have one model, and there are plenty of other models that have been suggested. And I think the antitrust subcommittee will look at just how individuals' information is controlled and used in the privacy area. And then lastly, we have this information flow and censorship and Section 230 immunity and other related issues. I think the approach has to be on all fronts at the same time, pushing to amend the laws and enforce the laws on these giant companies."*[73]

73 Interview with Congressman Ken Buck, January 27, 2021, via phone.

With the 2020 election and the censorship of President Trump in clear coordination, Silicon Valley has shown a propensity to work in tandem to move the country in particular directions. I asked the congressman how he planned to combat any efforts he and his team planned to combat Big Tech when the industry is so coordinated:

> *"I think it's a cultural issue to a large extent. You've got to see the Silicon Valley culture for what it is: clearly left of center in their thinking and the unspoken word in their actions. [On Donald Trump being blocked from Twitter] there may have been phone calls between tech companies, but there may not have been phone calls because of the culture that exists, once one of them moves, the others are going to react very quickly. And so, I think that if you got Jeff Bezos and Mark Zuckerberg and Tim Cook in a room, you could ask them about a hundred different issues. They're going to agree on ninety-eight of those issues. They're not socially or financially or politically different in how they see the world."*[74]

Our conversation turned towards the future for Republicans in the House. I asked the congressman if he is hopeful about how the next few years without Republican control will go and how the GOP can win back the narrative:

> *"[Over the next four years], there's things that you point out to the American people. And I think in two years, the House will certainly move back to the Republican side. History tells us that it's very likely that that would happen. The only time it didn't happen was in 2002, after 9/11. But for the most part, we have a small margin now in the House. And I think the*

74 Interview with Congressman Ken Buck, January 27, 2021, via phone.

> ***House will flip. And so, the House will be able to slow that tide."[75]***

And overall, the congressman is hopeful about the direction of the GOP. In fact, he disagreed with the basis of my question that the GOP was fractured when I asked how we unite as a party:

> ***"I disagree with your premise. We gained seats in the House, and we did better than expected in the Senate. A fifty-fifty Senate was not what anybody predicted six months ago. And so, I think that while we lost the White House, you could look at Trump's first debate. You can look at a lot of issues that occurred in his campaign and during his administration. Wonderful policy, but really some personality challenges with communicating to the American people. And so, I think that overall, Republicans did fairly well after the fact that four-year run and especially the first two-year run of the Trump administration. I think the people have accepted our policies and approved of our policies. And they had some problems with some personalities. I expect that the American people will be back on board in two years. And there is nothing that unites a party or any group more than winning. And so, I think you're going to see more unity going forward in the Republican Party. But I don't think there is disunity. I think there is a healthy debate right now about what our priorities are. And you will see a healthy Republican Party in these midterm elections."[76]***

Congressman Buck knows the importance of narrative and the perception the media wants to espouse that the Republican Party is broken beyond repair. On disagreements

---

75 Interview with Congressman Ken Buck, January 27, 2021, via phone.

76 Interview with Congressman Ken Buck, January 27, 2021, via phone.

within the party, "I agree that we are a family. And we should have a family discussion, and we should keep it inside the family and not perpetuate the myth that we are so broken that we can't move forward, because I think we will move forward very strongly."[77]

This year, Congressman Buck has been hard at work on antitrust reform to reign in Big Tech taking aim at breaking up the monopolistic practices of Amazon, Apple, Facebook, and Google. "This legislation represents a scalpel, not a chainsaw, to deal with the most important aspects of antitrust reform... We're giving the Department of Justice and the Federal Trade Commission the tools they need to restore the free market, incentivize innovation and give small businesses a fair shot against oligarchs like Jeff Bezos and Mark Zuckerberg," he argued before the Judiciary Committee earlier this year.[78] I, for one, will be doing everything I can to make sure he is successful in his efforts.

Congressman Madison Cawthorn

I have liked Congressman Cawthorn's work and the way he fights for his constituents. I think he's a very sharp guy, and he wants to be of service. While he knows Washington is a game, he is very good at finding the balance between getting things done and throwing red meat to the media and to his voters. In this partisan gridlock, Republicans won't get much done, so he's been particularly successful at self-promoting and building his brand.

Congressman Cawthorn has led Congress in social media engagement and placed an emphasis on connecting with the American people. I asked him why this is so important to his mission in Washington:

77 Interview with Congressman Ken Buck, January 27, 2021, via phone.

78 Justin Wingerter, "Ken Buck Is Staring Down Big Tech companies. And Powerful People in His Political Party," Denver Post (June 27, 2021), https://www.denverpost.com/2021/06/27/ken-buck-amazon-facebook-google/.

> *"The American people deserve direct, uncensored access to their elected representatives' thoughts and ideas. The mainstream media despises our message, and they will never champion the ideals that made our country great or empower the forgotten men and women of America. Social media offers me the opportunity to connect with an extraordinarily large audience across the nation and receive their encouragement, support, and constructive feedback. Social media is the 'fireside chat' of the twenty-first century, and it's essential to our messaging strategy that we connect directly with Americans without the polluted worldview of biased journalists."*[79]

This connection with the American people through social media led to the success of his campaign. He told me:

> *"Social media is a powerful medium that can make or break a political movement. Our campaign combined social media, grassroots momentum, and clear messaging to deliver a stunning victory for the people of North Carolina's 11th district. They sent me to Congress to be a fighter, and part of that battle is being fought on social media platforms. I want to set the standard for effectively communicating in the modern political arena, and social media is a crucial component of that strategy."*[80]

However, social media can be a gift and curse; Congressman Cawthorn is constantly talked about online, and often times the media is trying to gin up scandal. I asked him how he goes about combating these attacks:

---

79 Interview with Congressman Madison Cawthorn, August 27, 2021, via email.

80 Interview with Congressman Madison Cawthorn, August 27, 2021, via email.

> *"The left cannot combat the right's ideas with legitimate, intelligent reasoning. Instead, they work to cancel the most powerful voices in the conservative movement. If I'm hated in Washington and in the media, it means I'm effectively fighting for the people of Western North Carolina. Their hatred comes out on social media through false accusations, misleading headlines, and outright lies. As conservatives, if we don't engage online, we've forfeited the narrative and surrendered to the left. Social media platforms give me the chance to call out the mainstream media, the radical left, and the fake news to their faces. Social media's crucial role in our modern political dialogue is also why it's so important to fight back against censorship from Big Tech platforms hell-bent on censoring conservative voices. If the left can silence us, they can beat us. They'll never beat us on principle or argument, and the Silicon Valley elites know that. Defending our right to remain uncensored on social media platforms is one of the most consequential struggles in our movement today."*[81]

It's hard enough with Silicon Valley altering your message, but as an outsider, Congressman Cawthorn faces significant threats from the Washington Establishment threatened by his plainspokenness and ability to connect to the common man. I was curious about whether his preconceived notions of the Swamp have been reinforced since arriving in DC:

> *"The Swamp is worse than I ever could have imagined. Washington, D.C. is not real America. There are so many bad actors in the federal government who are only interested in furthering their own careers, furthering their own financial success, or furthering*

81 Interview with Congressman Madison Cawthorn, August 27, 2021, via email.

> *their own false agendas. (If you want to see all three of these collide, I have some members of Congress I'd like to introduce you to.) Nothing should ever come before the American peoples' interests. The Swamp fears patriots like President Trump who govern with the men and women of America on the forefront of their minds. America needs more patriots in Washington who fight for the future of America and not their own selfish gratification."* [82]

And Madison is a fighter. The congressman is only twenty-six years old and propelled himself from a car accident that left him partially paralyzed to the United States Congress. He is an inspiration to all of us. So I asked him how he would counsel conservatives to join him in the fights our country is entangled in:

> *"America cannot be replaced. Our great American experiment must be protected from those who seek to radically change our country. There's nowhere to turn if we lose our nation, our home. We all have unique individual struggles, and we all experience hardship in our lives. But even with our struggles and our flaws, there is no other nation as great as America because We the People are captains of our own destiny.*
>
> *America is still the shining light to all the world, the standard among the nations. We do not have the luxury of sitting idly by in comfort and ease while our country falls apart. The left wants to fundamentally alter the fabric of our nation and change America into another failed socialist experiment.*

82 Interview with Congressman Madison Cawthorn, August 27, 2021, via email.

> ***We are on the forefront of the battle for America's soul and the future of our nation. Do not grow weary in fighting the good fight. When you look up from the battle you will see men and women like you and me passionately fighting for freedom and liberty. Press on, hold the line, and help define tfr4we=908ohe conservative movement."*** [83]

Congressman August Pfluger

Congressman August Pfluger of Texas' 11th Congressional district has been a leader in Washington on energy and an agenda that protects American small businesses. The Congressman has also been particularly concerned about foreign powers coopting our social media companies to disseminate their radical agenda in the United States.

At the time of my interview with the Congressman, Texas had been struck by a storm system that knocked out power for a lot of Texans. Concerned with narratives from the left that came out of that weather system, I asked the Congressman what the left got wrong in the days and weeks after when discussing and crafting narratives around what Texans went through:

> ***"It was absolutely false. Any suggestion that we had a weather system that came through and knocked out our energy, our ability to provide energy for folks because we didn't have enough green energy is completely inaccurate. We have a baseload capacity problem and we're digging through the facts right now. But initial thoughts on it suggest that one of the issues is that over the last decade, we have mis-incentivized certain forms of energy. We have incentivized certain***

83 Interview with Congressman Madison Cawthorn, August 27, 2021, via email.

> *forms of energy at the expense of others that are reliable and that when it comes to the capacity to provide baseload energy, you have to have certain things that are going to be reliable 100% of the time. Wind and solar do a great job of adding marginal capacity, but they're not baseload. They're not. They're not capable of desolate production. So the storm highlighted that people didn't know anything about the electrical grid. Any suggestion that it was due to not having enough green energy is false. We have more wind energy in my district than the entire state of California, so we don't need a lecture on wind energy or renewables. We have a tremendous amount of solar and wind in Texas, and that's great and we're going to need all of all of the above. But the storm highlighted the fact that before you can get real excited about renewables, you need to make sure that you're real good on the reliability piece."*[84]

His concern about the narrative is a profound one being from one of the greatest energy producing states in the U.S. The Left has attempted to command the narrative as if support for fossil fuels is mutually exclusive from supporting green energy:

> *"Pushing this narrative that fossil fuels are bad, and that we for pushing for their use and the jobs they create are therefore bad is abhorrent. If you don't believe in 'climate change', if you don't believe in the Green New Deal, or that particular green policy, well, then you're bad. I would push back against that. Hold on. Let's talk about the one billion people over the last ten years throughout the world that have been raised out of poverty because of affordable, reliable energy.*

84 Interview with Congressman August Pfluger, March 11, 2021, via phone.

> *As such, this narrative is very much virtue signaling. 'I'm good because I'm green and I'm green because I believe in wind energy.' Well, we believe in wind energy, too, but we also believe in affordable, reliable energy, which happens to come from baseload capacity, such as natural gas and nuclear and coal. You can have both of these things. The narrative that we're seeing on social media is it's a one or a zero, if you believe in green energy, you are completely against fossil fuel, which is just terribly, terribly inaccurate."*[85]

I asked about how the market has reacted to the evolving energy needs. The Congressman told me:

> *"About 22% of Texas electricity comes from renewables. But we haven't built any new coal or gas or nuclear plants in years, and there are no plans to do so. But we've got a thousand people moving into the state every single day, which tells me that our demand is going to continue to grow. Where's that energy going to come from? There's a lot of concerns that we have. The federal government has subsidized wind and solar and that has priced out natural gas and coal and nuclear."*[86]

As I have asked some of the other interviewees, I wanted to know what the gap is between what is happening in Washington versus what is happening on Main Street. Congressman like Congressman Pfluger bring a fresh perspective and earnestness reflective of their constituents in their hometowns in Texas rather than the interests of Washington. The Congressman said:

---

85 Interview with Congressman August Pfluger, March 11, 2021, via phone.

86 Interview with Congressman August Pfluger, March 11, 2021, via phone.

"There is a disconnect between policy that's being passed in Washington, D.C., and what my district believes. Look, let me start there. Does social media have an impact on that? Certainly, it does ... but mostly, people are fed up with $1.9 trillion [of government debt]. They don't want their guns taken away. They want to make sure that our border is secure. They don't want the federal government running elections and doing away with ID requirements ... The people in my district are feeling that the country is being taken away from them." [87]

Congressman Byron Donalds

Congressman Byron Donalds has been fantastic. It's always tempting when you get to Washington to fall into the status quo, but Congressman Donalds has held his own. He does his own thing. He is dynamite. He has the most TV hits of any freshman member so far, and he is great on social media. And while he wants to avoid being a token, Congressman Donalds wants to grow the party. His vision excites me. Byron is a fighter. Byron is in a deep red state that's only getting redder. He only supports the Trump agenda, and he knows all the right issues and what to say.

I had the pleasure of speaking with Congressman Byron Donalds via phone in January, following the events at the Capitol and on the day Speaker Pelosi had called for a vote on President Trump's second impeachment. While he closely watched the debate on the House floor, Congressman Donalds spoke with me about the future of the GOP, Black Lives Matter, Antifa, and how conservatives can reach minority voters.

87 Interview with Congressman August Pfluger, March 11, 2021, via phone.

Congressman Donalds represents Florida's Nineteenth Congressional District. He is a newly elected member of Congress in 2020 and an avowed member of the Freedom Caucus.[88]

An African American man, Donalds was immediately attacked by Black commentators early into 2021 for his support of President Trump. One CNN pundit, Keith Boykin, tweeted, "Byron Donalds, of Fort Myers, Florida, was the only Black person to join in Trump's congressional insurrection yesterday. He voted to disenfranchise Black voters and to block a Black woman from becoming vice president. @ByronDonalds should resign in disgrace."[89] Donalds, a man of conviction, punched back, "I don't vote based on my skin; I do so in allegiance to our Constitution & to always follow the Rule of Law. Blue checkmarks live to delegitimize my right as a free Black man to act, think, & vote based on my convictions rather than skin color. Also, it's Congressman to you."[90] In a different age, conservative politicians might have feared criticism from CNN and its contributors, maybe even pandered with virtue signaling to appear as if there is no daylight between him and the Black community, a community he is, in fact, part of.

But Congressman Donalds is a principled conservative, and it's precisely due to this courage that I wanted to speak with him about tweeting his conscience rather than basing his worldview purely on his skin color. I asked him what he thought of blue check marks trying to drive a wedge between him and the Black community simply because he is a Republican.

He told me, "I don't really care that [the Left] says that, number one. I've got to point out the hypocrisy in some aspects of the racism behind these commentators, the Black

88 https://www.foxnews.com/politics/pro-trump-rep-responds-cnn-pundit.

89 Keith Boykin (@keithboykin), Twitter, Jan. 7, 2021, 6:29 a.m., https://twitter.com/keithboykin/status/1347188520612458498?s=20.

90 Byron Donalds (@ByronDonalds), Twitter, Jan. 7, 2021, 7:48 a.m., https://twitter.com/ByronDonalds/status/1347208536862896130?s=20.

man against the Black man. I think the issue is that he has a wrong assumption. It's my blackness he called into question."[91] For Congressman Donalds, his skin color isn't a domineering characteristic of his individuality and participation in our social order but rather a contributing characteristic.

We spoke about Black Lives Matter, a group in which he respected their initiative but perhaps disagreed with their tactics and overall approach:

> *"You had to give them credit for their marketing because no one disagrees with the terminology Black Lives Matter. Of course, I get that absolutely one hundred percent. The problem is that of intention and not of reality. And virtually all political debate and cultural debate that happened last week [the week of the Capitol riot on January 6, 2021], you have members in the Democrat caucus and people on TV who are calling the white protestors racist. In my view, the riot was basically an insurrection because they were going through a constitutional process at that point in time. But by a similar logical construction, we hear all the time that any reforms to our election laws are racist that somehow all laws are disenfranchising Black people. But if you go by that logic, then what you're saying is that Black people vote for people only based upon race. They did not vote for Donald Trump. And this is the problem with the Left, because their entire political strategy is steeped in using race as a marketing tool to try to nullify a political agenda or the means upon which to accomplish their political agenda. That's the problem we face."*[92]

The congressman understands how important it is for conservatives to engage with communities of color better and

91 Interview with Congressman Byron Donalds, January 13, 2021, via phone.

92 Interview with Congressman Byron Donalds, January 13, 2021, via phone.

more comprehensively: "If we don't take the opportunity to truly understand the culture of the minority community and fully understand some of the ideas that make us as a nation, that's a political decision, not of the elected officials of people or political parties. It's going to be very difficult for us to message. That is going to be very difficult to communicate. How can you communicate with somebody if you don't even understand where they are in life?"[93]

Obviously, the Democrats have possessed the narrative to win Black votes over the past thirty years, and groups like Black Lives Matter (with the help of the half-hearted All Lives Matter rebuttal from some Republicans) have solidified that most minority votes go to Democrats. However, I asked Congressman Donalds if there was an opportunity for Republicans with minority voters.

> *"There's too much analysis, and* ***there's too much paralysis of analysis going on about this whole thing.*** *You have consultants who want you to hire them. They say, 'You've got to put this into a [focus] group' or, 'How do you put this on some kind of an elastic approach?' The first thing you do is to just start talking to people. Forget that you're trying to start and just start going and trying to solve the problems these communities are concerned with. Number one is education. And number two is health care. And actually, number three is a bit of a hybrid: maintaining a strong police force because many people in the community want the police to be there. At the same time, they would like to see some reforms in policing. There is not one or the other. Actually, both. In order to understand that, you got to get these communities to be able to do that from your conservative side. It's easy for a white person to*

93 Interview with Congressman Byron Donalds, January 13, 2021, via phone.

> *message to people who grew up in those communities to kind of understand the nuances of the valuable things, the banks and insurance companies and what you're talking about, because that's how you grew up. That's the community you've evolved in. It is difficult to have that same person then shift their messaging strategy into a community they've never spent time in. Hang out and just play together and actually talk to people. It's not just about messaging, it's actually having an understanding of what actually happens in these communities. Don't just drive through. Get out of that car, because you can't have a relationship without a conversation."*[94]

I asked the congressman how we heal as a nation from the very divisive 2020 election:

> *"Americans are trying to get past all this. To be able to change. And that was a tragedy for our country. But at the same time, I think Americans want to get back to life, the politics of the day. I think that's one of the things that's critically important. This whole thing where our politics has become life is exhausting.... People have a shelf life for politics. Most people do. This is just another meeting after another meeting or another rally or after another rally or another article of legal analysis from another that people just came by to say, I'm tired of this, and I just ignore this for now and go back to my life. I think people in America actually spoke out about it. I think people want to go to sporting events and go back to work.... The vast majority of people across the political spectrum completely denounce what happened on January 6th, completely unacceptable."*[95]

94 Interview with Congressman Byron Donalds, January 13, 2021, via phone.
95 Interview with Congressman Byron Donalds, January 13, 2021, via phone.

We actually spoke to the congressman the morning of the impeachment vote of Donald Trump in the House—a historic moment. It was humbling to be on the phone, listening to the congressman weigh his forthcoming vote:

> *"No one is giving credible evidence that the president contributed directly to an insurrection on the Capitol. I know everybody is a huge fan of the flames and stuff. And the election was stolen, blah, blah, blah. It's overly dramatic and especially a problem because we're all the victims of what happened, and it's clearly a problem because you'd never have a victim in the jury box.... This is a travesty of our Constitution. This is a complete misuse of impeachment."*

Looking to the future, I asked the congressman what he hopes to accomplish during this session in Congress:

> *"I'm trying to get things done. Information, technology, space. We do have a serious issue of businesses.... It's very tough to get things done since Congress isn't talking to each other. They act like children and have shouting matches in the tunnel [under the Capitol building]. And I believe it's a very emotional time. And there is value in your feelings about a lot of things. But if you're going to do this job, you've got to take that message and be sober and mature, frankly. You've got to focus on the actual issues and not have your emotions cloud your judgment. And I think they now have a lot of emotions that are part of a lot of people's judgment."*[96]

As I hung up the phone with the congressman, it was hard not feeling that the GOP is in great hands.

96 Interview with Congressman Byron Donalds, January 13, 2021, via phone.

The Candidates

I really don't have much downtime. The moment one election is over, another begins. It's not uncommon for me to be driving from West Palm Beach to Atlanta for a fundraiser, only to find myself needed in Washington, then Chicago, all in the same trip, and then rushing back to Mar-a-Lago for a fundraiser over a weekend.

As we head towards 2022, the outlook doesn't seem to be slowing down at all. My firm will be involved in at least forty races across the country. We're going to be working from coast to coast. As of this writing, I am looking at my client list and pipeline, and we will be traveling all over: to Illinois, Texas, Ohio, North Carolina, Florida, Nevada, Washington State, Texas, Kentucky, Tennessee, New York, Colorado, Georgia, Massachusetts, New Hampshire, and California. (I still need to work on my Hawaii and Alaska client list.) It's a blessing to be busy.

About five years ago, when we first started the company, we didn't turn down any candidate who came our way. We needed to prove growth, and in business, beggars can't be choosers when it comes to the work. Now we are fortunate enough that candidates come to us, and because of the values of the company, we have turned down many who have approached us. It's because now that we have made it on the scene, I have had the opportunity to travel to all parts of this country and see candidates run in races that they never would be able to win, and they still ask for money. And during the pandemic, when people were struggling for money, I viewed the proper allocation of political resources differently. It's really the difference between people who understand middle-class America and the party of the Maxine Waters or Nancy Pelosi types who care only about remaining in power. I am now all in the business of helping elect conservative winners and conservative leaders. We care more about activism than we do about business.

That makes working with and preparing candidates very important and requires honing a strategic focus. Many of the people we work with already know how they want to pitch their public identity. They have taken the time to assess what they bring to the table: if they're a businessman, prior accomplishments, whatever it is that they can sell to an audience. If they haven't self-assessed, then we do the assessment. But it has to be something particular, relatable, and simple. For example, was the candidate a former Trump administration official? Air Force pilot? Owner of a multimillion-dollar business? We help them promote this identity, and at first, this requires a narrow, disciplined approach.

It's also important that candidates share the views of the voters. The adage was that "all politics is local"; that might be true for the local coroner election, but on most issues in most districts now, politics has become very national. This means that on most issues, we are reacting to and tying messaging to what's happening nationally because voters are plugged in. And despite what blue check Twitter or CNN would have you believe, the average American is paying attention and is angry with the direction radical Democrats are taking this country.

And as we have discussed in previous chapters and will cover later in cancel culture and Big Tech chapters, it's no small feat to run for Congress. As a conservative, it takes a lot of guts and grit. That is why I thought it would be helpful to hear from a few candidates I have worked with and what has made them successful.

Joe Kent

The Republican bench is really deep with leaders rising up to take on the radical Left and the Establishment. One such hero is Joe Kent. Joe is a retired Green Beret who has thrown his hat in the ring for Congress in Washington's First Congressional District. He is an America First republican and has become active online with a surging presence after President Trump's endorsement in recent days.

I chatted with him through email about the book, and he was eager to provide his insights in the early days of his campaign.

As campaigns have largely gone online, I asked how successful candidates navigate relying on their online presence to raise money and awareness about their candidacy:

> *"My online game is not sophisticated, I'm going for authenticity so I post my stances & opinions on news via Twitter. As awful as twitter is it's where the national conversation happens so by staying informed & commenting on critical issues I have been able to attract earned media & a decent following.*
>
> *I have gained a good deal of traction by posting 2:20 videos on Twitter of me talking about a specific issue. This shows people that it's actually me expressing my ideas & I think that authenticity has resonated. None of my opponents do that.*
>
> *I stay abreast of local issues on Facebook and try to push my content from twitter there because most of my constituents are on Facebook, not Twitter."*[97]

I asked him what online strategies he employs are particularly effective, and he told me that "posting videos addressing issues or answering questions has been very effective." [98]

---

97 Interview with Joe Kent, August 30, 2021, via email.

98 Interview with Joe Kent, August 30, 2021, via email.

Obviously a patriot and someone concerned about the direction of the country, Joe has been clear about his message to voters:

> *"2022 is absolutely critical for our nation, we can't stand 2 more years of the left having total control. My message is simple, I'm not a politician & I'm here to fight. Adjudicate the 2020 election, secure our elections, our borders, on shore our industries, school choice, break up Big Tech, & end endless wars."*[99]

He brought up Big Tech, so I asked him whether conservatives are fighting a losing battle against a corporate/social media monopoly. He responded, "We are losing, unfortunately there's no 'start your own twitter.' The tech sector is out of control and the Government must break up Big Tech." [100]

No stranger to adversity and fighting in hostile territory, Joe stays encouraged in a hyper-liberal state:

> *"My state is blue but my district is red and we are fighting daily. Getting out and meeting people really fires me up. People want to take back our nation.*
>
> *The memory of my late wife, our kids and all the friends I lost in combat keep me moving forward, their legacy is in our hands, we cannot let our nation fail."* [101]

Anna Paulina Luna

Anna exemplifies what it means to be a strong candidate. She is certainly one of the strongest messengers the GOP has right now. I've known her for four years now, long before she

99 Interview with Joe Kent, August 30, 2021, via email.

100 Interview with Joe Kent, August 30, 2021, via email.

101 Interview with Joe Kent, August 30, 2021, via email.

ever considered running. She and Charlie Kirk joined forces, and ever since, she has been a strong voice and champion for American values. As a result, Hispanic voter turnout has been through the roof for Republicans.

She ran a smart and important race against Charlie Crist, a former governor with virtually unlimited campaign resources and many allies both on the left and Establishment Republicans. She was supposed to lose big but instead came very close to winning. She can raise the money. And she can put up one hell of a fight.

In May 2021, she announced she would run again in Florida's Thirteenth Congressional District.[102] (Poor Charlie Crist is running for governor, where he's about to get demolished by DeSantis. Fun fact about Charlie: he's lost in statewide races as a Republican, as a Democrat, and as an independent. If you're going to lose, you might as well lose across the full spectrum.) But Anna is a winner, and she's going to be a member of Congress. And when she gets there, people are going to try to pigeonhole her because she's effective and because she's a Hispanic woman who doesn't think how the Left thinks she should. But she's going to be a difference-maker and a very powerful voice.

I talk to Anna a lot, but we were able to sit down and discuss her last election and what advice she would give to would-be candidates. Anna spoke of her constant battle against social media companies censoring her and her campaign, which she attributes to creating significant hurdles on the campaign trail:

> ***"The problem was with my social media, though. I was, even in my primary, the only candidate that was censored. But I still managed to make it through the primary being censored. Big Tech was preventing me***

102 Kelly Hayes, "Anna Paulina Luna Announces Congressional Bid in FL CD-13," *Florida Politics* (May 4, 2021), https://floridapolitics.com/archives/426475-anna-paulina-luna-announces-congressional-bid/.

> *from posting my fundraising links on different platforms. The only way that I was able to get around this barrier was by working that much harder off social media."*[103]

Anna told me that grassroots was pivotal to being competitive in her race. "I had a really strong grassroots game. If I didn't have that, I would have lost the election, period. And I know that a lot of people say, 'Oh, yeah, you gotta knock on a lot of doors.' But it wasn't just that. It was actual grassroots activism."[104]

As I have written before and Anna echoes, money is vital, and Big Tech worked to cut against her fundraising efforts:

> *"So if I [hadn't been censored] thanks to the help of Big Tech, there's no doubt in my mind that I probably would have been able to raise maybe three times the amount of money. But again, when you're censoring the way that I've been censored, it makes it hard. So what I would tell the candidates who are looking at getting involved is: it's not going to be glamorous work. You really just have to bite the bullet, put in the elbow grease, but also, the name of the game is fundraising."*

I asked Anna if she had reached out to Twitter and Facebook about censorship. She told me:

> *"I have about ten emails back and forth with Twitter and with Facebook and Instagram. Facebook kept telling me that that it was a bug. And then I messaged them, and it finally stopped. But Twitter's really been, I think, my archnemesis in all of this. And what it was and what it is, is that I am the most prominent conser-*

103 Interview with Anna Paulina Luna, December 10, 2020, via phone.

104 Interview with Anna Paulina Luna, December 10, 2020, via phone.

> *vative Hispanic voice in the country. And I happen to be someone who ran for office. And I'm a political commentator, I guess, but my brand as a whole kind of transcends into the activist world. And for my voice to be weaponized, it's a threat to the progressive ideology. So, what I truly believe is that this is suppression of minority voices. I believe that there's no difference between this and segregation, honestly, because of the fact that if you are a minority that's not conservative, you're put on a pedestal. But if you are conservative, you are treated less than and, as someone who ran for office, I mean, they wouldn't verify my account. They were preventing me from running my ads. They were saying that my ads were a danger to the community, which was completely false. There's nothing dangerous about my ads. It's my story about growing up and really what my family went through."*[105]

On an intersectional level, Anna told me that she was a target of criticism by reporters for her Hispanic heritage:

> *"How the media treated me as a whole was reprehensible. I remember I had one reporter tell me the extent of my Hispanic identity because of the fact that I'm lighter skinned, which to me is totally prejudiced. So I think that there's deeply ingrained suppression of minorities within tech and within the progressive ideology, and that's why I was censored."*[106]

As happened in the 2020 election, minorities are leaving the Democrat Party. I asked Anna why she believes this is happening:

105 Interview with Anna Paulina Luna, December 10, 2020, via phone.

106 Interview with Anna Paulina Luna, December 10, 2020, via phone.

"But the only reason that the minority community is leaving the Democrat Party is not because the Republican Party or the Republican Party's messaging, it's because of Trump and the fact that Trump is, like most people, not a politician. And that's deeply respected, at least within the Hispanic community, I can say. Let's talk about something as simple as the mask. No one ever thought that the mask versus anti-maskers would be a political stance. But it has become one because of government overreach. And if you have an entire demographic of people, for example, the Hispanic community, very large families, and you're in somewhere like Philadelphia where you can only have ten people in your home, that's crazy. And so, people as a whole are realizing that even now, when they start to post things that aren't political, for example, mask stuff or complaints about the lockdowns, that they're being censored. And because of that, it's creating a rejection of that narrative by people as a whole, specifically minorities. And in general, I think it's also a generational thing—you have your entire life been told you need to vote a certain type of way, or you see how your community treats you. If you think outside of the box, I think that we are the right type of minority. I wouldn't say that we're the wrong type of minority. I think that people are just realizing now because of the phone access and because of how much we interact with people on a regular basis, whether we realize it or not, that there are more people out there like us and some just shut down mentally simply because of ignorance."[107]

107 Interview with Anna Paulina Luna, December 10, 2020, via phone.

Anna is convinced that without Big Tech interference and had the campaign been run slightly differently, she would have won:

> *"I think that if things had played out a little bit differently, I would have won. What I would have done differently is I would have announced earlier, because, mind you, I only had a two-month election from the primary to the general, and that's two months I was able to still outraise Charlie by several thousand dollars. But he was already sitting on three point something million because he was in a non-contested election for his primary. So I would have gone in earlier so I could fundraise. And I think, now, I'm not saying that politics is closed for me, but I do know for a fact that if and when I do decide to run again, that I know that because of my name ID, which is really the name of an election, that I have a really, really good shot at completely bringing this home. So getting in earlier, this was never symbolic. It was definitely to win. But I think that the message that's resonating with people, especially now during COVID and with everything else that's happened in 2020, is: Do you want your government telling you what to do? And that's really what it's come down to."*[108]

A key takeaway from all of our candidates (especially echoed by our female interviewees) is that you have to put aside fear to run or put yourself out there politically:

> *"When you decide to use your voice, you have to check your feelings at the door. I constantly hear from candidates or people considering running, 'Oh, well, I'm afraid of what they're going to say about me or my family,' or, 'I'm less than perfect.' Well, you're*

108 Interview with Anna Paulina Luna, December 10, 2020, via phone.

> *not expected to be perfect. You're expected to have a backbone. Not callous or rough. But you have to really have a sense of who you are. You have to be able to communicate. You have to be up with tech. So it's not just Facebook, Instagram, or Twitter. It's finding other avenues, for example, like the one thing that got me through my primary when they were literally making stuff up about me. And what I was able to do is I was able to go to my social media and post, 'Hey, this is a lie, here's the truth.' And I was able to directly communicate with the voters. And I actually took that playbook right from President Trump. That's exactly what he does with the American people on his Twitter. And so, I was able to do that. And that really got me through. So I feel like good lines of communication and then definitely going back to the grassroots game, you have to make sure that you can organize and that you can put together events that are outside of the box and really connect with people as to what's happening in their community, but also to the trending topics of the day. So, during the lockdown, they're saying that you can only do political acts rather than day to day. So, I was doing protests instead. And that actually, I think, gave me a strong grassroots game. And I had a ton of protest and protest work, and we protested socialism. We protested a bunch of things. But I was able to move and adapt to the times."*[109]

I tell all of my candidates that in this space, you either adapt or lose. And Anna, learning from her past elections, stands to win big in 2022.

---

109 Interview with Anna Paulina Luna, December 10, 2020, via phone.

Catalina Lauf

I have been working with Catalina Lauf, who is running for Congress in Illinois's Sixteenth District. My firm has been assisting with her social media and messaging, and we have been thrilled to work alongside her as she seeks to bring Illinois values to Washington.[110] If she wins, Catalina stands to be one of the youngest people ever elected to Congress. And just by her candidacy alone, she lends particular insight into running to attract new voters to conservatism and brings a fresh perspective to Washington. She is taking on current representative Adam Kinzinger, who has completely betrayed his voters and the Trump base. His soft conservative values are exposed daily with every appeasement he makes to the Left. Catalina hopes to change that.

With the help of our team, she launched a video to kick off her campaign where she revealed herself to America as a patriot and woman aiming to hit the ground running in Washington. She professed an inclination towards Main Street and holding onto American values in the face of a global landscape hell-bent on gaslighting us into the third world. Her message in that video and since in her social media posts and TV appearances has been raw and real, authentic and passionate.

I spoke with her about her social media strategy and asked her about striking the proper balance of authenticity and how that translates into online behavior. "Social media is a double-edged sword for politicians, as we know," she told me. "There's an opportunity to really unite people, but I do hate how divisive it can be."[111] She gave me an example of how social media can unite people on certain topics. "The scandal going on with Governor Cuomo right now and the Lincoln Project, those two issues are very serious but are

110 Catalina Lauf for Congress 2022, https://www.catalinaforcongress.com/.

111 Interview with Catalina Lauf, February 19, 2021, via phone.

bringing people together towards a pressure campaign that is beyond Republican and Democrat.... It's forcing people to come together on what's basic right and wrong. And I think that without social media, we wouldn't have the ability to find this common ground, find these issues and commentary, and unite behind them."[112] For Catalina, it's also about balance. "I think that there are ways to be more open and to talk about other things that aren't political. I try to post either on Instagram or other platforms. But I try to put things other than politics on social media just for the sake of recognizing that we're all human. People want to see authenticity, and they don't want to just be berated by politics all the time."[113]

Catalina's strategy of authenticity and mix of politics and regular life has been refreshing, and she has been rewarded with follows and engagement. "When it comes to politics, everything right now is total warfare. We are in a culture where we're in political warfare. It's important to fight and push back and to make sure our voices are heard in a way that breaks the PC laws. We have to fight back against the culture warriors. But at the same time, I've made so many friends, digital friends, on social media who are influencers. And strangely, we have found each other because we both like a meditation app, or we both liked the same article...something outside of politics. That is what connects us as people," she says.[114] To her, social media platforms can be unifying. "Sometimes these platforms just turn into a political battlefield, nobody listening to each other. And I think we need to try more to break those artificial barriers and find what unites us aside from the fighting in politics."[115]

Unification is admirable, and for Catalina, finding conservative coalitions has been a hallmark principle of the strategies we employ for our candidates. I asked Catalina about her

---

112 Interview with Catalina Lauf, February 19, 2021, via phone.
113 Interview with Catalina Lauf, February 19, 2021, via phone.
114 Interview with Catalina Lauf, February 19, 2021, via phone.
115 Interview with Catalina Lauf, February 19, 2021, via phone.

efforts to be a unifying force and to build coalition. She told me, "I think a majority of Americans love our country. And it's something that we might have our own ways of wanting to change the world or wanting to make things better here. You go to places like China, or you travel the world, and you see the worst of humanity because they are so driven by this kind of really dog-eat-dog mentality. We live in the greatest country in the world, the most innovative and most capitalistic society. And commerce is supposed to unite our people. Doesn't matter what your political beliefs are, you can change the world with innovation and an open marketplace."[116]

I asked her to self-reflect on her brand and how she pitches herself on social media. "I'm an optimist, and I think it's very hard right now to be a positive force in politics. I always wanted my campaign and who I was and my brand to be positive. And I always wanted to be authentic because I think that politicians have for far too long on both sides of the aisle been so fake and phony and out of touch with the average American."[117] She continued, "I grew up in a really small town. I come from a diverse background that is very different from the average Republican, or at least that's what the media will tell you. We can better message our side that we're actually the most compassionate, we want people to thrive. We want people to be able to build businesses and be whoever they want to be."[118]

Catalina's social media footprint has been rightly credited for her fundraising and gain of followers. I asked her about her strategy and why she thinks social media will play a big role in her campaign's success. "I have so many people now that probably did find me through social media over the last year, that maybe didn't know who I was back when I first ran, and I've kind of built those relationships because

116 Interview with Catalina Lauf, February 19, 2021, via phone.
117 Interview with Catalina Lauf, February 19, 2021, via phone.
118 Interview with Catalina Lauf, February 19, 2021, via phone.

of this networking tool that is Twitter and Instagram. To be successful, you have to have solid commentary on different topics and know where you stand on a variety of issues."[119] Catalina's campaign was kick-started with an ad from our team that was really successful. "I had an ad for my first one that we posted on social media that really kind of made my campaign. Fox News picked it up on Twitter right away, and that's why I got interviews. That's a huge component of social media, too, is literally making people [famous] overnight. It's odd, too, because when you're an athlete and you have, say, five to ten years to build your brand. But when you really become a media sensation overnight, there's a huge mental and emotional component to it."[120] She cautioned would-be candidates, "People lie all the time about me now. But in the public eye, it's an open forum. You have to develop thick skin immediately."[121]

Kimberly Klacik

Kimberly Klacik is a TV commentator and ran for Maryland's Seventh Congressional District in 2020. She is one of the many Republican women standing up to the radical Democrats and breaking norms. She is also actively recruiting many Republican candidates across the country, using the power of social media to help them win. She's been very helpful to Catalina, and I am confident she will use her voice to help other Republican candidates across the country.

Kimberly also knows the power of social media and launched into the national spotlight with an ad that went viral. "The ad idea itself was actually Benny Johnson's idea. He told me that he thought he could take my message and put it into a three-minute ad. It took us about four hours on the hottest day ever, and it cost roughly six thousand dollars. But it was

119 Interview with Catalina Lauf, February 19, 2021, via phone.
120 Interview with Catalina Lauf, February 19, 2021, via phone.
121 Interview with Catalina Lauf, February 19, 2021, via phone.

doing something different. We thought we'd focus on the infrastructure, all the things that we talk about succeeding in my campaign. But we're going to do it while walking around West Baltimore," she said.[122] "But I just decided to wear what I usually wear, what I always have, dresses with the red shoes that day. And we noted the stark contrast between the red dress and heels to these dilapidated homes. [Benny said], it kind of worked."[123] She was stunned by how well the ad came out, though she was saddened by the ultimate message. "That's basically what Baltimore looks like, unfortunately."[124]

It went viral. "I think that in the first seventy-two hours, we raised about two point five million dollars on that ad."[125]

Kim echoed many of our other interviewees that battling it out in the modern political game is a no-holds-barred type of sport. "You got to be kind of tough, but if you're running for office, you've got to be tough and be persuasive."[126]

A key note that I want people to take away from this book is how critical it is to be a team player on the conservative side. There are real issues at stake, and nitpicking each other is unhelpful. Kimberly is a team player. I have seen her campaign for and donate to people and causes she believes in. I asked her about the coalition mindset on the right. "I think that's what the Democrats have over us. We've got to come together to be a team and have a strategy to do this the right way so that we can attack it from all angles. Democrats are really good at getting voters out. And they have people that are team players. We should be supporting each other."[127] She continued, "Obviously, like you were saying earlier, building a brand is important. But I think sometimes you do it at the expense of other conservatives. And so, I will see conservatives fighting on Twitter and think the internal fight was over the

122 Interview with Kimberly Klacik, January 15, 2021, via phone.
123 Interview with Kimberly Klacik, January 15, 2021, via phone.
124 Interview with Kimberly Klacik, January 15, 2021, via phone.
125 Interview with Kimberly Klacik, January 15, 2021, via phone.
126 Interview with Kimberly Klacik, January 15, 2021, via phone.
127 Interview with Kimberly Klacik, January 15, 2021, via phone.

top. But the Democrats love to see that because they could see that we're not together. And we need to stop doing things just for the sake of personal gain. We need to get organized and come together."[128]

Kim is also wary of the Democratic Party's propensity for identity politics. "Your gender or race does not make you qualified for a particular position. That's not how we should be dividing people up. We should look at what they could bring to the table, what their ideas are."[129] She cautioned that Republicans "should not counter [identity politics] with identity politics. I don't think we should play it at all.... We need to talk a little bit more about the fact that we are a big-tent party. We welcome everybody. That would be great."[130]

Kim created a whole new style, and she was a trailblazer. So many of my clients come to me now and ask: "How can we make a Kim Klacik video?"

Scherie Murray

Scherie Murray ran as a Republican for New York's Fourteenth Congressional District in the 2020 election.[131] Congresswoman Alexandria Ocasio-Cortez currently represents the district in Washington.[132] Though a long-shot race, Scherie is another example of someone who launched their candidacy on social media and, through the frenzy and excitement of her ad, garnered millions of followers overnight and raised tons of money. However, Scherie's candidacy was plagued by ineptitude from her consultants. (They didn't even file the paperwork to get her on the ballot.) But I wanted to include her in the book because, yet again, she exhibits the national appetite for

128 Interview with Kimberly Klacik, January 15, 2021, via phone.

129 Interview with Kimberly Klacik, January 15, 2021, via phone.

130 Interview with Kimberly Klacik, January 15, 2021, via phone.

131 Official campaign website for Scherie Murray for Congress, visited December 1, 2020, https://scheriemurray.com/.

132 Official Congressional website for Congresswoman Alexandria Ocasio-Cortez, visited December 1, 2020, https://ocasio-cortez.house.gov/.

new, minority voices within the Republican Party, garnering immediate national attention due to social media.

We sat down for an interview. "Getting the national reception was quite overwhelming. Our campaign was part of a small sliver of other African American conservative candidates who threw their hat into the ring and carried the torch for the party."[133] We have seen an uptick in the number of African American candidates who are running as Republicans. And I asked her how we attract more people of color to the Republican Party.

> *"The Republican Party needs to change its outreach to communities of color and to minority communities by starting to show up and lend a hand at the local pantries for example or coming out to support the local not-for-profit, whether they see a winnable seat or not—just being present is key: you cannot expect someone to vote for you if they don't know who you are. So, if the party doesn't show up, they're never going to garner the vote of the community for which they seek.... I've knocked on doors, and I've knocked on a lot of Democratic doors. And I've had a gun pulled on me. I've had doors slammed in my face. And I have also met some really great people, Democrats who I've reregistered as Republicans. And so, to your question, it's really about getting the work done and delivering those results."*[134]

I asked her about the importance of narrative to winning over voters to the Republican Party:

> *"You have to tell the story from the perspective of someone like myself. When you have elected officials that dominate the seats in local communities,*

133 Interview with Scherie Murray, December 1, 2020, via phone.

134 Interview with Scherie Murray, December 1, 2020, via phone.

> *and they come around and they blame the Republicans for everything that they don't accomplish. And if you hear that every single time, time after time, they've basically succeeded in demonizing our party at the local level. And until the party structure really understands how to connect with communities of color, minority communities, communities that they don't see as winnable seats—Republicans won't win races in a city like New York City. My campaign certainly set a precedent, and that's why you saw campaigns like Kim [Klacik]'s really take that viral moment and take it to the next level. Unfortunately for me, I had some hiccups, but fortunately for Kim, she was able to really demonstrate what that level of support partnered with mobilization on the ground and just that genuine appeal could do to win support within the community. Those markers, I think, have to work in tandem."*[135]

She mentioned missteps in her campaign and being a resource for candidates to learn from others. And I asked her what she would have done differently:

> *"I certainly learned a lot. And I think for every experience, if you don't take away something from it, then it wasn't meaningful. I mentioned that my campaign did almost raise a million dollars, having national support for an African American immigrant straight from Jamaica. It was very humbling. And I'm forever grateful to America and to its citizens for believing in me and my campaign. And it needs to come from everywhere, not us, friends and family. It has to come from the grassroots. But when you really talk about grassroots, you have to talk about voter education, and so, run a campaign to try to educate your commu-*

135 Interview with Scherie Murray, December 1, 2020, via phone.

nity. But, party bosses, party leadership also plays an intricate role that you may be well aware of, that that connection is integral to really making an impact." [136]

The Guys Behind the Scenes

Your team is everything. Any politician or candidate has no future in politics without the proper support behind them. It's like a boxer and their trainer. That's a relationship where if you have a bad trainer, you're not going to be prepared to mount the best fight of your life. (This goes for life as well—some free Alex life lessons for you: you're only as good as who you surround yourself with.)

In Washington, many people work as staffers and have developed sharp skills that give candidates and politicians broad expertise and insights into key issues.

Donald Trump's novel use of social media disrupted politics as usual. Running a lean campaign required guys like Brad Parscale behind the scenes running strong, intelligent digital campaigns that broke through to the voters in ways that traditional campaigns could not. We spoke to Brad for this book and his reflections on their campaign and how they are and will continue to be successful.

It would be impossible to talk about social media and Capitol Hill without talking about and to a guy like Matt Whitlock. Matt was a former staffer to the now-retired Senator Orrin Hatch and helped to curate a voice for him online. Matt is a great example of someone who understood the issues and blended his knowledge of the issues with social media narratives of the time. This permitted Senator Hatch to be on the cutting edge of the conversation either in serious policy narrative or in jest mocking the latest craziness of the

136 Interview with Scherie Murray, December 1, 2020, via phone.

Left. Staffers should emulate guys like Matt if we are to make serious progress in elections going forward.

Another conversation I wanted to have for this book is with Stephen Moore. Stephen puts out a newsletter that every Hill staffer in the Republican House gets that is basically his thoughts on what's happening every day with the economy. And Steve has advised presidential campaigns from Rand Paul to Donald Trump. He's advised many members of Congress. Steve is really wise, and he understands these issues. A lot of people don't understand this, but politicians, at least the good ones, are jacks of all trades—not many are policy experts on a broad range of issues and require staff with a wide knowledge base. When I learned how Washington works, I realized that all these politicians do is vote and voice issues. It's really their legislative and policy teams behind the scenes who call the shots and can make or break your success in office. (Except for Donald Trump. Like most things, he did things a bit differently.)

As I say, the guys behind the scenes make or break you, so as you can imagine, getting the best guys is tough. From the best being gobbled up by top leadership to natural attrition away from Washington, good staff is hard to come by sometimes. What's worse, strategic staffing takes place on the Hill all the time. For example, when new members come to Washington, they have no idea who is good and who isn't, and as I say if they hope to accomplish anything, they have to have people who know the ins and outs of the halls of Congress. So, exploiting their immaturity in terms of Washington politics, a new member might hire a staffer recommended to them by someone who is the antithesis of their policy agenda or aims. In effect, the seasoned member of Congress has a tool within the new member's office. And so, that's how the Swamp grows.

I always tell my clients that you need to have your chief of staff locked in right away. This allows a member to maintain the heading of their office and champion the ideas they claimed to espouse on the campaign trail. There's a lot of bureaucracy, to be sure, but having someone you trust at the head will make for a strong and lasting career. Having someone fresh with your vision is also necessary, as oftentimes career DC staffers will look at the work as more of a job rather than activism. This means that their loyalty is to their mortgage in Washington rather than protecting the economic well-being of the average American.

In terms of the future, conservative groups are organizing to improve staffing for America First leaders, but change is going to take time. Hopefully, cultivating better staffers will lead to more effective politics for us on the right.

What follows are a few conversations I have had with guys who are doing it right on the Hill. Working with these gentlemen has certainly strengthened my approach to social media and my clients and undoubtedly can improve your social media approach as well.

Brad Parscale

Brad Parscale served as a senior advisor to President Trump during his 2016 campaign. He is the brains behind the digital strategy for the president and leveraged social media on behalf of Trump to vault him into the White House despite Hillary Clinton outspending President Trump significantly.

I caught up with Brad during the writing of this book to learn from the best in the game on how to advise candidates and take advantage of social media to achieve electoral success.

"I changed the rules forever," Brad told me.[137] Credited with the digital genius of the Trump campaign and much of the grassroots campaign that originated online, Brad tells me that Facebook has changed the game now to prevent the lightning in the bottle of the Trump campaign from happening again:

137 Interview with Brad Parscale, January 29, 2021, via phone.

> *"Facebook changed the algorithms for videos because I utilized the video so strongly. They even changed how payments were made to someone.... I was the largest digital player in the world in 2016. I spent many millions a month for one hundred million dollars in three months, which was the most play they'd ever seen. The CMO of Facebook said of the campaign that it was the best campaign ever run in the history of the platform. And they started to look and see how I manipulated their algorithms and the things they were doing to get such expansion. But I started with one person, and by the time I had harvested their attention and I harvested forty million people out of the platform, it's our own contest. So they had to really change things because I was running such emotional ads to people. Facebook was allowing us to share our ads that would reach one hundred thousand people for free from all over the world. And so, it just created a visceral experience."*[138]

I asked him about how the Trump campaign went about crafting political messaging and content:

> *"I was testing my creative approach across my audiences to see how they were statistically moving people and then using real-time feedback and programmatic responses to try and tie to efficiency and the release of information. And in doing so, I was efficiently or effectively moving people at a higher rate into our coalition.... I would focus on algorithms geared to determine keywords, key phrases, key elements, key emotional things, the behavioral science, to create an outline of what behavioral science needs to do, then*

138 Interview with Brad Parscale, January 29, 2021, via phone.

create ads that targeted and impacted the audience when looking for the news tied to those ads."[139]

With crackdowns on conservatism and the president himself from social media giants, I asked what's next for political activism online:

"They've got to go direct. They're going to have to spend millions of dollars and build up and go back to mail, email, text. We're going to see phone numbers become more static. I believe we can get people to sign up to groups. And I think that you'll be able to get tens of millions of people in these groups, and the effectiveness of them will work. The problem is that President Trump was almost four years too early for the technology and how some of these platforms are going to merge together.... The new difficulty will be in the apps where harvesting and processing that portion of the politics funnel for Facebook will become more difficult. And then that political process, however, will also be difficult for the Democrats. So they'll have the same growth problem. So that's why I believe right now the most important thing, and I'm trying to launch this, is a grassroots initiative to keep the forty-seven million people we already have on the 'list' to continue to grow and collect that personal information to reach our voters."[140]

Some of the work that Brad and others are doing in aggregating contacts on the right is hugely helpful going forward despite what Trump decides to do in 2024:

"We continue to grow, and once we reach a critical mass, I could fund large-scale advertising.... We only spent

139 Interview with Brad Parscale, January 29, 2021, via phone.
140 Interview with Brad Parscale, January 29, 2021, via phone.

> *a few million dollars on persuasion. And building and finding out the user base was then matching them across all platforms by…emails and their phone numbers. And we got millions and millions and tens of millions in front of us…. If you have a grassroots movement with a leader, a platform's not the problem. Censorship is always going to be an issue. But once you can go direct, no matter the censorship, you have somebody saying we're going to somewhere else."*[141]

We touched a bit on the 2020 campaign. Brad notes that the COVID-19 epidemic sank the campaign and noted that all indicators prior to COVID-19 pointed to a huge victory for President Trump. However, Parscale added that Trump could have won in 2020 with a single viral moment: "I have to say a bit critically, I think if you stick with the data, you don't have to say you made a mistake. But if you write about his loss, it comes down to one simple line: if he had walked out of a hospital, looked at the camera, starts a little bit, get teary-eyed, and said 'the whole force of this government is behind you. And I'm going to try to save as many lives as I can.' If that's on tape, he wins."[142]

Which was a bit surprising because Parscale notes how much the president works the media. As many suspected, Trump knows how the media works and played them like a fiddle. "The funnel of information online doesn't control the media narrative. But they pay attention. So it's what the president was doing on Twitter. He wasn't talking to his people. He was talking to the media…. I thought there were times where we really needed to change the media narrative. And so, I would post things that sometimes people don't want to post that it was almost better to have the media talking about

141 Interview with Brad Parscale, January 29, 2021, via phone.
142 Interview with Brad Parscale, January 29, 2021, via phone.

something I did to overshadow some stupid thing the president did. And so that was useful for a national campaign."[143]

Looking to the future, Brad says, "What's really going to happen in the next few years is complicating messaging. They'll decentralize the communication among conservatives. I think it's going to go away like Bitcoin. [Big Tech is] going to decentralize the communication ability."[144]

Matt Whitlock

Matt understands trends. He reads Twitter. He gets what issues are popular and understands the best way to get the message out. He is particularly good at building online friends (and offline), and those friendships build a collective wall of support for the ideas he champions, which are frankly those that serve the American people the best, in my view.

I caught up with the former communications director for now-retired Senator Orrin Hatch from Utah. As I said, he is the brain behind the ingenious communications plan of translating Senator Hatch's quirkiness and humor into the social media age. Although he expressed a tremendous amount of humility when I asked him about his role crafting Senator Hatch's "brand" online: "I have an advantage with [Senator] Hatch. He already had a good sense of humor, a great personality, and an established brand. And I could build out and mold around issues of the day and the fights of the day."[145]

I asked him what advice he would give to his younger self:

> ***"My guidance to younger communications staffers on the Hill or even just conservatives rolling up their sleeves in this fight is everyone needs to find their voice and find what makes their perspective valuable in the conversation of the day. [For Senator Hatch],***

143 Interview with Brad Parscale, January 29, 2021, via phone.

144 Interview with Brad Parscale, January 29, 2021, via phone.

145 Interview with Matt Whitlock, November 17, 2020, via phone.

> *we were able to pinpoint issue areas of leadership for him based on his experience and his career. And we were able to use that with bits of his personality and his sense of humor and things that he liked to really make that work. And so, the value of establishing that foundational voice is good. You can comment on news of the day—that's something that like a [Senator] Ted Cruz does really effectively now so when there's a cultural discussion happening, he can weigh in and rally more people to his cause because they see that he's more well-rounded than just the narrow issues that they might see him discussing on C-SPAN. And so, looking for opportunities to round out that brand, the issues that they're working on and engaging on, I think it's really valuable."*[146]

I asked Matt if and how he could replicate the work he had done for Senator Hatch for other members of Congress on the Republican side:

> *"I do think that that could be replicated. And members of Congress and political leaders and just regular people start to consider what they're using social media and political communications tools for, or you're trying to reach as many people as possible. And not every single person is going to like every message that you have to say. But for us and for [Senator] Orrin Hatch to be able to build an audience that included younger people, he would have young people come up to him in the street in Utah and say, 'Hey, I don't agree with everything you say, but I enjoy following you because you have a fresh personality online, and you make the political debates of the day more accessible.' To me, that felt like an accomplishment. It felt like we*

146 Interview with Matt Whitlock, November 17, 2020, via phone.

could take debates from the halls of Congress that are a little bit stuffy and perhaps distant or abstract from normal people and help kind of break them down and make them easier for a normal person to engage with. And that's really been a big, long-term focus of mine, because I think that what the Left has done effectively is mobilize a larger base online where the conversation is happening, and it allows them to amplify more quickly. And they basically have an echo chamber between the media and their footprint on social media being mobilized very quickly. And so, for conservatives to compete in the messaging wars of the day, we have to be able to mobilize more quickly around simpler messaging. That's something that I think we try to model early on. But I think in a lot of cases we found good success, particularly during Supreme Court confirmation battles, during the #governmentshutdown a few years ago. That in itself was exclusively a PR and messaging war. And even more recently, when we've had these large debates over coronavirus relief, when we're able to explain why what they're doing is wrong and what we're doing is right in the simplest way possible. I think we're able to rally people who are close and, in the end, affect a good outcome, because when there's a major national clamor, this is a part of how the CARES Act[147] passed earlier this year when Democrats tried to block it. [Speaker of the House] Nancy Pelosi came up with an outrageous list of demands that included things like every airline needs to publish their carbon emissions for each individual flight. It was so crazy that when we blew that up and got national media attention on that, rank-

147 CARES Act, H.R. 748, https://www.congress.gov/bill/116th-congress/house-bill/748/actions.

> *and-file Democrats were so embarrassed they dropped that proposal and agreed to the CARES Act without any changes, really from what Republicans had proposed. So that is an example of winning messaging wars, one simple fight and one simple message at a time."*[148]

Matt Whitlock told me that their work in the National Republican Senate Committee has evolved since the 2020 general elections and that the average voter is concerned about the direction of the country and the Democratic Party:

> *"One thing that we learned ahead of the November 3rd general elections across the country is that normal voters, independent voters, and even moderate Republicans and moderate Democrat voters have very strong concerns about the overall direction of the Democratic Party. It started with socialism but has really gone far beyond that. And so, we have seen whether it was Theresa Greenfield,*[149] *an Iowa Senate candidate, Sara Gideon*[150] *in Maine, Cal Cunningham*[151] *in North Carolina; they stood for much more liberal policies, and their voters really weren't prepared for it. We focused really hard on highlighting their positions that were out of the mainstream. In the end, I think voters decided that they did not want to move that drastically to the left. We have that same model ready to follow in Georgia, where Jon [Ossoff]*[152] *ran a much more moderate campaign for the [Georgia] Sixth District in 2017.*[153] *Now that he's running statewide, he's talking about a public option plan, which is a*

148 Interview with Matt Whitlock, November 17, 2020, via phone.

149 Theresa Greenfield for Iowa, https://greenfieldforiowa.com/.

150 Sara Gideon for Maine, https://saragideon.com/.

151 Cunningham for U.S. Senate, https://www.calfornc.com/.

152 Jon Ossoff U.S. Senate, https://electjon.com/.

153 "Georgia Election Results: Handel Defeats Ossoff in U.S. House Race," *New York Times* (June 21, 2017), https://www.nytimes.com/elections/results/georgia-congressional-runoff-ossoff-handel.

> *Trojan horse to socialized medicine. He's talking about how funding for police departments should be on the line, things that some voters soundly reject across the country. Raphael Warnock[154] has a lot of comments on the record from his career that show that he's very far out of the mainstream. Following the model that we established ahead of general election around the country, we see a baseline strategy of making sure people know that these two Democrat candidates are not your grandparents' Democratic Party and Chuck Schumer's radical 'change America' party."[155]*

I asked Matt what has happened to the Democratic Party and how this impacts down-ballot Republicans:

> *"We discovered in this election cycle that offensive messaging against your opponents, nationalizing them and tying them to national Democrats, helps. For messaging focused on your own candidate, our messaging is really focused on local and I think that one thing that has really helped this clash of incumbents be able to understand what is mainstream and understand where their voters are ideologically at any given time; for example, [Senator] Susan Collins has a better understanding of the pulse of voters in Maine than anybody else, probably in the history of the state. And I think you could say the same thing for [Senator] Joni Ernst of Iowa. These senators have spent so much time with their constituents, really hearing what they care about, so they hear people saying, [defunding the] police really scares me, they hear people saying they don't like the idea of packing the courts. Sounds like a terrible idea. I don't like that. And so, they have sort of a built-in sounding board*

154 Reverend Raphael Warnock U.S. Senate, https://warnockforgeorgia.com/.

155 Interview with Matt Whitlock, November 17, 2020, via phone.

for their actual constituents. Whereas Democrats have spent a lot more time listening to what people are saying on social media. I think an incredible example of this is look at the last presidential campaign and how many large policy decisions they made based on what people were saying on Twitter. I think you have to have that, really engage closely with your constituents so what their priorities are and how to make sure your work is reflected. But if you show them that their opinion matters to you, it is playing a role in the way that you represent them. I think there's a lot of value there. And so, I do think that that's one advantage Republican candidates have."[156]

Though Matt concedes that conservatives have an uphill battle with the media sometimes: "I wish the media would treat [conservative wins] with a bit more well-rounded coverage and reaction than just reporting on the public reaction. But I do think we've gotten a lot better at mobilizing than we were before. I think we've still got a long way to go, but I think that we are on our way."[157] Matt proposed a different strategy that I agree is 100 percent correct. "Conservatives can do better figuring out how to work effectively with the media. Even with adversarial media outlets, I think becoming better judges of what is good faith in what is seen working with the media when they're working with political leaders and political sides. I think there's a lot of times where we mistake negative coverage that we don't like with our side and sometimes in making negative comments that we deserve."[158]

Overall, Matt is hopeful about the future of the conservative movement: "I think we've got a bright future. Conservatives have figured out a lot of things, and they're still going to keep learning a lot of things. But we look at the House

156 Interview with Matt Whitlock, November 17, 2020, via phone.
157 Interview with Matt Whitlock, November 17, 2020, via phone.
158 Interview with Matt Whitlock, November 17, 2020, via phone.

races, and when you look at our current Senate makeup and the coalition building behind them, I think we've got a lot to feel optimistic about."[159]

Stephen Lawson

Former communications director to Florida Governor Ron DeSantis and Senator Kelly Loeffler and current president of Battleground Strategies, Stephen Lawson, gave his account of working behind the scenes:

> *"I started my career at a boutique research/communications firm with some of the guys who worked for Rick Scott's first gubernatorial campaign. And they really focused on opposition research and really finding and identifying the vulnerabilities and other candidates, and really finding and creating narratives and synergies to kind of go after an opponent, whether it was the actual opponent or some tangential thing that we wanted to try to get to. So that's sort of my genesis in terms of getting into politics, is understanding how lethal and how potent information can be and the ability to shape and craft and create and utilize that research, that information to one's advantage."*[160]

I asked him to talk me through some examples of strategic remessaging and crafting narratives that beat back the Left.

> *"One of the areas for DeSantis was the environment. Republicans for so long have just let the Democrats win on the issue. But [Governor DeSantis] flipped the script on that narrative and shifted that paradigm in terms of: here's somebody who is going to be an effective steward for the environment, who's*

159 Interview with Matt Whitlock, November 17, 2020, via phone.
160 Interview with Stephen Lawson, June 2, 2021, via phone.

> *going to be a smart conservationist, who's going to really go out and message and fight to clean our water, to clean our air. And in a state like Florida, it is paramount.... He pushed back on that conventional wisdom that Republicans have to take a backseat to Democrats on the environment."*[161]

He also gave an example from working on Senator Loeffler's campaign:

> *"The most poignant example was her basketball team. She was a co-owner of the WNBA team the Atlanta Dream. And the league decided that they were going to force this league-wide initiative to give financial contributions to BLM. And I think that didn't sit well with Kelly. I know that it didn't sit well with our team because, your readers and we all know what the organization stands for, but that the organization is very different from the statement that Black Lives Matter. Of course, every African American life matters, but this organization is so divisive and has supported things like defunding the police and abortion. (And, as you know, obviously, their now-disgraced CEO has resigned because it was a total grifting operation.) But on the campaign trail, we decided to stand up and say something that as a co-owner of a basketball team, she didn't feel like the league should be standing for an organization like that. She stood up and spoke out and, unsurprisingly, the media, the Left, the league, everybody came after her. She has been completely vindicated in what she said. And she got a lot of respect and encouragement and support from both conservatives and independents who said, you're right, we need less, not more politics and*

161 Interview with Stephen Lawson, June 2, 2021, via phone.

> *sports. But we also need people like you who aren't afraid to stand up and say something about it, who aren't afraid to stand up and say no. As a team owner, we should be standing for the national anthem. We should be standing for the flag. We should not be standing for divisive political organizations. And our sports people are tired, and people are sick of it. I think that that ultimately was one of the reasons she ended up winning the primary. But she didn't do it and we didn't do it because it was the politically expedient thing to do. She got a lot of backlash for it, but she did it because it was the right thing to do and somebody needed to step up and say something about it, and that's why she did it."*[162]

I asked for some inside baseball of the behind-the-scenes strategy sessions, what they look like and the focus that's required:

> *"It's March of 2020. Kelly and her husband, he being chairman of the stock exchange, her, being in fintech and having come from that world from the New York Stock Exchange, she obviously has to go through tons of rigorous transparency in terms of filings and procedures related to her finances.... When she came into office, any of the positions that either her or her husband had were managed by a third-party manager, and had to be filed and submitted through the Senate Ethics Committee, and that's sort of the back story. The Daily Beast, a glorified left-wing blog, published these filings and concocted this total conspiracy theory and ended up calling Kelly's office, I think at like nine o'clock at night or something ridiculous. And then with this conspiracy theory based on a few trades*

162 Interview with Stephen Lawson, June 2, 2021, via phone.

that Kelly's investment manager made, they obviously publish the story without confirming any of this information that they have, verifying any of it, getting a comment, anything. So they published a story like thirty minutes later and then wall to wall, it is picked up by the mainstream media on social media, as a matter of fact, blindly without stopping or asking any questions. And it just went viral. We are sitting there, scrambling, knowing none of this is true.

But it's also very complicated. And, we're not going to say anything that is going to be factually inaccurate because that would just make the situation worse. So we put out a statement later that night basically refuting the claims, but it didn't stop the mainstream media. The next morning, we got to work compiling the facts and trying to factually show why this bogus narrative that The Daily Beast had concocted was totally wrong. For the next few weeks, [there were] hours and hours of conference calls with lawyers putting together fact sheets on exactly the nature of the trades and exactly what happened and why neither Kelly nor her husband had any knowledge of any of these transactions.... But we know that the mainstream media and the corporate media aren't going to stop. They're going to continue to just recirculate these bogus claims. But I said we've got to continue with our head down, putting out the facts, exposing why they're wrong. Because when this comes out that Kelly is vindicated when it comes out that neither she nor her husband have done anything wrong, we will have created a narrative arc, and we will be able to say, I told you so. And it was there were a lot of long days....

But the mainstream media once again looked like a bunch of clowns.... We as conservatives, when we see this misinformation that the Left is pushing and that the corporate media is just taking as fact, we've got to be more aggressive in pushing back on some of those narratives quickly."[163]

Stephen Moore

I sat down with Stephen Moore, author of *Trumponomics*, co-founder of Club for Growth, and economic advisor during President Trump's 2016 campaign.[164] Stephen's been in politics for twice as long as I've been alive. People come to him from all over the political spectrum for his advice and counsel, as he is the predominant expert on the Hill for economics. You don't stay relevant in Washington for as long as he has if you're not respected or taken seriously. He co-founded Club for Growth, which is one of the most influential super PACs in the nation. Every Republican member interviews during their candidacy, begging them for their highly coveted endorsement.

Talking to Stephen was like talking to a sage and economics professor at the same time. For example, I spoke with him about the importance of narrative, and this was his response, "There's an old saying, we think with our heads, but the music is within our hearts. And that's a problem because people vote with their hearts, not their brains. [Republicans] don't tell stories, and that's a failing of our movement as we use statistics and [those on the left] tell stories."[165]

I asked for examples of areas where Republicans need to tell better stories and where we succeeded the past few years but didn't necessarily translate into successful political messaging.

163 Interview with Stephen Lawson, June 2, 2021, via phone.

164 Interview with Stephen Moore, December 15, 2020, via phone.

165 Interview with Stephen Moore, December 15, 2020, via phone.

"This economic nationalism is something, I prefer to call it putting America first, it's a sound and sane and sensible backdrop. It's absurd to me that the Left doesn't agree with that. They really believe in a multilateral global kind of approach to problems. And we believe you solve problems at home and local government in your state government and under national governments, but not in a global way. That's just not practical, and it's not constitutional," he said. "It's contrary to American ideals. I believe that the Republican Party has shifted in favor of Republican government. Now, the Republican Party is the party of small business, Democrats are clearly the party of big corporate America. Republicans are the party of the little guy of the working class, and the Democrats are the party of the very rich and the very poor.... We need to be the party that fights for working-class, blue-collar workers. And we need solidarity with that because this is a middle-class country. And that's a point that really emphasized Americans are with Trumpism, which has also turned away from the neocon idea of America as a global police force."[166]

Even before Biden took office, Stephen expressed grave concerns, many of which have borne out in this administration. "A lot of people voted for Biden thinking everything's going to be just fine. They're in for a rude awakening. The Left has taken over every nook and cranny of our government. This is not going to be a moderate administration. It's going to be a far-left, radical agenda. And the only thing that's holding up the economy and the stock market now is that investors believe that Republicans, through checks and balances, will prevent them from doing what they want to do."[167] He's been exactly right. Joe Biden himself has vowed to be one of the most progressive presidents in history.

As states across the country struggle with high taxes, high fuel prices, low wage growth, battling for people to go back to

166 Interview with Stephen Moore, December 15, 2020, via phone.

167 Interview with Stephen Moore, December 15, 2020, via phone.

work rather than living off endless government checks, I am still struck by how smart one of Stephen's remarks was: "It's a very simple concept. Never do something for someone that they can do for themselves. That's a very wise doctrine to live by. Charity is necessary, but you're not being charitable by doing something for someone that they can do for themselves. It's the teach a man to fish."[168]

168 Interview with Stephen Moore, December 15, 2020, via phone.

Chapter 4:
THE MOVEMENTS

SOCIAL MEDIA MOVEMENTS ARE incredibly important to the direction of our country and have realigned politics, in many cases, permanently. The world before social media is unrecognizable both in its politics and mechanics of how politics get done today. And there is no turning back. Movements, even those in recent months, have led to legislation, corporate refocus and restructuring, firings and hirings, changed the way we speak, changed the way people think, and examined the very fabric of this country. Knowledge of how movements work, who the players are, and how to create a movement are essential learning if Republicans hope to be successful in maintaining the culture that we love and cherish.

Sometimes (all the time) what passes for fact on social media and triggers social change requires serious scrutiny by conservatives. Republicans need to do a better job understanding what is real and what is inflated and manipulated instead of reacting knee-jerk to any movement. While I normally counsel being timely and reactive, for movements, conservatives need to wait for the facts to come out and sniff out leftist ideologues masquerading with good intentions in a movement. What I like to say is that the Democrats were on the wrong side of the civil rights movement, and to rectify this, they turn every little cultural moment into a civil rights movement. March for Our Lives, climate change, Black Lives Matter, you name it, all of these movements that, despite the merits or lack thereof of the underlying situation that precipitated them, have become literally "the greatest threat to democracy." They'll leverage these local moments into national movements, and Republicans typically fall victim to or play into their game.

In addition to playing defense, conservatives have to play offense. Championing a movement, leveraging its success, members, and momentum is vital to creating wholesale change. And unlike in the past with gradual change, seizing on the speed of a movement can make significant and swift change. Some take these opportunities for substantial societal progress, some latch on for personal or financial gain, and others just enjoy the ride of chaos. It's every bit as important to know who is along for the ride as it is to know where you are going.

Lately, these movements have been catastrophic for conservatism and Republicanism. The Right has failed to either craft narratives that gain a large enough following for substantial change or have failed in the instruments of success such as utilizing free media, organic growth, or lack the fortitude to push beyond basic barriers to entry. Republicans, at least elected ones, are often timid, weak, and afraid of being shouted down or receiving bad press. The Right also faces a unique challenge in the face of social media giants and tech companies who have demonstrated a willingness to censor and curb conservative speech and growth through their algorithms and speech police (more on this later in Chapters 9 and 10). The Democrats get away with a lot because they have the media and every institution in the system on their side, whereas Republicans lack institutional support.

These movements organize under hashtags that are on their face, irrefutable: #BlackLivesMatter, #MarchForOurLives. To better understand these movements and hashtags, I am going to highlight for you how these movements translated from simple hashtags into global movements through strategic uses, users, language, and timing.

You likely recognize well-executed leftist movements like #MarchForOurLives, the movement for unencumbered gun control after the Parkland school shooting, or the #MeToo movement, which led to the canceling of men guilty or accused of sexual harassment or assault. And also movements and pseudo-organizations like Antifa or #BLM/Black Lives Matter who act like go-betweens among organizations, movements, and as Joe Biden would say, its own ideology. These movements have made a profound impact on our society in many cases for the worse, and the Right needs to be better at constructing and championing movements unless we are comfortable watching the civil society and world we know disappearing into leftist chaos.

#MarchForOurLives exposed some of the timidity of some Republicans. Elected officials sat on their hands and got bulldozed. The leftists found children, and Twitter helped amplify their social media accounts. The media gave them twenty-four-hour news cycles. They had meetings with all of the major politicians. They had President Obama, now-President Biden, and different celebrities in their corner. Meanwhile, Republicans sat idly by wondering what happened.

That was until we started platforming people like Andrew Pollack, Hunter Pollack, and Kyle Kashuv. We will hear more from them later in this chapter, but I will just say here that I often tell people they and President Trump single-handedly saved the Second Amendment. I and others spent the time after the Parkland shooting getting the facts and learning what actually happened (it's always amazed me how quickly the leftist media can find child spokespeople for leftist talking points and how slowly they find the underlying facts of these crucial moments in our history). So, while our counter movement was slow—fact-finding takes time—we were more effective from a policy-making standpoint. But perhaps we were not as effective at disseminating the counternarrative. It's nasty business, but sometimes we have to play their game, and the Republicans have to get in the ring.

From educating our children to the lack thereof during the coronavirus, movements and narratives that disseminate information do so quicker than ever before, and conservatives have to be prepared to provide a cohesive counternarrative, or society will take what the Left says as undisputed fact.

What follows are a few movements and moments that I believe expose some of the countervailing narratives that the Left has pushed out to the public. Education has been a battle for centuries, but in the digital age, the access and streamlined uniformity of the Left has reached unprecedented levels. At all levels of education, there are ridiculous narratives that are taught to our children (countless to name, so I will highlight a few). I also wanted to discuss the Parkland shooting, which serves as a case study in the leftist response to school shootings. I spoke with men who embody the very spirit and intellectual tenacity necessary among conservatives for responding to a rabid Left. I address the COVID-19 pandemic and the many narratives espoused by the Left and put out to the American people that resulted in needless job loss, hysteria, and damage to our institutions and children.

Where the Right has had some success, I will try to highlight those aspects that were well executed and people and techniques that created real, effective change. There is lots of work to be done because, as you will see, left-wing organizations have the backing of social media companies and, therefore, benefit tremendously from having a stronger and less encumbered microphone.

Education

The culture war starts in the classroom. You get indoctrinated at a really young age. And I like to applaud my friends at Turning Point USA for acknowledging this and taking the fight there. They have been effective at pushing back at movements in college and high schools, and I appreciate that because I've been subjected to liberal indoctrination my whole life. I got to the point where I really hated school. I had history teachers who were just raging leftists and taught their deranged philosophy rather than the past. When I was in sixth grade, I remember sourcing a Fox News article, and my teacher got mad at me and would not grade my assignment because she said Fox News wasn't a real news source. I'm not alone, and trust me, if you experienced the same thing, you're not alone either. This has been happening nationwide.

We need to combat it. Nothing in this playbook will be effective without addressing the role of education and what future generations are learning now in the classroom. The battlefield over what our kids are learning and use as their educational foundation when engaging with real issues is a problem when those fundamental building blocks are flawed, incorrect, or overly stilted towards a political philosophy wholly inconsistent or at odds with a realistic engagement with the modern world.

Republicans need to get into the mindset of "Why would the Left stop doing these things if they're never going to face repercussions?" Republicans like to complain, but the dirty little secret is that Republicans raise more money out of fear and anger than they do when they actually legislate and lead. It's a terrible thing. So, it's hard for them to justify making constructive moves when being in the peanut gallery in the classroom is more efficient for them to retain power than taking an active role in removing leftist craziness from our students' curriculum.

I hope you read this book and start helping elect Republicans with guts because education, as it has been for decades now, is not worth defending. Let's start with the universities. Universities are a breeding ground for a lot of the soft PC culture that we live in today and the radical leftist culture. It's been like that for a long time, but in terms of the speed that social media has expanded this off the quad and into corporate America, five years ago, we were laughing about the safe spaces that the social justice warrior kids whined about. Now, these kids have graduated and joined the payroll of Twitter and Facebook and have created safe spaces to block out opposing opinions.

For years now, college campuses have boxed out conservative speakers from Ann Coulter to Ben Shapiro, fires, riots, you name it. Even Tomi Lahren was so dangerous (!) that she got kicked off campus at Clemson.

It's a terrible thing that's happening in this country, and it's because of these universities. And so, what are the Republicans doing about it? Nothing. And there are many easy solutions here. And it's called slashing their endowments, financially punishing these institutions, stop allowing them to be considered nonprofits, strip their nonprofit status. There's no reason that they should have a nonprofit status when they're charging the rates that they're charging, bankrupting a generation, and then teaching them to blame the one percent for their problems so that useless degrees go to waste.

I want to give Congressman Madison Cawthorn some credit. He recently helped to pass a piece of legislation that gives veterans the opportunity to use some of their G.I. Bill money to learn a new trade or skill instead of going to college. This is a really important fight. But the only way that we can really take on the schools and stop this liberal indoctrination is one, to stop teaching our kids that going to school is the only way to be successful, and two, to financially punish these universities that don't permit all viewpoints.

What do I mean by indoctrination? Over the past few years, the public relations teams for socialism and communism have been working overtime. According to Gallup, Millennials and Gen Zers express a nearly 50 percent positive view of socialism while capitalism has taken a sharp decline among the same generations, down from 66 percent in 2010 to 51 percent a little less than a decade later.[169] A generation of students is being indoctrinated with left-wing propaganda and conditioned to either be silent in the face of a radical, vocal minority or worse, joining the crazies, being openly hostile to different viewpoints.

On the ground, this is a reality for a lot of students. I spoke with conservative influencer CJ Pearson about what his generation faces now on college campuses. He told me, "It's a hell of a lot easier being at the University of Alabama. But the stories I hear from so many other kids at Ivy League schools and other public schools: it's insane. They say to me that they will hide their conservatism in papers, that they pretend to be liberal. Then they can get a good grade. We're not paying professors to be political parties; we're paying them to be teachers and educators."[170] I hear these stories every day. It's so commonplace now that it's predictable. You know that your teachers, administrators, and employers likely lean left or are vocally left, so you have to police your speech, thoughts, and actions to avoid repercussions or demerits. None of that is true in the inverse.

Leftist campuses have become dangerous to the conservative agenda. The scary thing is college campuses are where a lot of the narratives we see played out in society are crafted. I spoke with former President of the Florida Senate Mike

---

169 Lydia Saad, "Socialism as Popular as Capitalism Among Young Adults in U.S.," Gallup (November 25, 2019), https://news.gallup.com/poll/268766/socialism-popular-capitalism-among-young-adults.aspx.

170 Interview with CJ Pearson, December 15, 2020, via phone.

Haridopolos and author of *10 Big Issues Facing Our Generation* who echoed how leftist campuses have become and how dangerous this is to the conservative agenda. He knows how important it is to win the narrative war:

> ***"College campuses are where a lot of the narratives are crafted and implemented in a lot of these young people's minds through these college professors. That's going to be a long-term fight. I don't see that turning around any time soon. And I think the Trump administration has done a pretty solid job of recognizing that and trying to move some people away from colleges that they don't think have to go there, whether it's apprenticeship opportunities, trade schools, you name it." [171] Over time, when these young people enter the workforce, the delusions of college professors are implemented.***

In my conversations and in the interviews conducted for this book, I have not seen much evidence to suggest this is turning around any time soon. And while I think the Trump administration did a pretty solid job of recognizing the danger on college campuses and giving people a lifeboat with emphasis on apprenticeship opportunities and trade schools, there is a lot of work to be done in one, recognizing the threat and two, addressing it head-on.

Education expert and CEO of CLT Exam, an alternative to the SAT and ACT, Jeremy Wayne Tate,[172] expressed to me his concerns with the direction of education. "Students are not being taught what capitalism is. And this all goes back to the classics. Nobody's been taught the Reformation. Taught about the merits of capitalism. It's the least selfish economic system. It's the only economic system that rewards people for solving other people's problems. You think of a product or service

---

171 Interview with Mike Haridopolos, December 10, 2020, via phone.

172 Jeremy Wayne Tate (@JeremyTate41), Twitter, https://twitter.com/jeremytate41?s=21.

to make things better for somebody else, and the market's going to reward you. That's not how capitalism is presented or taught altogether. It's dismissed as greedy," he said.[173] This is only concerning so far as conservatives have grown accustomed to this being the predominant view for young people and changing when kids become adults. We have seen this time and again as foundational principles are briefly dismissed in college and then returned to afterward when real-world responsibility returns. The difference is, there is not that foundation nor are students returning to conservatism after college. David Spady, a media and public relations consultant, expressed that "if you look at the application of how people's worldviews are formed in their youth, which we'd expect will change over time as they begin to pay taxes or have certain responsibilities, they take on roles as parents that may change their views of the world. But instead, they're starting with that view of the world, and they're having to undo, unwind that. So when you look at our education system, public school education system, it's synonymous with the values of the Left, a sort of groupthink."[174] And when there is a predominant monoculture coming out of culture, there is serious concern that reversing or undoing this becomes borderline impossible. "It's almost like a mob mentality in line with the thinking of the elitists of the culture, your Hollywood types, and your education establishment. There's a groupthink in the elitist popular spaces that if you're outside of that, you're not part of the program. And so, it's almost a peer pressure thing. And that affects younger people differently than older people. Peer pressure is a bigger dynamic with young people. So, it's done maybe in subtle ways with entertainment. The progressives have figured out a way to influence impressionable younger people better than conservatives have. And they do that through entertainment."[175]

173 Interview with Jeremy Wayne Tate, January 12, 2021, via phone.

174 Interview with David Spady, December 7, 2020, via phone.

175 Interview with David Spady, December 7, 2020, via phone.

Like many of my other interviewees, *Trumponomics* author, Stephen Moore, expressed that education is largely to blame for the voter movement to the left: "This has been a pretty pampered generation that hasn't really had to deal with hardship. I think that they believe prosperity just happened, so they take it as a natural course of events, but it's not. Liberals in general place a much higher premium on things like security over liberty and freedom. And that's problematic because it is freedom and free markets that lead to prosperity."[176] He correctly notes that the battle for the classroom is key to long-term prosperity: "We are now paying a high price for letting this liberal organization spend six hours a day with our kids. And I'm talking about the teachers unions. And that indoctrination is really now doing substantial damage. We're seeing a whole generation of kids who know nothing about American history, nothing about economics or finance or history. And Americans appreciating America just doesn't exist with a lot of millennials."[177]

The lack of emphasis on basic civic education is partly to blame. Polls repeatedly show the average immigrant to our country knows more about basic civics than the average American. There was a great video from a few years ago where a Fox News reporter walked around New York asking people to name a Supreme Court justice, and the answers were... something. Jeremy Tate told me that "the total breakdown in teaching basic civics, constitutional knowledge, and understanding of America's founding is concerning. That's really the basis of whether a student is grounded and understanding the Constitution of America as the greatest document for a system of government in the history of the world that ensured more freedom to more people."[178] He also cautions that we should stop being shy about this. "It's fine to tell kids about Amer-

176 Interview with Stephen Moore, December 15, 2020, via phone.
177 Interview with Stephen Moore, December 15, 2020, via phone.
178 Interview with Jeremy Wayne Tate, January 12, 2021, via phone.

ican history. All of it. But if you don't have basic grounding for American exceptionalism because the Constitution is exceptional and accepting of the very best ideas about government from the Enlightenment, then we will have an entire generation of students who lack the fundamentals in how to maximize human freedom."[179] As Winston Churchill once said, "Those who fail to learn from history are condemned to repeat it."[180]

Narrative in education is especially important now more than ever. And narrative is something the Left has been fighting to win in education for quite some time. It's not too long ago that liberals told us that money in education was the problem, that conservatives were being racist and dismissive of minority communities by withholding funding or fighting funding to school districts with minority majorities. Yet, as history played out, cash infusions into troubled school districts did little to improve test scores and educational outcomes. In fact, conservatives resorting to their principles, those of limited government and self-determination, found solutions in providing alternatives to failing schools rather than paying for failures.

We are currently seeing a fierce battle playing out in public education nationwide regarding critical race theory. The flawed theory is that "racial inequality is woven into legal systems and negatively affects people of color in their schools, doctors' offices, the criminal justice system and countless other parts of life."[181] The idea being America is a fundamentally flawed and deeply racist nation so much so that it is actually "systemic." While teaching our kids to be critical thinkers is important, teaching kids as young as kindergarten that our

179 Interview with Jeremy Wayne Tate, January 12, 2021, via phone.

180 Winston Churchill, Speech to the House of Commons 1948, as quoted by the International Churchill Society, Oct. 21, 2018, https://winstonchurchill.org/resources/in-the-media/churchill-in-the-news/folger-library-churchills-shakespeare/.

181 Marisa Iati, "What Is Critical Race Theory, and Why Do Republicans Want to Ban It in Schools?" *Washington Post* (May 29, 2021), https://www.washingtonpost.com/education/2021/05/29/critical-race-theory-bans-schools/.

nation is systemically racist is wholly untrue, intellectually dishonest, and strange public policy. America has flaws, sure, but educating on solely our weaknesses and not our strengths can only result in young people thinking that if the system is fundamentally flawed, we need to destroy the entire structure, which would have devastating consequences for the United States and our children and our children's children.

Likewise, during the age of coronavirus, conservatives have actually seen some success in seeking alternative narratives from a leftist regime preaching the successes of public education. The Left, with unions who are largely responsible for our kids being out of schools for months beyond the actual threat to their health and safety from COVID-19, is deeply afraid of threats to an institution like public schools they wholly control and can use to indoctrinate children. Jeremy Tate put it well when he said, "Public education may be beyond recovery, may be beyond saving. There is this exodus. There is a renaissance of classical education across the whole school world. Catholic school enrollment is actually up as is enrollment in new charter schools. There are great things happening in charter schools and classical schools and Catholic schools, private Christian schools and homeschool. I worked in public schools for ten years, and I went to public school. The irony is the government, when they want something done well, they look to the private sector. This is why Northrop Grumman and Lockheed Martin, multibillion-dollar companies, handle a lot of production for our military, the creativity of the private sector to do things well. Why don't we do this with education? And I think the Trump administration was the first to do that."[182] He's right, despite the bullying and insane double standards applied to Secretary of Education Betsy DeVos, the Trump administration actually delivered more autonomy to parents in choosing the education for their children.

182 Interview with Jeremy Wayne Tate, January 12, 2021, via phone.

The scary thing in public education, COVID-19 exposed how interconnected politics was with education. Jeremy told me of an observation by his brother-in-law: "He's the head football coach at the local public school. And he shows me this map back in September. And I said, well, it looks like the Electoral College from 2016. He says that's the map of where they're allowed to play high school football right now."[183] Not surprising because the Left has been quarterbacking the coronavirus as a political maneuver since nearly its admission to the United States in early 2020. The educational outcomes won't be seen immediately, but let's check back in a few years when these kids grow up and compare the insane leftist Zoom regimes of California with public school out for months versus Florida public schools, which reopened quickly and got kids back in classrooms.[184]

As I have driven around the country during the 2020 campaign, I have spoken with parents deeply concerned about how their school districts have failed their children during the coronavirus, from an unwillingness to return to school, to inadequate resources, to just plain bad teaching. The scary thing is, our public educational system was already failing in many ways, and the inability to be in person for educational instruction has only exacerbated this trend.

I spoke with Lisa Michelle Britton,[185] a writer and feminism scholar, about the concerning educational gap developing between boys and girls and her views on the feminist movement, a movement she considers as having been commandeered to "push a victimhood mentality."[186]

To Lisa, the unhealthy intersection of modern feminism with education has created a notable gender intelligence gap that is growing. "Society realized it was doing something

183 Interview with Jeremy Wayne Tate, January 12, 2021, via phone.

184 "Where Schools Are Reopening in the US," *CNN*, https://www.cnn.com/interactive/2020/health/coronavirus-schools-reopening/.

185 https://www.amazon.com/Lisa-Michelle-Britton/e/B07YCT2YZF%3Fref=dbs_a_mng_rwt_scns_share.

186 Interview with Lisa Britton, January 12, 2021, via phone.

wrong with gender education disparities. They started making big changes. But there was an overcorrection. Now boys are far behind academically. But instead of blaming society, we're blaming the boys themselves. And we're dismissing the issues and charging them with accusations of male privilege and then doubling down on girl power in schools. When you look at the facts and statistics you see today, it's the boys who truly need our help today. But all they're doing is doubling down on girl power, and that worsens the problem with our boys today. So I believe that it's important to educate people on these perspectives on how society has it. But at the same time, you can't be so biased in pushing an ideology when what you see has happened over the past few decades."[187]

She went on, "It's almost like an otherwise good movement was hijacked because they wanted a different outcome in society and thought, 'Well, if we can make everybody resentful and angry, we can push for this new society we want.' And when I talk to many feminists, they tell me that you got to break a few eggs to make an omelet. And I think if you believe hurting innocent boys today is OK because it results in the omelet in the end, I would argue that you shouldn't be surprised if the omelet doesn't taste too good in the end. I don't think they will like the way that society is going to evolve in this way."[188]

She's right. Women are graduating high school at a much higher rate than men.[189] Women are graduating college and post-graduate school at a much higher rate than men.[190] And college-educated women make up more than half of the US

187 Interview with Lisa Britton, January 12, 2021, via phone.

188 Interview with Lisa Britton, January 12, 2021, via phone.

189 Richard V. Reeves, Eliana Buckner, and Ember Smith, "The Unreported Gender Gap in High School Graduation Rates," *Brookings* (January 12, 2021), https://www.brookings.edu/blog/up-front/2021/01/12/the-unreported-gender-gap-in-high-school-graduation-rates/.

190 Alana Semuels, "Poor Girls Are Leaving Their Brothers Behind. As a college education becomes increasingly important in today's economy, it's girls, not boys, who are succeeding in school. For kids from poor families, that can make the difference between social mobility and a lifetime of poverty." *The Atlantic* (November 27, 2017), https://www.theatlantic.com/business/archive/2017/11/gender-education-gap/546677/; see also: "Fast Facts," National Center for Education Statistics, https://nces.ed.gov/fastfacts/display.asp?id=40.

workforce.[191] That, combined with any analysis of dating and relationships, paints a rather terrifying picture. Researchers have realized that women, being the most educated, are looking for an equitable partner.[192] The *Wall Street Journal* cites data compiled by Hinge engineer, Aviv Goldgeier, quantifying "attractiveness in terms of an economic asset.... Economists use a measure—the Gini coefficient—to estimate the level of inequality in an economy. The nearer the number is to 0, the more evenly distributed the wealth. The closer it is to 1, the more unequal it is. It turns out that the Gini index for males is 0.542—a high level of inequality. A small number of men hold most of the attractiveness assets. For women, in the eyes of men, the attractiveness assets were much more evenly spread—a Gini index of just 0.376. Grim confirmation: a much smaller number of men are considered eligible by women than is the case for women as viewed by men. They're wanting an equitable partner. The gap is worsening."[193]

Lisa Michelle Britton confirms this from her own experience talking to women. "Research shows that the more educated a woman is, the more likely she desires a man who earns more than her. It's kind of like wanting their cake and eating it too. For decades now, we've shamed men on a massive scale to change their gender expectations for women and for themselves. But we haven't asked women that if they want this kind of equal society, they're going to have to change their expectations too. You can't have it both ways. You can't

---

191 Dani Matias, "New Report Says Women Will Soon Be Majority of College-Educated U.S. Workers," *NPR* (June 20, 2019), https://www.npr.org/2019/06/20/734408574/new-report-says-college-educated-women-will-soon-make-up-majority-of-u-s-labor-f#:~:text=Women%2C%20ages%2025%20and%20older,more%20bachelor's%20degrees%20than%20men.&text=Since%202000%2C%20the%20college%20enrollment,female%20students%20has%20outnumbered%20males.

192 Gerard Baker, "A Good Man Is Getting Even Harder to Find: The Future of Mating Looks Grim as More Educated Women Compete for Fewer Eligible Males," *The Wall Street Journal* (October 4, 2019), https://www.wsj.com/articles/a-good-man-is-getting-even-harder-to-find-11570200829.

193 Gerard Baker, "A Good Man Is Getting Even Harder to Find: The Future of Mating Looks Grim as More Educated Women Compete for Fewer Eligible Males," *The Wall Street Journal* (October 4, 2019), https://www.wsj.com/articles/a-good-man-is-getting-even-harder-to-find-11570200829.

change men and then, when it comes to women, say that men can't tell women what they desire," she told me.[194]

Lisa is seeing this play out in real time. "Just last year, a flurry of articles came out saying that women are upset because there aren't enough economically attractive men for them to date. And all of the articles framed it as if there was something wrong with young men. 'What's wrong with these young men?' it asked. I look at it, and I think for thirty-plus years we've been saying the future is female, boys don't need encouragement. Girl power, women, women, women. For three decades, we've put boys on the back burner. And I see the marriage rate going down. I have so many friends right now who are in their thirties or forties, who are single. And [my female friends] are panicking. They tell me that they could put off having families, and they are realizing that their compatibility isn't there due to lack of choices and due to elevated expectations."[195] What was once a reality, men were more educated, employed, and in committed relationships is no longer the reality. Yet, the narrative used by the Left to generate a divide between men and women very much so looms large and is having massive societal consequences. This is precisely what happens when you allow for reckless narratives to take root and grow without regard to their underlying factual basis and foresight of their outcomes.

I asked Lisa what can be done to remedy this: "We need balance moving forward and how we encourage and empower women because it's very one-sided right now. The results are not going to be good."[196]

And it's not as if Lisa is not a feminist, but she is rightly concerned about the direction of modern feminism. She recalls that "in 2017, I decided to go down to downtown LA and check out the Women's March. I went down, and I

194 Interview with Lisa Britton, January 12, 2021, via phone.
195 Interview with Lisa Britton, January 12, 2021, via phone.
196 Interview with Lisa Britton, January 12, 2021, via phone.

saw a father walking with a little girl on his shoulders. And she was carrying a sign. And I just stopped, and I realized right then that they were instilling resentment in young girls rather than saying to them, 'You can do whatever you want with freedom.' You're telling them at a young age that 'You're a victim, you're a victim.' We're not empowering girls and women. We're instilling in them and then motivating them by that instilled resentment. So that's not empowering at all because that just gives way to division and hatred. And I believe that's kind of the goal: to divide and control every aspect of what's happening today."[197]

That is why social media and the narratives it generates are so important. From equal pay initiatives to #MeToo to viral tweets about inequalities between men and women, you'd believe modern American society is *A Handmaid's Tale.*

On empowerment, I believe that there are obvious rebuttals that the Left is, in fact, empowering women by giving them this knowledge of power structures that have been in place and have had asymmetrical outcomes against women. Definitely informing people of how human civilization has been and evolved and everything like that is important because to say feminism is all bad is incorrect. Inequality between men and women is real and has existed since the dawn of human history. But the narrative doesn't meet the reality anymore, and it's the job of conservatives to stand up and maintain balance and parity with the truth.

Much of the solution to this is to realize that conservatives need to remain steadfast in their narrative that Americans are individuals and not a cog of the collective. Assembling people neatly into racial or gender groups, like the leftists do, makes people easier to manipulate. Instead, as Lisa Michelle Britton argues, "I believe that we should teach children that they're individuals. We should teach them to embrace personal accountability in life and teach them we need to stick to the

197 Interview with Lisa Britton, January 12, 2021, via phone.

facts. We should teach them not to be ashamed of who they are. We should teach them to embrace personal accountability so that they can do whatever fulfills them in life."[198] She also is hopeful about restoring confidence and growing together, men and women. Rather than lifting one group over the others, "We need to encourage our boys, tell them it's okay to be a boy. It's about masculinity. It's time to bring it back to center where we motivate everyone the same. And so, I think it's important as conservatives to start putting into schools to have compassion for others."[199]

Parkland and #MarchForOurLives

School shootings are a tragic reality in the United States. The nation has grappled with decades of violent attacks from truly deranged people, from Columbine to the shootings that will undoubtedly occur once lockdowns are lifted and more and more students return to the classroom. And as predictable as the sun rising in the east, when violence occurs, there is a thirsty portion of our political electorate and elected officials who seize on the opportunity to profit or politically benefit. It's gross. It's nasty.

But it's in the nasty business amidst the chaos and bloodshed that some of the most grotesque and liberty-abusive policies are enacted. It's why during times of upheaval, conservatives have to be the most vigilant. Democrats never let a good crisis go to waste.

The morning of February 14, 2018, a madman, Nikolas Cruz, entered Marjory Stoneman Douglas High School and murdered seventeen people and injured seventeen others.[200]

198 Interview with Lisa Britton, January 12, 2021, via phone.

199 Interview with Lisa Britton, January 12, 2021, via phone.

200 Elizabeth Chuck, Alex Johnson, and Corky Siemaszko, "17 Killed in Mass Shooting at High School in Parkland, Florida," *NBC News* (February 14, 2018), https://www.nbcnews.com/news/us-news/police-respond-shooting-parkland-florida-high-school-n848101.

While school resource officer Scot Peterson cowered in fear, true heroes rose up to protect others.[201] Assistant football coach Aaron Feis used his body as a shield.[202] He would die later during surgeries from his wounds. Others rose up that day to defend their teachers, classmates, and friends.

Immediately, the Democratic media apparatus descended upon Parkland. Students, some of whom weren't in the school at the time of the shooting, were plucked out to puppet talking points of the gun control Left. Calls from Hollywood, New York, and the media screamed "no more" as if they were the only adults in the room who cared about school shootings even before the facts came out. CNN hosted a town hall in Florida with seemingly the sole purpose of allowing angry parents and students to lambast Senator Marco Rubio.[203] His Democratic colleagues were given glowing treatment and asked what could best be described as softball questions. Also, never mind the fact that the facts of Parkland were still coming out. I believe that the Constitution was written to stand the test of time, and I am a firm believer in the Second Amendment, but who cares about something that was written hundreds of years ago when there's a social media hashtag? Facts be damned when there is a narrative to be crafted.

And those students who were the most "effective" at questioning Senator Rubio or eliciting emotion were thrust into the media spotlight further and thus began #MarchForOurLives.

---

201 It's worth noting that former resource officer Scot Peterson now faces charges in Florida: "The criminal charges against Peterson stemmed from an investigation by the Florida Department of Law of [*sic*] Enforcement, tasked by former Gov. Rick Scott to examine the response of law enforcement to the worst school shooting in state history. Peterson was charged with seven counts of child neglect, six of them felonies, in connection with the killing of seven underage students at the school. He was also hit with three misdemeanor counts of culpable negligence and one misdemeanor count of perjury for lying during questioning by investigators." Miami Herald, "Former Marjory Stoneman Douglas School Resource Officer Scot Peterson Arrested on Charges of Child Neglect," *Tampa Bay Times* (June 4, 2019), https://www.tampabay.com/florida-politics/buzz/2019/06/04/former-marjory-stoneman-douglas-school-resource-officer-scot-peterson-arrested-on-charges-of-child-neglect/.

202 Lisa Ryan, "These Are the Heroes of the Florida School Shooting," *The Cut*, (February 15, 2018), https://www.thecut.com/2018/02/parkland-florida-school-shooting-heroes.html.

203 David Choi, "Marco Rubio Gets Booed and Slammed as 'Pathetically Weak' at Parkland Shooting Town Hall, but Hints He Might Shift Some on Guns," (February 22, 2018), https://www.businessinsider.com/marco-rubio-cnn-town-hall-parkland-shooting-2018-2.

The movement structured a day of speeches in Washington, DC, to attack Republicans, the National Rifle Association, and President Trump as if one, two, or all three of these parties were responsible for school shootings nationwide. This is where the Right fails. But the Left understands this—they center the issue. This is the crisis. These are the people. We need the platform. I think the closest moment that we've had to losing our Second Amendment rights was the Parkland school shooting movement. And had we not had Donald Trump as president, I think we would have, or at least our Second Amendment rights would have looked very different.

While Hollywood and New York lectured through the mouths of babes tired, gun control talking points, others rose up, wanting to make sure this never happened again. I talked to some of these patriots about how they pushed back in the press and on social media against falsehoods and excessive power grabs under the guise of school safety.

What I remember from the horrific day of the shooting is seeing a picture of a man, Andrew Pollack, who was wearing a Trump 2020 T-shirt. He was going to the school to see if his daughter, Meadow, was alive, and he held up a picture of his daughter, and the media captured some images of it. Those pictures went viral on social media. The comments were ruthless, lots of anti-gun, anti-humane as if because he's a Trump supporter, his daughter deserved what happened. It was disgusting.

I think the Pollack family single-handedly countered the prevailing liberal narrative. They took on the corporate media, the entertainment industry, and Democrat politicians. They cared.

Andrew Pollack, father of Meadow Pollack, a victim of the Parkland shooting, told me that unlike the media, "I didn't jump to any conclusions just yet. I just wanted to know how this could happen—how I could drop my daughter off at school and she get murdered. I was angry. I'm still angry to this day that this happened. And I wanted to know the facts. I didn't jump into anything right away until the facts started coming out. And I started hearing some students at the school saying they knew this kid was evil, and he said he was going to be the shooter. I took a step back. We started interviewing people and doing our own investigation."[204] In the months and weeks that followed, Andrew pushed back and wrote about his own investigation in a journalistic and personal effort to understand what happened in his book titled *Why Meadow Died: The People and Policies That Created the Parkland Shooter and Endanger America's Students.*[205]

Combating the narrative to actually cover what happened was not only essential to Andrew Pollack and the memory of his daughter but to the countless future children who would be lost if conservatives and moderate Democrats didn't come together to find common sense solutions to gun safety. "I owed it to my daughter to get the truth out. She wanted me to—I had a voice telling me, 'Daddy, you tell everybody what happened to me, and you hold all these people accountable.' And from the get-go, that's what it's been for me is accountability. And we've been getting it little by little. We went after the sheriff. He was removed. We have a wrongful death case. It's all about accountability. Most of the media didn't want to know the truth. They didn't want to know anything. What happened at Parkland, they just were going after a semiautomatic rifle. Their counter movement to #MarchForOurLives is very simple, a two-word hashtag, #FixIt. Basically, all we wanted to do was increase school safety. And we ended up getting a commission set by President Trump to review school safety. We got different states adding more school resource officers to their payroll. And that was one of the more important hashtags that I've been a part of."[206]

---

204 Interview with Andrew Pollack, November 16, 2020, via phone.

205 Andrew Pollack, *Why Meadow Died: The People and Policies That Created the Parkland Shooter and Endanger America's Students* (Post Hill Press, September 10, 2019), https://www.amazon.com/Why-Meadow-Died-Policies-Parkland/dp/1642932191.

206 Interview with Andrew Pollack, November 16, 2020, via phone.

The Left, seeming to be in the dark on gun control or willfully ignorant on the issue, seems to prey on gun violence to go after guns. And while the good guy with a gun trope is the obvious rebuttal, I know it gets tired. But these people are relentless. They act as though universal illegality of firearms would somehow eradicate gun violence in the United States. We know that to be false. Common sense and any cursory observation of any area of the country plagued by gun violence does not bear this out.

Hunter Pollack, seeking to lend his voice to the debate of the moment and grieving the loss of his sister, Meadow, was shut out of the #MarchForOurLives event at the last minute. "The only reason they didn't want me to speak was because I didn't mention 'gun control' in my speech. And then they alleged that they had a brief meeting, but I was never invited. I think they were just totally shocked because my speech didn't align with the narrative of that day."[207] Imagine how disturbing this is, the brother of a victim of extraordinary gun violence wasn't allowed to share his perspective—all because his story wouldn't align with the message of the day.

I found this to be reprehensible. So I said, "Hey Hunter, record your speech on my phone, and I'll make it go viral on social media." And that's exactly what I did. He recorded on my phone, and I put it on Facebook, and it went viral. It received more than four million views overnight on Facebook and lots of views on other platforms.

I was determined to get his message out there, because it was just horrible. Here I was listening to a brother do what no brother should have to do: publicly mourn his sister taken far too young and in such a terrible way. It should not have happened. I knew that I had the opportunity to give them a megaphone. I was heartbroken for them. Hunter and his sister were very close in age—about the same difference between my brother and me. The Pollacks were brave, and

207 Interview with Hunter Pollack, October 27, 2020, via phone.

they set themselves to the mission to make a difference in Meadow's name. And they did it.

Hunter is keenly aware how sensitive but necessary the battle is to win people over online and especially when it comes to hot button issues like guns. "Social media engagement reaches people that you can't simply reach just walking door to door and sharing your story. Having social media gives you the power to expand your voice and make your presence more known throughout the country and perhaps throughout the world," he explained.[208] "What I wanted to share was my personal experience: exposing information that not everyday people know or that everyday people could easily find in their own research."[209]

That is why offering alternative narratives and not giving an inch to the radical mob is paramount. Social media only exacerbates radicalization on the left. Leftist posts on gun violence juxtaposed with images of children are meant to scare the American people towards safety versus freedom. In the immediate aftermath, they know that social media without any counternarrative can shift the Overton window so far to the left that any explanation to the contrary means that you necessarily don't care about children.

The Democrats controlled the narrative until we created a counternarrative. And the counternarrative was the superintendent of the school board was handpicked by President Obama to be put in charge of the fourth-largest school district in the country to run a pilot program. The pilot program was to stop the "school to prison pipeline." What does that mean? It means if you committed a crime at school, instead of being reported to the police, you go to this little special program where you're hand-held, and you don't get reprimanded.

The deranged Parkland shooter was part of this program. He had serious problems: he brought knives and bullets to

208 Interview with Hunter Pollack, October 27, 2020, via phone.
209 Interview with Hunter Pollack, October 27, 2020, via phone.

school. His classmates reported him to the police and to the FBI. But the school never did anything. And the FBI didn't follow up on any of the claims. The issue with Parkland was that by the time we came out with these facts, we were too late. The news cycles had moved on.

But despite the short attention span of the media news cycle, Andrew Pollack knew how detrimental the policies in place at Broward were to students. "There were policies in place in Broward County that allowed students to commit misdemeanors during the school year without ever getting introduced to law enforcement; there were programs in place that you could assault a teacher or student, drugs, etcetera and never get introduced to law enforcement," he said.[210] "Democrats think they're helping children by not holding them accountable for their actions or not introducing them to a program where law enforcement's involved to help mentor these kids. They believe in their mind that they're going to send these troubled kids to a healing circle.... They think not holding these kids accountable is going to set them up for success," he explained. He went on to note exactly what we see play out every day, that any policy that the Left doesn't like gets lambasted with the typical, tired attacks—it's racist, homophobic, the typical laundry list of lazy attacks. Andrew Pollack contends that President Biden has already said he is going "to end the school to prison pipeline ... if you look up statistics, teachers are getting assaulted more than ever right now because of these programs. So the fighting gets in the public schools," while "school to prison pipeline" is a nice bit of branding, what we know is that Donald Trump allowed schools to hold students accountable and the Left is scared to police lest they be labeled a racist.[211]

And while the Left is busy name-calling and engaging in bad faith activism, Andrew Pollack created software to

---

210 Interview with Andrew Pollack, November 16, 2020, via phone.

211 Interview with Andrew Pollack, November 16, 2020, via phone.

make police response more efficient. School Safety Grant is an application that Andrew has given to police departments and sheriff's offices throughout the country.[212] The program "allows police or sheriff department to link to any entity that has cameras within five seconds. So, if someone calls 911 from the school that has connected to cameras, we will have every camera up in real time in the crime center in the sheriff or the police department. The same thing goes to implementing them in places of worship, temples, churches, mosques. Hospitals are implementing the technology. We're able to better protect these places. So I look forward to working with law enforcement to make them more efficient and to save lives. The software will cut minutes off response time.... I don't care if their parents are Democrats or Republicans or independents, I want to help make these kids be a lot safer at school."[213]

Kyle Kashuv was a student at Marjory Stoneman Douglas High School when the shooting happened. I respect Kyle a lot because he had the maturity to shy away from being called a Parkland school shooting victim or survivor because, as he has attested many times before, he was on the opposite end of the building when the shooting happened.

That being said, Kyle saw the way that his classmates were being used and knew that he needed to get involved—not for fame or a platform but to ensure that this never happened again. I asked him how he got involved, and he told me:

> ***"It's been my mantra since I started speaking out. It's the combination of having maturity and focus. When I first started out, I would meet with anyone. I met Senator Chuck Schumer and Congresswoman Nancy Pelosi, Senator Chris Murphy, Senator Cory Booker. I had meetings with many more. I don't think I've ever talked about this publicly, but I've had a meeting with***

212 School Safety Grant, "Our Mission," https://schoolsafetygrant.org/mission.

213 Interview with Andrew Pollack, November 16, 2020, via phone.

> *Kamala Harris. (Bernie Sanders still hasn't responded to my emails.) But I was willing to meet with anyone. Because the end goal isn't for partisan politics. The end goal is to make schools safe."*[214]

He also told me about his meetings with Republicans:

> *"I met with Congressman Kevin McCarthy, Speaker of the House at the time Paul Ryan, Congressman Steve Scalise, Senator Tim Scott, Congressman Matt Gaetz, and Senator Ted Cruz. And I would have met with anyone who would have spoken with me. The end goal is getting policy passed."* [215]

Kashuv focused on policy changes and noted the distinction between his effectiveness and that of his peers who took to social media and TV channels was that he didn't go to Washington to "berate" politicians. Instead, Kashuv encouraged "working together to get a bipartisan school safety bill passed."

I asked Kyle why the Right fails in the gun debate, and he explained that we have to come back to "common sense.... I think the average American can resonate with that. You want to be able to have a gun to defend yourself, right?"[216]

Time has revealed that the facts didn't match the narrative of the Left immediately after the shooting. Kashuv told me:

> *"We saw extreme levels of government corruption that allowed this to happen.... What happened in my school was by far the most preventable school shooting in US history. The FBI knew this would happen. The sheriff's department had dozens of tips on the shooter. The school officials had boxes and boxes on him. So really, it was in large part an issue of government corruption or at least extreme incom-*

214 Interview with Kyle Kashuv, November 30, 2020, via phone.
215 Interview with Kyle Kashuv, November 30, 2020, via phone.
216 Interview with Kyle Kashuv, November 30, 2020, via phone.

> *petence. The school resource officer who stood outside and didn't do anything. There were millions of dollars in funds that weren't used to protect our schools. And though this was looked at as a gun issue to appeal to the American people, this wasn't a gun issue. And even more so, the policies proposed by the Left on this tragedy with gun control would only hurt average citizens and wouldn't have prevented the shooting."*[217]

The narratives that arose following the shooting didn't comport to what students like Kyle uncovered in the weeks and months afterward. However, Kyle notes as I have discovered in an early career in politics that sometimes facts be damned if you have a good narrative. Kyle is cognizant of that as he tries to convince others to his bipartisan school safety, self-protection agenda. "Why did this happen? Well, this happened because the school board failed. This happened because the school safety officer failed. This happened because the FBI failed. And then looking at the legislation, the issues that arise once you start talking about complex legislation and gun statistics, sometimes people drift off, and I don't blame them," he noted. The difficulty is combating the leftist anti-gun agenda with that of a similar but contrary narrative that cuts against the radical notion of an absence of self-preservation. "Why are we making it so that a single mother of two kids shouldn't be able to defend herself? Who happens to be nineteen? Or twenty-six? That doesn't make sense. And that's something that I think the Right doesn't do well enough, is that at the end of the day, there is a large emotional component to a lot of people and how they vote and how they think. And the Right, in large part, has almost entirely abandoned that for statistics, which is fine for some part, but you need to be able to talk to the people and break it down to a level that people are willing to

---

217 Interview with Kyle Kashuv, November 30, 2020, via phone.

listen to and understand. They obviously can if you spend hours on end explaining statistics. But most people aren't going to spend three hours listening about guns."[218] And even further, and to put a finer point on Kyle's comments, there is an important distinction to be made that conservatives can't make narratives that stem entirely from "this is a statistically unlikely event"—there is a sensitivity to certain political issues that ought to make conservatives rally to the side of self-preservation and dignity rather than surrendering wholesale rights to the government out of an incident of fear and pain.

Kashuv was pleased with how the Trump administration handled the Parkland shooting. He met with the president in the Oval Office. "I thought the president was great. He had a seventeen-year-old kid sit down in his office and talk about what changes I wanted to see and how we can make our schools safer. He listened. And I genuinely think that this administration has taken school safety to the forefront. They had lots of the parents come and meet with members of the administration. They took school safety seriously, created a task force, and oversaw bipartisan accomplishments that have made schools safer."[219] Hunter Pollack echoed a similar sentiment. "With President Trump, what you see is what you get. He's like what you see on TV: personable, empathetic, compassionate, caring. We were able to achieve just so much when we first went there in February of 2018. We discussed that in the Oval Office, and he saw the whole picture. He said he loved that idea. And he invited us back two more times, and he acted on what we discussed."[220]

Kashuv noted that partisanship plays a major role in effectiveness on the Hill. He told me: "I think more [legislative accomplishments] could have been done had we not

218 Interview with Kyle Kashuv, November 30, 2020, via phone.
219 Interview with Kyle Kashuv, November 30, 2020, via phone.
220 Interview with Hunter Pollack, October 27, 2020, via phone.

politicized this issue so much. When I met with Nancy Pelosi, all she wanted me to do was to get Paul Ryan to bring a gun debate to the floor [of the House]. And I was thinking: I'm here to talk about a bipartisan bill that eighty percent of all of us can agree on. Let's get that done. Let's get the eighty percent that we all agree on and then we can have that twenty percent gun debate. But let's do all the things we can agree on. And that's just not what the intentions of some were."[221]

I asked about the significance of social media versus the traditional means of targeting voters and canvassing. Kashuv responded, "The ability to target a specific area in Georgia, versus going door to door knocking, that is an unbelievable disadvantage if you're not able to do that on Facebook. So, Big Tech matters, and making sure the conservatives answer them is important, and some say we'll just go to Parler. Great. Make a new platform. That's fine. But the power of Facebook and Instagram is that there are more people there who may be slightly political. Maybe they're apolitical, maybe they're apathetic to politics, but you're able to message and contact them. And even maybe someone throws it on their friend's social media, and they see it. And they agreed. Right. It's not necessarily direct ad campaigning. It's the ripple effects of having a strong conservative user base on that app. And once these people get banned, you're not able to message to get to people even naturally or buy ads. And the second thing is that we've seen with this election that Democrats have become the party of the managerial elite and Republicans have become the party of the people. And we need to take that to heart."[222]

That is key, but for gentlemen like Kyle Kashuv, Andrew Pollack, Hunter Pollack, and a few others, the prevailing narrative, both from a public policy perspective and on social media, would have been the eradication of "assault weapons" and avoidance of the really concerning issues—the failings

221 Interview with Kyle Kashuv, November 30, 2020, via phone.

222 Interview with Kyle Kashuv, November 30, 2020, via phone.

of the school system, school resource officer, and the FBI—instead favoring the lazy approach: "Guns are bad." As people in the United States are already experiencing, with the lack of policing due to reckless Democratic campaigns, possessing the right to self-defense now comes at an all-time premium. The necessity for conservatives to combat incorrect social media campaigns with facts, figures, and boldness is crucial. The men I highlighted in this book are bold, coalition-minded, and created a network of conservatives to push back. They honor the victims every day when they focus on real solutions and make our schools safer.

COVID-19 and the Lockdown Hysteria

"China hasn't paid enough for unleashing the pandemic on the rest of the world."[223]

- Tom Cotton

The COVID-19 pandemic is still a tragic, ongoing situation. While hot takes from pundits continue to this day to sour as more science and research comes out, what we have learned from the pandemic is how dangerous government can be when given unfettered access to power and the media when they are rewarded for delivering a daily dribble of gloom and doom.[224]

Heading into a crisis that no one alive has ever endured, politicians, including President Trump, relied heavily on the medical community for consent and knowledge on particular

223 Tom Cotton (@TomCottonAR), Twitter, Jun. 1, 2021, 7:56 a.m., https://twitter.com/TomCottonAR/status/1399741737707491334?s=20.

224 I want to credit my friend Jack Posobiec for being the first person I can think of who was sounding the alarm around January 2020 that this was going to be a big deal.

issues related to public health. What we found out is that the Centers for Disease Control and the likes of Dr. Fauci are wholly bereft of the ability to communicate cohesively with the American people. Coupled with a media hostile to President Trump, these failings generated a crisis.

Conservatives much more in tune to the pandemic have documented and will relay the specific instances of hypocrisy, misdirection, and misinformation for you.[225] Those books will be coming, and thankfully, there are accounts that have threaded together this information to see in real time. But for this book, what I want to point out to you about the pandemic is how narratives were formed and became gospel to huge parts of the population. I want to draw out a few examples and enumerate them in this book before the Left memory-holes their failings, as they are prone to do.

First, let's remember how the public health community started their messaging. We needed to stay inside and socially distance for "fifteen days to stop the spread."[226] The aim was to prevent hospitals from being overrun and our resources from being depleted. The vast majority of people followed CDC guidelines. The media ran article after article and tweet after tweet about how we were going to run out of ventilators. They published fear porn like this absurdity from the Center for Public Integrity, "State Policies May Send People with Disabilities to the Back of the Line for Ventilators."[227] Never mind the fact that, according to Politifact, "a ventilator has been available for every patient that needed one," and, "our

225 Drew Holden (@DrewHolden360), "I have a sneaking suspicion some people are gonna look real silly for writing off the idea that coronavirus could've come from a high-tech virology lab, run by a secretive autocratic regime, overseen by a bat expert studying coronaviruses, in the city where cases first appeared." Twitter, Apr. 21, 2020, 11:51 a.m., https://twitter.com/DrewHolden360/status/1252671364844204032?s=20.

226 Centers for Disease Control and Prevention, "Stop the Spread," archived webpage, https://www.cdc.gov/coronavirus/2019-ncov/communication/stop-the-spread.html.

227 Liz Essley Whyte, "State Policies May Send People with Disabilities to the Back of the Line for Ventilators," *The Center for Public Integrity* in partnership with *The Daily Beast* (April 8, 2020), https://publicintegrity.org/health/coronavirus-and-inequality/state-policies-may-send-people-with-disabilities-to-the-back-of-the-line-for-ventilators/.

research found that most states have procured enough ventilators to match the demand."[228]

Also remember that President Trump was monitoring the situation and closed the US border to Chinese citizens. Meanwhile, the Left seized on this to call him a racist; Nancy Pelosi was in Chinatown saying that Trump is a xenophobe. In fact, while Trump was focused on the coronavirus, the media and Democrats were focused on impeachment, impeachment, impeachment.

And that's when the hysterics started. Every news network put up a ticker about the deaths and positive tests. Fifteen days to stop the spread became flatten the curve to, "We can't go back to normal unless everyone is vaccinated." All in the span of a few months.

Meanwhile, the elites decided to play by different rules than they set. Andrew Cuomo used the pandemic to bolster his career and national spotlight. California Governor Gavin Newsom ordered Californians to stay home while he enjoyed one of the nicest restaurants on the planet with friends. The list goes on.

The media coverage was also disgraceful. By just watching the mainstream media alone, you would have believed that Andrew Cuomo was single-handedly protecting the country from the coronavirus, but, in fact, he was one of the worst governors, sending our elderly to their early deaths in nursing homes. During the pandemic, he did MSNBC and CNN hits, basically doing a buddy comedy with his brother, Chris Cuomo, on CNN, and pretended to be this success story. He even wrote a book about his "accomplishments." The contrast against this glowing treatment to that of Governor Ron DeSantis of Florida could not be more stark. "DeathSantis" trended on Twitter, the media regurgitated lies from the *60*

228 Bill McCarthy, "Can Anyone Who Needs a Ventilator Get One? So Far, It Looks Like It," *Politifact* (April 24, 2020), https://www.politifact.com/article/2020/apr/24/can-anyone-who-needs-ventilator-get-one-so-far-it-/; first quote is from Colin Milligan, director of media relations at the American Hospital Association.

Minutes report that turned out to be completely false about the success of the Florida vaccine rollout and platformed liars who falsely accused Ron DeSantis and his administration of impropriety. But that was then. The media's memory of their ineptitude is very short, indeed.

The point is that the Left used hysterics to their advantage. Hysteria and social media are a match made in hell because hysterics spread like wildfire on Twitter. Fear and anger sell on social media. It's very hard to get a positive movement started. So it was difficult to say that President Trump took necessary precautions and did the least restrictive measures to keep people safe while enjoying the liberties afforded Americans. It's much easier to fearmonger and craft a narrative of "blood on the hands" of your opponents.

A guy who was consistently battling the narrative on COVID-19 was Buck Sexton, the radio host taking over for the beloved Rush Limbaugh,[229] who cautioned that a big part of pushing back on the coronavirus "experts" was that "there will be consequences, especially online with the social media giants, the monopolists. Speaking the truth has reached a point where the truth itself is not actually truth anymore. The old saying is that the truth is an absolute defense against slander allegations. That if you say something that's true, you can't be guilty of slander. But with tech monopolists and Big Tech in general, if you're correct, it doesn't matter because they punish you for going against the approved narrative, and there's no making it right after the fact. Everyone needs to understand that even when you're right, you may suffer consequences.... You speak out against these narratives, what I call the Fauci consensus because, otherwise, it just feeds on people's complacency and unwillingness to stand up and say what's actually true."[230]

229 Anne Steele, "Rush Limbaugh's Radio Show to Be Taken Over by Clay Travis and Buck Sexton," *The Wall Street Journal* (Mar. 27, 2021), https://www.wsj.com/articles/rush-limbaughs-radio-show-to-be-taken-over-by-clay-travis-and-buck-sexton-11622127616.

230 Interview with Buck Sexton, June 1, 2021, via phone.

As the party who acted during the coronavirus, we have the opportunity to reclaim the narrative in 2022 and 2024. Bold leadership and governors stood up to the radical Left during the coronavirus and kept their states safe and open. And their economies boomed as a result. The American people saw that leadership and voted with their feet by moving to Florida and Texas and places that had children back in schools and people back to work. At the time, the media and the "experts" called these governors reckless and dangerous. The American people didn't elect Dr. Fauci. In 2022 and 2024, if we use the tools in this book correctly and mount a vocal defense, we can ensure the crazies who blindly followed the radical Left don't wield power over our day-to-day any longer.

The 2020 Big Tech, Democrat, and Media Coordination

I was in the West Wing on election night. I built out a social media war room. We had four TV stations on, MSNBC, CNN, Fox, and CBS, to watch the election results come in. We were super pumped. It's about 10:30 p.m., and Bill Hemmer of Fox News is at the Magic Board at the election desk. He's going through the state of Pennsylvania, and he's saying, "Donald Trump's margin of victory is looking greater now than when he beat Hillary in Pennsylvania." I was in the room with some of the smartest people I know in politics. We're looking at what's happening in Wisconsin and Kenosha County. We're up huge. Then the counting stops.

It's 10:30 at night, after Florida had just been called, and I'm scrolling through Twitter and all these leftist accounts I follow on Twitter were freaking out, saying it's over.

Then Fox News calls Arizona.

In the confusion and chaos of the ensuing days, we were determined to combat narratives until the official election results were announced.

Trump ultimately lost.

But the scary part wasn't the fact creepy Joe is president, but the fact that every institution in the United States was working in coordination to ensure that Trump lost. Corporations were working in cahoots. *Time* magazine put it covertly, they "fortified" the election for Biden.[231]

Take, for example, the work done to bury the Hunter Biden story. Let's not forget that Tucker Carlson reported about possible corruption by Joe Biden's son, Hunter Biden, by his business associate, Tony Bobulinski. "I have heard Joe Biden say he has never discussed his dealings with Hunter. That is false. I have firsthand knowledge about this because I directly dealt with the Biden family, including Joe Biden," Bobulinski said.[232] And as I discussed earlier, Big Tech spent ample resources suppressing this interview and reporting by the *New York Post* about apparent corruption and bad faith negotiation by Hunter Biden with the Chinese, raising numerous questions about Biden's loyalties and the elder Biden's ties to Beijing (Beijing Biden does have nice alliterative effect...).

Always convenient to note that less than a month after the election, CNN is reporting that the US Attorney's Office in Delaware is "examining multiple financial issues, including whether Hunter Biden and his associates violated tax and money laundering laws in business dealings

231 Molly Ball, "The Secret History of the Shadow Campaign That Saved the 2020 Election," *TIME* (Feb. 4. 2021), "There was a conspiracy unfolding behind the scenes, one that both curtailed the protests and coordinated the resistance from CEOs. Both surprises were the result of an informal alliance between left-wing activists and business titans...-a well-funded cabal of powerful people, ranging across industries and ideologies, working together behind the scenes to influence perceptions, change rules and laws, steer media coverage and control the flow of information. They were not rigging the election; they were fortifying it." https://time.com/5936036/secret-2020-election-campaign/.

232 Ebony Bowden and Steven Nelson, "Hunter's Ex-Partner Tony Bobulinski: Joe Biden's a Liar and Here's the roof," *New York Post* (October 22, 2020), https://nypost.com/2020/10/22/hunter-ex-partner-tony-bobulinski-calls-joe-biden-a-liar/.

in foreign countries, principally China, according to two people briefed on the probe."[233]

(I guess the embargo on reporting on Biden malfeasance is over.)

The power that the media, social media companies, and the Democrats have together is something that the world has never seen before, that our country has never seen before. They control what you hear. They control what you see. They control what you want, what you can say.

We'll cover some of these themes later on in the book as well, but it's worth noting here, too, that every pro-Trump movement on Twitter was censored, with accounts disabled or throttled, and every anti-Trump movement was amplified.

We have to fight back. We can't just let this happen.

It's Time to Move

To win elections in 2022 and 2024, we need to start demanding our elected officials actually fight for our values and beliefs. We have to stand up to these tyrants in corporations and the media. We need to understand that the media is hell-bent on promoting leftist agendas and destroying America as we know it. Wealthy Republicans need to start getting tough and putting their money behind movements we believe in. Democratic billionaires are always looking for good activism. Bloomberg owns one of the largest media corporations in the world. Bloomberg has thousands and thousands of writers. They produce thousands of pieces of content every day. Jeff Bezos owns *The Washington Post*. Zuckerberg. Dorsey. The list goes on and on. Every platform and content-producing medium is owned by leftists. And so, Republicans need to get tough. They need to infiltrate some of these boardrooms.

233 Evan Perez and Pamela Brown, "Federal Criminal Investigation into Hunter Biden Focuses on His Business Dealings in China," *CNN* (December 10, 2020), https://www.cnn.com/2020/12/09/politics/hunter-biden-tax-investigtation/index.html.

I want to charge the everyday Republican voter to keep track of what their lawmakers are doing and make sure their lawmakers are being held accountable.

We need to get tough. We need to elect conservatives who are not going to shy away from the culture war and who will be on the front lines every single day, fighting for our values and our freedoms. If we don't, these movements will shift the direction of this country.

Chapter 5:

THE ORGANIZATIONS

GRASSROOTS ORGANIZATIONS ARE A key driver in American politics. Politicians are informed, briefed, and funded by organizations. An organization like Club for Growth or Heritage may put their blessing on a candidate that allows them to accelerate through a crowded primary. A poor score from the National Rifle Association may stifle donations to a candidate or place a target for future primary challenges on a politician. Other groups like Turning Point USA or Log Cabin Republicans take more organic approaches to politics, seeking to draw in constituents through humor and community. But no matter the organization, groups have had to take their work online. The popularity and ability of social media to spread messages, garner donations, and raise awareness on issues have made effective use supremely important.

And I want to continue to note that the deck is stacked against us. As Mike Davis notes, "The Left has powerful allies in the media, against you. They've got allies in Big Tech against you. They want every powerful institution in this country, including even corporations."[234] This is a tall ask for many organizations to compete with at their onset.

234 Interview with Mike Davis, November 30, 2020, via phone.

TPUSA COO Tyler Bowyer correctly noted the value of organizations saying that TPUSA "set the narrative and completely reset the entire list of talking points for the entire country. We've done this numerous times, and we don't publicize that. We don't share that information with people. But we have, and a lot of times, we've been the only defense mechanism to or we've been one of the starting defense mechanisms against the Left when they start up their fake news cycle against President Trump."[235] As a narrative matter and translating that narrative into action, organizations like the Article III Project were instrumental in ensuring President Trump's success. Mike Davis, former head of the Article III Project told me, "President Trump campaigned on the promise that he would transform the federal judiciary with judges in the mold of the late, great Justice Scalia. And he absolutely delivered on his campaign promise with the appointments of Justice Gorsuch, Justice Kavanaugh, Justice Barrett, and near all-time record appointments of federal circuit court judges and over two hundred district court judges. We have a website called JudiciaryTracker.com, and it shows President Trump's historic success in transforming the federal judiciary."[236] Scott Parkinson, the vice president of Club for Growth, speaking in his individual capacity and not as a spokesman for Club for Growth, told me: "Conservatives have done a good job at leading on economic policies when the cards were sort of stacked against us during the Obama administration…if you can understand the parallels with social media and the way that groups like Club for Growth got the messaging out and also conservative leaders on Capitol Hill who were trying to catch lightning in a bottle to reach a new audience that they really never had access to before…social media allows groups to fact check things in real time and question political rhetoric in real time. So it's kind of shifted in the way that politicians

235 Interview with Tyler Bowyer, December 28, 2020, via phone.

236 Interview with Mike Davis, November 30, 2020, via phone.

would use social media than ten years ago. But they know that they have to use it in order to reach a really large number of people and also to be a part of the media narrative."[237] These organizations crafted a narrative and used social media to disseminate it. We need more of these organizations doing this work. That is why, as a true believer, I wrote this guide to give you the tools you need to build out your organization.

Many of my tips apply equally to organizations. Through our work and following these tips, I have helped my clients see growth on Facebook, Instagram, and Twitter, taking them from zero followers to over 450,000 followers in the span of a year. But I want to separate this chapter because I think there are some organizations that are particularly doing things well and others that are getting left behind. Like any major shift in politics—in this case, to online—to remain relevant, organizations must adapt to these changes.

As I said about being coalition-minded, it's going to take all of us liberty-seeking people, working collectively, to make the necessary changes to keep society free and safe for conservatives. We work with a number of organizations and have seen their work and efficacy increase as a result of some of the tips and tricks I have outlined for you below.

Be Online and Offline

Seems simple, but you'd be surprised how many organizations with massive volunteer bases spend little if any time curating an online following or organizations that are very online put little effort into offline activities. I've seen it in my business, where organizations will come to me and ask how they can grow their social media, and I ask, "How many events have you had this month? How have you reached out to your followers in person?" Oftentimes, the answer is zero or very little.

237 Interview with Scott Parkinson, November 24, 2020, via phone.

To grow in both, you must do both. Develop a social media following by being online and offline.

Andrea Catsimatidis, chairwoman of the Manhattan GOP, knows this all too well and echoed how surprised she was about how the Manhattan GOP was operating before she got there. I asked her about her experience putting their organization on the map:

> *"Even though Manhattan is a hot zone for the liberal boogeyman, we don't have really any elected Republicans in Manhattan. In the past, nobody really cared about Manhattan. Republicans weren't focused on us at all. But one thing that we've done really well is I have been very attuned to social media and have developed a social media following. So I was able to bring attention to all of the crazy things that liberals are doing in New York that I thought that people would be interested about. And now all of a sudden, people that normally wouldn't be focused on Manhattan are now focusing and telling other people to pay attention. Through social media and our events, we brought attention to our issues, raised outrage when we needed to breed outrage, helped our candidates, got volunteers for our candidates, raised money, and have just been out there and able to draw attention to things."*[238]

Andrea works with a number of other ancillary groups who focus almost exclusively on throwing events for Republicans in Manhattan, typically with speakers and exclusive access to big names for off-the-record discussion. The social events she promotes on her socials provide a community for Republicans in the city and thereby reinforce her social media growth and that of her group.

---

238 Interview with Andrea Catsimatidis, January 12, 2021, via phone.

Charles Moran is the spokesman of Log Cabin Republicans,[239] the nation's oldest and largest organization of LGBTQ conservatives and their allies. He similarly bragged about his amazing team and members, that the great work they do and "the energy of the organization comes from the people. And I think that's the reason we have succeeded, and these other organizations have failed: they just don't have the grassroots support from their members. And we do. And we have a track record of accomplishment, achievement."[240] Moran says that he regularly speaks with chapter heads and ensures that Log Cabin Republicans both promote events and raise awareness on key issues to draw in more conservative LGBTQ community members. Moran and his organization were some of the key informers from the Right on LGBTQ issues, often reminding the mainstream media that "Donald Trump, who really had a really long-standing history with the LGBT community of being in support of our community and our issues like HIV, AIDS, and employment nondiscrimination; he really was almost like a new Ronald Reagan because he had friends that were gay, and he socialized with people who were in our community."[241]

Be your own best advocate and develop a community, one that grows online by the feedback loop of offline content. While everyone has become a keyboard warrior, people are drawn to groups that encourage real, in-person exchanges of ideas and want to build lasting relationships with those who share similar goals.

Did I Mention Content?

I've said it before, and I will say it again: if you're not making content, you will not grow.

239 Charles T. Moran (@CharlesTMoran), Twitter, https://twitter.com/charlestmoran?lang=en.

240 Interview with Charles Moran, December 17, 2020, via phone.

241 Interview with Charles Moran, December 17, 2020, via phone.

"Create content that matters," says Tyler Bowyer. "At the end of the day, it's content, content, content. Don't be afraid to post things and know that there's some flexibility there online, where we can remove it quickly or make adaptations and changes quickly because it's digital." Creating a fierce base of support for an organization immediately requires large blocks of content. People don't know what you don't show them. I often tell my organizations that it's also effective to put faces to an organization early—a lot of them. Far too often organizations tie their group to one person, and the entire success and failure of the group is reliant on the success or failure of that person. However, broadening the brand to true believers, everyday people who want to give you content or show how XYZ policy works on the ground, are great ways to expand, build community, and increase support.

Being a first mover on content is also important. In our discussions with multiple individuals with close ties to social media companies and our own experience, being the first to market ideas makes you more likely to go viral. Not just for the obvious reason of being first, but because web crawlers that exist in each of these social media platforms are able to distinguish unique content from not, whether an image or video or specific words. If you're not first and instead are recirculating something, it has a much lower chance of going viral. That's why some organizations that recycle a lot of content tend to have lower views and engagement.

Having a unique style is also key. Tyler Bowyer describes TPUSA's approach:

> *"I come from a background where I worked very closely with individuals at Google and in the social media space for a long time, specifically on the political side. And what I realized really quickly was that the conservative movement was lacking. [TPUSA] has been a pioneer, pretty much the way that everybody frames*

> *their videos. We used a very specific font, the style of fonts that was topical. We started launching Turning Point USA social media sites a few years ago. Nobody was really getting it right at all in the political space. And nobody had really made themselves known as a viral content creator. And we taught them everything they needed to know, which is that, in order to have a successful social media strategy, particularly in politics, is that it can't look like it's too polished, and it has to be something that people feel like they can share. And so, that's really been the basic strategy behind everything that we've ever done: don't look too polished. Polished enough where people know it's coming from a legitimate source, but not too polished where it looks like it's corporate, and then also creating ideas and speaking up on behalf of people that don't have a huge following, where other people, they feel like, well, that's organic."*[242]

Creating a unique "look" also distinguishes your group from the other players in the space.

Conservative organizations also need very specific, community-based content campaigns. These are social media movements focused on lots of different people telling different stories within the same theme. Morgan Zegers is the founder of Young Americans Against Socialism, a grassroots political organization devoted to educating young Americans on the perils of adopting a socialist worldview.[243] My team has worked with her on numerous content campaigns to grow their audience. In the interview for this book, she stressed the significance of those video campaigns. "We make educational videos, and we focus a lot on firsthand testimony and emotional communication. We focused on peer-to-peer

242 Interview with Tyler Bowyer, December 28, 2020, via phone.

243 Morgan Zegers (@MorganZegers), Twitter, https://twitter.com/MorganZegers.

communications."[244] Another example is Charles Moran who spoke to me about GetOutspoken.com. "I had writers and researchers on staff who were doing the work and writing the pieces that make the conservative arguments and provide the context on a number of LGBTQ issues.... Log Cabin is in a position to lead that conversation because we can help conservatives articulate arguments without sounding like a hater or not inclusive. Our members and our surrogates out there are leading these conversations and articulate those arguments for straight allies."[245] This was a breakthrough campaign for Log Cabin, as Charles describes it. "We had chapters, but we didn't have any digital way for people to engage with our organization. If you didn't live in a state or a city that had a chapter, there was really no way for you to easily engage with Log Cabin. So by creating a 'Get Outspoken' campaign and doing the type of work we did by having those meetings and the videos and the shareable information and pushing back on the lies that the Left pushes out, cancel culture, giving people that voice to step up and say, 'I've never been involved in the Republican Party, I've never been involved in the conservative movement, or I've never even been involved in politics. But these people speak for me, and they help amplify my voice. And there is a way for me to participate and engage with that.' We've never had anything. These are being powered by Log Cabin Republicans to draw in these people and to create this new voice and to start to take back the narrative that if you're proud and gay, that you've got to be this crazy lefty."[246] Connecting with individuals at an organic level was immensely successful for the Log Cabin Republicans and should be a blueprint for others.

The quantity of content doesn't matter if the quality isn't there. We have found that combating narratives head-on is the most effective tactic for social media growth. It's not

244 Interview with Morgan Zegers, December 1, 2020, via phone.
245 Interview with Charles Moran, December 17, 2020, via phone.
246 Interview with Charles Moran, December 17, 2020, via phone.

enough to say taxes are too high or regulations are bad, but you must specifically comment on news of the day issues and relate information back to ultimate policy aims.

Daniel Turner is the founder and executive director of @PowerTheFuture, an organization devoted to American energy advocacy and "exposing the socialist radical green political movement."[247] Daniel is particularly familiar with leftist organizations commandeering language surrounding the environment for their benefit: "The Left is winning in the environmental space because it has us all conditioned to see the world as a binary choice or to see this issue as a binary choice, meaning you either support fossil fuels and coal and oil or you want to clean the earth."[248] Power the Future pushes back against these narratives by "reclaiming language and not being afraid to engage in these battles."[249] Daniel and his group know the power of social media. "Facebook and other socials helped promote our stuff, which our main content was drawing out the logical consequences of what these policies would do. Comedy works, charm works, appeal works. We did a series of photos of what America covered in solar panels would look like, what America covered in wind turbines would look like. It is really important because people need to see these issues sometimes in a vacuum. Climate change is seen in one dimension, 'We just have to do X, and it will go away.' But that action does have an equal and opposite reaction, and that's the consequence that we never talk about. So that's one of the most important things to do.... For example, there was a video, one was my most popular tweet, with kids skipping school on a Friday, all saying, 'Hey, hey, ho ho, fossil fuels have got to go.' And every kid had a cell phone and a water bottle in their hand. And I pointed out that they have no idea

247 Power the Future, https://powerthefuture.com/.

248 Interview with Daniel Turner, December 11, 2020, via phone.

249 Interview with Daniel Turner, December 11, 2020, via phone.

what they're even thinking about."[250] And what groups like Daniel's do particularly well is expose the hypocrisy—liberal groups that Daniel goes up against never realize that their tactics "never hurt some of these other geopolitical foes of ours. They just hurt the US and make our position competitively disadvantageous."[251] (I also just loved this take: "It's alarming to see how willingly people that have never traveled anywhere or think that, like Europe is some role model for us. You just sort of shake your head, wondering what's going on there."[252])

And never forget, consistency is king. Tyler Bowyer knows this all too well. "You got to remain consistent. You've got to have good, quality content every single day. It's a mixture of cross-promoting well and using brands and relationships that you have. We did this well when we started a number of years ago and that really helped start kick our organization off. And that's why we've become more effective and bigger than anybody else."[253] He went on to say: "People like that consistency on Twitter, if they're going to be able to visit it and get that same brand every time they go and visit a page. And that's part of the thing with the content piece that we're going to detail with, because this is everything, all of these social media companies, everything is based on consistency."[254]

Texas Public Policy Foundation has also seen success with videos on social media exposing real-world outcomes of policy. Chief Executive Officer Kevin Roberts[255] described to me, "We decided to do one- to two-minute videos.... One that was really successful was of a younger woman who we showed during her day, twenty-five or thirty different things she uses for makeup, her pants, what she puts in the car, all products we advocated for and represent Texas' interests.

250 Interview with Daniel Turner, December 11, 2020, via phone.

251 Interview with Daniel Turner, December 11, 2020, via phone.

252 Interview with Daniel Turner, December 11, 2020, via phone.

253 Interview with Tyler Bowyer, December 28, 2020, via phone.

254 Interview with Tyler Bowyer, December 28, 2020, via phone.

255 Texas Public Policy Foundation, https://www.texaspolicy.com/about/staff/kevin-roberts-ph-d/.

It's sort of a soft message that it is also very upbeat, which I think is strikingly appealing for younger viewers. And we deployed this tactic in Colorado when they wanted to ban fracking. We weren't directly involved in that campaign, but we used our audience segmentation techniques, and roughly over a period of three weeks, give or take a few days, we moved females to support our opposition to a fracking ban, something like fifteen percentage points, and it was directly correlated to what we invested to boost that video, as well as some folks out there who are working. And so that's one example. The point in microcosm of what our strategy is, which is to find segments of the audience, to move them, to talk to them about the importance of petroleum in their everyday lives, rather than be in the impossible position of trying to defend how the Left has framed the narrative, which is that oil and gas people are bad."[256]

As we discussed before, knowing your audience is key. For the Texas Public Policy Foundation, they "determined which segments of the population to target.... We do polling.... We poll issues rather than candidates."[257] He continued, "So three years ago, we were probably pretty good at the typical digital advertising that groups are doing. In fact, most people thought we were ahead of the curve. We hired some people from the true political campaign world.... But what we did differently was we basically did a focus group on steroids.... And we were due to add testing that you're familiar with, with our digital campaigns so that we could have targeted messages for segments of audience."[258]

Being successful is going to require consistent content with a targeted approach. We must be ready and willing to reflect on what content is and is not working and make necessary adjustments.

256 Interview with Kevin Roberts, December 15, 2020, via phone.
257 Interview with Kevin Roberts, December 15, 2020, via phone.
258 Interview with Kevin Roberts, December 15, 2020, via phone.

Networking 101

I have worked with organizations with basically empty checking accounts, no Twitter prowess, no real following or media contacts, certainly no political contacts. To be a successful organization starting out, you have to be prepared to work hard and be 110 percent dedicated to building your movement and your mission. Relationships are everything. Find dynamic, interesting people and establish relationships with them off of social media. As I have addressed numerous times in various parts of the book, the success of a movement is dependent on who is promoting and how it is being promoted. An electric idea with no believers is a tweet. A good idea with a network is a movement.

TPUSA prioritizes networking. "Our ambassador network, which essentially is our digital activists, we have now almost three hundred ambassadors for Turning Point USA. They're unpaid, but we invite them and bring them in for events and then provide them with content and opportunity, a unique opportunity to get our content and then network with one another that really never existed before," says Tyler Bowyer, "and so, a number of those people have been on TV, news personalities or fitness gurus or their own political brand or athletes. We seek these people out every single day."[259]

Look around and see who is doing something similar to you. Coordinate with them, collaborate on projects, content, and events. Remember, we are coalition-minded on this side of the house. This also means never turn down media (at least early on). Be prepared to get up early to do a TV hit, even if for a random local news station. Early on, all press is good press. Every opportunity that someone gives you to freely promote your work, you have to take. You also never know who you'll meet when you do a TV or radio hit, and those connections can be invaluable later on.

259 Interview with Tyler Bowyer, December 28, 2020, via phone.

It's Not about the Money, but Kinda

At a certain point, we all have to get paid. Organizations struggle constantly from lack of funding, and many suffer from inefficiencies, unnecessary largesse, and unfocused missions. One inefficiency is organizational spending on social media when it's not efficient. Most of my clients want to toss money at Facebook ads and think that will get them the results they desire. This is not always the case.

Keep in mind conservatives are wildly outspent in advocacy. "We have to punch above our weight.... On the energy issue, for example, we're outspent about twenty to one.... But conservatives are spending that money more efficiently. And therefore, with even more money, our policy outcomes could be even more efficient and more persuasive and broad-based."[260]

Organizations have to break out of traditional spending to be effective. "I think that organizations that are successful in the end have had the ability to raise enough money so they could invest in additional platforms like digital and social media."[261] But as Stephen Moore says, "The mission is to get people something. And I think another lesson is people want to feel like they're part of something. If you give twenty dollars or fifty dollars or one hundred dollars, you're just spitting into a big ocean. But if you do it in combination with a thousand other people, you're making a big impact. So people like to feel like what they're doing is having an impact on something, and the Club for Growth model was training people of like minds together."[262]

Donations will come when all the other steps are achieved. But stay away from groups with a history of reckless spending.

260 Interview with Kevin Roberts, December 15, 2020, via phone.

261 Interview with Scott Parkinson, November 24, 2020, via phone.

262 Interview with Stephen Moore, December 15, 2020, via phone.

Chapter 6:
THE "INFLUENCERS"

"We are losing the cultural war and the cultural values; we've been losing for a long time. Politics certainly plays a role in all that, but I think politics is downstream from the broader cultural dynamics of the entertainment world. And so, what Hollywood has done to advance their cause, to change the narrative and really change people's values and how they view things is probably the most powerful and influential component of that."

- David Spady [263]

BEYOND POLITICIANS AND POLITICAL organizations is an entire cadre of people labeled "influencers" for their ability to shape public perception and policy. The influencer class has been particularly effective with their political discourse on social media by being removed from the actual political fight and the need to be elected, which

263 Interview with David Spady, December 7, 2020, via phone.

permits candor, authenticity, and the ability to be more direct (and brutal) to progressives. The mere attention of a particular influencer to a particular political issue has often created an outsized political response that has caused politicians and organizations to respond accordingly.

For decades now, Hollywood and New York celebrities have added their two cents to progressive politics and furthered the liberal agenda. In recent years, conservatives have had a growing rebuttal with conservative influencers able to garner significant media attention and followings on social media.

Reading this book, you might yourself want to accumulate enough followers to become an influencer. Good. From memes to TV punditry to rapid-fire tweets, we need more conservatives wielding all the tools and identities and backgrounds we can to connect with as many folks across our nation and the world. The big tent has got to cut across a lot of different mediums. Being influential is really just creating an audience and getting people in the door. It doesn't matter if that is Twitter engagement, a TV audience, or getting people to come to the Big Top to see the political circus.

In my work, I help candidates, politicians, and organizations, but I also work with influencers in their own growth and promotion to help them find their audience and keep them coming back for more. What makes me and guys like me so helpful is that some folks don't know (at least at first) what is going to make them, *them*. The one viral moment that defines a career can happen in an instant or come slowly from years of diligent, consistent work.

What I know is that conservatives in the influencer space have to work together. It's a symbiotic relationship that brings us all up. I know in other parts of the book, I talk about the importance of the individual, and I do so in terms of individual liberty. But what I mean here is that we have to be about the mission, the activism. Working in tandem and with a conservative movement in mind gets more eyeballs on our content and, in my case and in my view, good content that drives our country forward.

We have to start elevating people who are actually about the work, people who are out there on a grassroots level, connecting with voters and making a difference, cleaning up neighborhoods, and carrying out the service that our nation calls for. And we need to obviously take down a lot of these people whose only contribution is selling their books on Fox News, making it seem as though they're out there being activists when they're doing nothing at all.

We talked to a lot of influencers—some you have heard of and some you might not have. All of them bring to the table something unique, something worth listening to, and if you want to emulate them, a lesson to learn.

Donald Trump Jr.

(6.9 MILLION TWITTER FOLLOWERS)

I want to start my look into influencers with perhaps someone who set out to be a businessman but was thrust into the national spotlight when his father entered the political arena on June 16, 2015. Donald Trump Jr., the eldest son of President Donald Trump, is outspoken, unapologetic, and enigmatic in his defense of what has made this country great. He continues to this day to be a strong supporter and advocate for his father and the policies that made him popular enough to be president of the United States.

Emulating someone like Donald Trump Jr. is obviously a tall task, as he is wealthier and more connected than most people. However, speaking with Mr. Trump is such a rare opportunity, and his insights by mere proximity to how our government works from the highest levels to the mistreatment at the hands of the mainstream media require his inclusion in this book.

I asked Donald Trump Jr. about how uses his social media accounts. "I probably check my Instagram and Twitter way more than I should, and I run both accounts myself. My Twitter is almost strictly political, as I use it as my primary source to follow and comment on the news of the day, whereas my Instagram is much less focused on politics and more about just having fun."[264]

As busy as he is, we noticed how important it is to the Trumps since President Trump has left office to point out how unfairly their family and his presidency have been treated. I asked him what he thought about the difference in treatment: "The great irony of the media's obsession with 'fake news' spreading on social media is that they themselves have been the biggest culprits of making verifiable lies go viral. They'll scream and demand 'fact checks' over joke memes I post on my Instagram but don't seem very interested in a self-reckoning when it comes to their own records of reporting 'misinformation.' We just saw an example of this with the *Washington Post*'s false reporting about my father's phone call with Frances Watson of Georgia's Secretary of State office. The *Washington Post* got caught red-handed lying about what was said in the call, but the damage was already done, and ultimately, the *Washington Post* won't pay any price for getting the story wrong. That's their playbook: Write a salacious lie using anonymous sources to drive whatever narrative they want to drive, let it go viral, and then if they end up getting caught lying, they'll quietly post a correction weeks or months later.... But the damage is already done at that point, and the reporters writing the lies know that. You also saw it with the false *Atlantic* piece, claiming my father disrespected members of the military. Despite the fact that numerous on-the-record sources denied it ever happened, that didn't stop the entire

264 Interview with Donald Trump Jr., March 31, 2021, via email.

corporate media from treating those smears as a stone-cold fact. There are virtually no consequences for reporters who get stories wrong, so long as those stories damage Donald Trump or conservatives more broadly. There's a huge gulf between how the media covered the Trump White House and what the reality was. There are so few major news organizations interested in presenting a balanced and unbiased product today, which is why I do think social media is the most effective way to combat lies from the Left."[265]

After President Trump was banned from Twitter, Donald Trump Jr. stated freedom of speech doesn't exist in America anymore.[266] "I understand the difference between the legal definition of the First Amendment and the principle of free speech on which the First Amendment was based. So while technically these Big Tech companies aren't violating the First Amendment, since that only applies to government, they are certainly knowingly violating the principle of free speech," Trump Jr. wrote to me.[267] He continued, "I think that's wrong. Our founders would be aghast at the idea that corporate conglomerates were shutting down the legal speech of everyday Americans. My views on this are really very simple. I believe these social media companies shouldn't censor legal speech. Threats of violence are illegal speech and should be banned, but if it's not against the law, all speech should be protected, no matter how repellent some of that speech may be. It amazes me to watch how the Left has devolved into puritans on the issue of speech and are willing to use Big Tech to enforce their dogma. It is anti-American, and conservatives need to understand that their ultimate goal is to erase all of our voices on the platforms that most Americans use. That's why I think it's important that we don't recede and leave the

---

265 Interview with Donald Trump Jr., March 31, 2021, via email.

266 Connor Perrett, "Donald Trump Jr. Says 'The World Is Laughing at America' as He Rails against His Dad's Twitter Ban, Saying 'Free Speech Is Dead,'" *The Business Insider* (January 9, 2021), https://www.businessinsider.com/trump-jr-free-speech-is-dead-controlled-by-leftist-overlords-2021-1.

267 Interview with Donald Trump Jr., March 31, 2021, via email.

big social media companies like YouTube, Instagram, Twitter, and Facebook because that's exactly what the other side wants. But at the same time, I think it's important to simultaneously build up non-traditional platforms like Rumble and Telegram who are actually committed to protecting the speech rights of all Americans."[268]

This isn't an uncommon refrain from those we have spoken to in this book. Undoubtedly, conservatives are under attack from social media companies. At a minimum, these companies are having a chilling effect on free speech. Donald Trump Jr. warned, "Conservatives aren't at war with Big Tech. Big Tech is at war with conservatives. They declared war on us when they decided they would do the Left's bidding and use their secret algorithms to censor conservatives and boost Democrats. They were obsessed with stopping my father's reelection in 2020 and have made clear that they will continue to do whatever they can to stop him or another conservative like him from ever winning the White House again. All we're doing is defending ourselves from their attacks. While at times it may seem like an uphill battle for conservatives, I believe that as cancel culture, censorship, and corporate blacklisting increase and affect more and more people, that more will wake up to how dangerous the masters of the universe in Silicon Valley truly are to our way of life."[269]

The more I have seen and spoken to Donald Trump Jr. about politics and his future, I couldn't let the opportunity pass by without asking his future plans. "I don't consider myself a politician and have no plans right now to run for elected office. However, I do care about the future of the country and want to be in the fight for conservative values."[270]

---

268 Interview with Donald Trump Jr., March 31, 2021, via email.
269 Interview with Donald Trump Jr., March 31, 2021, via email.
270 Interview with Donald Trump Jr., March 31, 2021, via email.

Charlie Kirk

(1.7 MILLION TWITTER FOLLOWERS)

Charlie has been a dear friend since I began on social media many years ago. He is a genuine guy and has been clearly successful in his still early career. Charlie founded Turning Point USA and grew the organization to a massive group with hundreds of chapters nationwide, conferences that draw thousands, and influence in elections and in the White House under the Trump administration. The president and his son Donald Trump Jr. consider him a friend, and there is a laundry list of people who can directly attribute their success in their careers, in their political positions, or on television to Charlie Kirk.

In addition to being gracious enough to provide the foreword to this book, Charlie gave me an interview as well.

Charlie has become known for particular (and very effective) tweet formats. I asked him how he created several tweet formats that are always going viral:

> *"This really is more of a history class answer than it is a current events answer at this point. Twitter has declined so dramatically in terms of its effectiveness for people who hold our views that what was is no longer what is.*
>
> *That said, there is a methodology to this. When I started campaigning with Don Jr. in August of 2016, I was unverified on Twitter and had 31,000 followers. By the end of the campaign, I was still unverified but had grown to 63,000 followers. Four years later, I was verified and had more than 1.8 million followers. Axios reported me as having one of the top five Twitter accounts in the world.*

While the specifics of my technique are proprietary, the approach I have taken is not. For starters, I have really worked at it. I would put in hours studying my successful tweets and ask myself, 'Why were they successful?' I would look at language, structure, timing, everything. I would try to recreate success and stay away from failure.

I would tweet roughly every forty-five minutes and throughout the news cycle. Staying timely and being present were keys. Nobody ever had to wonder and wait for too long to find out what Charlie Kirk thought about what was going on.

I would also push boundaries, but I would do so factually, not with over-the-top rhetoric. This approach has become increasingly important, as censorship on Twitter has reached a level that would have been hard to envision just a few years ago.

In short, effective use of Twitter is like anything else. To be successful, you really have to work at it. There are no shortcuts. There is nothing about me inherently that made my Twitter success inevitable. I was also not a celebrity. I just made a deliberate and dedicated effort to figure it out."[271]

TPUSA continues to be instrumental in steering legions of conservative youth away from socialism. Charlie explained how he has adapted his messages to meet the interests of each generation of students:

"You have to stay on top of what concerns them. When we started TPUSA, it was all about limiting big govern-

271 Interview with Charlie Kirk, March 4, 2021, via email.

> *ment interference in a free-market economy. We had themes like 'big government sucks' and 'capitalism cures.' Our focus was very similar to that of what you would associate with a traditional sort of libertarian platform.*
>
> *Today, all of that has changed. Students are far more concerned with the cultural issues we are experiencing, such as cancel culture, the imposition of critical race theory in schools and businesses, Big Tech censorship, and so on. While the original issues like debt and deficits, taxes, and health care are still near and dear to me, they are not what energizes the movement. If we failed to adjust our focus, we would quickly become irrelevant.*
>
> *That is the difficult part about organizations that are bound to fixed principles but without current adaptation. While principles are indeed timeless, their level of applicability and their relative importance vary. In our work at TPUSA, we try to not forsake principles, but at the same time, we insist on staying relevant. If we fail in the short run, we won't be around to prevail in the long run."*[272]

Based on a number of metrics, Charlie has one of the most engaged-with accounts on Twitter.[273] I asked him how he goes about reflecting on his brand and what role he thinks he plays in simultaneously combating left extremism while building a coalition on the right:

> *"With regard to what is termed 'left extremism,' it is fairly easy to combat because it is very easy to*

---

272 Interview with Charlie Kirk, March 4, 2021, via email.

273 Axios (@axios), Twitter, Feb. 22, 2019, 9:52 a.m., https://twitter.com/axios/status/1099004062039-789568?s=20.

see. There are also well-established philosophical arguments against it that have been developed over centuries, going back to Aristotle. The key is simply to understand the arguments and to apply them to current times and in current language.

Building a coalition on our side, however, is a little more intricate. The key is to first recognize and admit that we also have extremists, just like the other folks, and that those extremists' views are every bit as dangerous on our side as they are on their side. That said, the question is how do we recognize them?

The answer is by making certain we know exactly who we are as individuals and for what we stand. We need a philosophical foundation of right and wrong. We need to know what we believe. If you don't know what you believe in, then you can easily be co-opted. We all know the person who sits in a meeting and has no strong position and who can change their mind on any topic depending upon who is speaking. We cannot let ourselves be that person.

If you believe in God, if you believe that someone's skin color doesn't matter, if you believe that all people have the same natural rights, then anyone who comes your way speaking differently cannot corrupt you. If you are just wearing your team's jersey, you will likely end up cheering for anyone who says they are on your team. If you're principled, if your premises are solid, you are much tougher to mislead.

Ultimately, the extremists will always reveal who they really are. You need to build a principled movement

> *that does not bend to them. If you do that, they will eventually 'snap' out of frustration. We need to flush them out, not fit them in. If we do that, it is easy to build a coalition around principled people sharing the same core values."*[274]

In addition to building his own brand, Charlie runs a successful organization full-time. I asked him about what has contributed to his account's and organization's success and how other conservatives can emulate what he and his team have done:

> *"This relates to the answer I gave to the first question. The success of any individual or organization's use of social media platforms is generated by investing the time and energy to become students of the platform and masters of the craft. It is almost that simple, and there is really no substitute.*
>
> *My team will tell you that I would spend an almost excruciating amount of time laboring over the word choice in every single tweet. I would start with a premise and just write it down. Then I would think through, word by word, the most effective way to say it. I would sometimes spend forty-five minutes wording a simple 130-character tweet. This painstaking process gradually became shorter and simpler the more I practiced and the more I learned what resonated.*
>
> *Social media gives us a unique opportunity to say more with less. How many times have you read a 1,000-word column and wondered at the end what the writer really was trying to say? If social media is used*

274 Interview with Charlie Kirk, March 4, 2021, via email.

properly, its tighter format forces you to consolidate your thoughts. How thoroughly and clearly you do that is up to you and how hard you want to work to become a subject matter expert.

I also truly believe that conservatives need to be more creative and have more fun in their use of messaging, not just with social media but overall. I started at this so young that, in some ways, I tried things where I might simply not have known any better. Whatever the case, my unorthodox and creative approach has seemed to resonate. So take a walk on the wild side and express yourself in ways that are not offensive but that can take hold with your audience. For a concept to really take hold, it needs to be understandable, actionable, sticky, and fun. Conservatives need to remember that last item in the string when trying to connect with any audience."[275]

Tomi Lahren

(1.6 MILLION TWITTER FOLLOWERS)

Fox Nation host Tomi Lahren took a break from kicking ass and taking names to speak with us about getting in the fight for conservatism. Tomi got her start super young and has been a public figure for a long time with tons of TV experience and experience advocating for conservatives across the country.

In her own words on becoming Tomi Lahren, she told me:

"I started my social media presence in my first job out of college at twenty-one years old. I had my own show. I was on national TV. It was so fast. I knew I

275 Interview with Charlie Kirk, March 4, 2021, via email.

> *would have to get pretty good at social media because that's the only way I was going to be able to grow in my career. That was the only way I was really going to be able to promote what I was doing. We used to cut the final segment of the show, we used to put them up on YouTube, on Facebook, and any social media. I would start with a little post on my Instagram back then. I really had to get creative in using social media to get awareness of what I was doing.... For me, it was really out of necessity to get online... and then [my clips] happened to go viral on their own just because of the content and because of the way that I deliver. And I think the passion people hear I'm talking about was effective. I think there are so many young people now who aspire to be influencers, aspire to be YouTube or Facebook personalities, or even aspire to be political commentators that look at a career like I've had or others that have followed me, and they want to just be viral immediately. They want to do and say things to get people's attention or be controversial for the sake of being controversial.... Sometimes people just say things to go viral. My advice is to build an organic following. It's just a gradual build. I've been able to sustain it and build that brand because I maintain those core values no matter what I was in and over time."*[276]

Tomi is a passionate talker and takes an unabashed approach to social media. She is a role model in many ways. I asked her about her approach to social media:

> *"I get accused of being too controversial or too radical. But I talk about supporting troops, supporting military, believing in God, believing that the American people have the freedom to open their businesses and go to*

276 Interview with Tomi Lahren, December 29, 2020, via phone.

> *work every day. So it's really a double standard when it comes to the Left and the Right.... I say things forcefully, and I say it passionately. I believe it to my very core. And nothing comes out of my mouth that I don't believe.... They like to talk about empowering women. But when women like myself have a strong and passionate voice, we are deemed controversial, radical shock jocks, attention seeking.... Being labeled has never bothered me because I know that that is a tactic of the Left, and it's a tactic we have to stop following you."*[277]

As we discussed earlier in the book, there is a premium on coalition building and creating a network. Tomi knows this firsthand:

> *"Conservatives need to band together and start sticking up for one another. Even if we disagree with each other, which is perfectly acceptable, and encouraged, I encourage conservatives to have disagreements among ourselves. But I do think we stick together and not fall victim to canceling each other. Sometimes that's easy to do because some people are trying to one up their careers. They want to silence the other conservative, which has been a big problem. I think grifting in the conservative base has been a big problem. Those who had realized that they can make a profit off of it or join an organization and make a profit off of it or get some fame off of it, that's been a big problem in the conservative movement."*[278]

Tomi is a content machine, constantly tweeting, putting out videos, and pushing her opinions. I asked her about her process:

---

277 Interview with Tomi Lahren, December 29, 2020, via phone.

278 Interview with Tomi Lahren, December 29, 2020, via phone.

"For those that want to get into this career, Twitter and Instagram and Facebook and TV appearances, and that is the totality of the life for me. I live and breathe this. So it's important to me to follow the news. It's important for me to put that out there. But it's not something that's a job for me. It's kind of just my life. But the reason I've been so successful, particularly on Instagram, is because I show more than just the political side of my life. I show all sides to my life. Really. I'm an open book. I show people what I do. I show people that I have fun. I think that's another way that we win. The culture war is that conservatives have to stop standing in front of a camera in a suit or dress, delivering their message and then going off and living their lives. And nobody has any idea what they do. And we just become a segment of the television or the screen. That's not me. I go out, I have fun, I have friends, I drink beer, I listen to rap music. I show people that. And that's one of the reasons that I have done so well, especially in the social media space, is because I'm not just this one-dimensional political robot that exists on Twitter or Facebook to argue with liberals."[279]

And because I value my readers and want to leave no stone unturned, I asked her what her favorite beer is, to which she told me, "Miller Lite."[280]

279 Interview with Tomi Lahren, December 29, 2020, via phone.
280 Interview with Tomi Lahren, December 29, 2020, via phone.

Chris and Dana Loesch

(1 MILLION TWITTER FOLLOWERS)

I spoke with the power couple Chris and Dana Loesch on their role in the conservative movement. Dana is a Second Amendment activist and former National Rifle Association spokeswoman. Chris is her partner in crime and chief of staff.

Dana is a regular on national TV and has made many tough appearances including being the heel at the CNN town hall to defend the Second Amendment immediately after the Parkland school shooting.

As an influencer and thought leader, big moments in the spotlight are where Dana has proved that she has intellectual strength and fortitude under pressure.

I asked Dana to tell us about her headspace going into the Parkland town hall:

> *"I don't think I ever had the chance to really sort of frame it in my mind and gain any kind of strategy beyond remaining the calmest person in the room because it was so, everything was very last minute. I think that when the town hall took place, it was on a Wednesday, and I found out that I was going the Tuesday before, and I didn't realize that I was going to be on stage. I just kept thinking it was going to be a more traditional town hall and the people that would be speaking who were directly involved, either as families or administrators or members of law enforcement who were probably responsible and involved with creating a security plan, for instance. I had to fall back on everything that I know to do up to that point because I didn't find out I was going to be on stage until the strike down the next day. And at that point, I didn't even realize that I was saying*

anything. And then I didn't realize I was going to be on stage actually speaking until I got there. I always expect the worst. So I was just anticipating to be completely railroaded, and there could not be a good faith discussion. ***I knew that I was going to be there for about two minutes of hate.*** *And I was kind of an avatar for gun rights, that they were wanting to stand me up to exploit a tragedy to push policy. And when I got there, that's when they told me that I was going to be on stage speaking, and I was going to be on stage with the sheriff, and I knew immediately what they were going to do. They were going to appeal to authority, and they were going to make it look as though I was up against law enforcement, and they were going to set up a double narrative of making him look like a sympathetic figure when in fact he was the cause of it because he was just absolutely incompetent, according to the Amnesty Commission. And that's just not what they concluded. Even his deputies had no confidence in him. They were making them not to be very sympathetic. And while at the same time making it was making me take the fall, making me the bad guy. When I just left, many people in America had only heard of the school district. But unfortunately, when this happened—and so you asked about my mindset going in there—you have to just be able to adapt very quickly. And I hate saying it because cynicism, especially in young people, is so awful. But you really kind of have to expect the worst and expect the absolute worst so that you can prepare for it and prepare for the worst possible outcome and know what kind of narrative they are wanting to put together. They're incredibly transparent because I*

> *think that they just felt as though that they were really brazen about it. They just felt overly confident that the activists knew that the media was going to help carry water for them. And it was unlike anything that I've ever experienced. And I've been in debates before, and I've been at rallies and protests and all kinds of stuff. But this was the first time that it was sanctioned on a national stage and broadcast on a major cable news network. And I thought that was kind of a turning point in political discourse."*[281]

Being on the national stage constantly can take a toll on someone. As a family that defends a really controversial issue in America, the Loesch family is subjected to a constant barrage of hate. I asked how their family handles the spotlight, because if you want to be an influencer, you need to be prepared:

> *"When we flew out there to Florida to do that event, I typically told my mother to not allow my kids to watch it within one hour, children watching what was going to happen on television, because we knew it was going to be pretty brutal, and they did anyway. And I have always sort of allowed them to come to their own conclusions on things. We educate them, we give them the tools. But then at the same time, we expect them to develop into thinking people to come to their own conclusions. We have family dinners and events. We're a very tight-knit family. I would say I was very worried initially, obviously, because, just for kids to see their parent in a position like that, it's tough. But I was also very concerned about any actions of grace that they would tell because it is really easy to see something like that. And you are very justified in having resentment and a really hard part to respond*

281 Interview with Dana Loesch, December 10, 2020, via phone.

> *to things like that. I can't begrudge people for being hardened by those experiences and seeing things like that. ...How we all need to match all of the rage and all of the hate and all of the resentment that was there, match it and nullify it by pushing back with as much grace."*[282]

Chris gave his perspective as well:

> *"We tell our kids you're going to see things on social media, you're going to hear things from people that maybe in your friend group periphery that are negative about your mom especially or myself sometimes. And you have to kind of let it roll off your back a little bit.... But I will say that preparation for that was a lot of prayer and understanding that people from the other side were going to be extremely coached and emotionally very charged... we knew that* ***you can speak the truth while also still being compassionate and sensitive to what is happening around you****."*[283]

The Loesch's echoed the message of authenticity:

> *"On social media, it doesn't matter how truthful the statement is. It just matters how many people repeat it. Your first new measure of authenticity. You know, unfortunately, and that's why there are so many people, including even some on the left, who are more classical liberal that are pushing back on this because they see the danger in it. And I mean, you have to know this was coming in a system that rewards the, I think, most strident with likes and thumbs up and everything else and comments and retweets or what-*

282 Interview with Dana Loesch, December 10, 2020, via phone.

283 Interview with Chris Loesch, December 10, 2020, via phone.

> *ever, that that was just the logical next step, the logical progression for all of this new state. I mean, especially now with things being manipulated and people on the left having to create a safe space for themselves because they can't offer a rebuttal to anything that conservatives are putting out there. So they want to limit the conservative side of it."*[284]

Dave Rubin

(988.7K TWITTER FOLLOWERS)

Dave Rubin, a former progressive and now a libertarian show host, built his following from the ground up with a unique style of just talking to people and being a good listener. He has become a firebrand on the right for his comedic style and wide-ranging conversations and demonized on the left for talking to people they consider political villains.

I spoke with Dave about free speech and how he has built his show:

> *"How I sort of became one of the central figures in this thing was different for me than the average conservative because I came from the Left. I was on the Young Turks Network. I was a Democrat my whole life. I was a Bernie supporter. I absolutely was a progressive. And when I started, now it's about five years ago, I started seeing some of this stuff; 'woke' was kind of creeping into everything. I started seeing how the liberals were calling to cancel people, not defending free speech. I was seeing this sort of new radical side of liberalism that seemed completely illiberal to me. I started saying the phrase regressive rather than progressive*

284 Interview with Dana Loesch, December 10, 2020, via phone.

> *Left.... A lot of young people especially, they don't want to be thought of as conservative. There's something old about it. It sounds kind of crusty and not that appealing.... But I think when they saw me, a regular person, clearly not an extremist, not an old guy, not someone that was angry, someone that was just kind of pleasant and decent, say, 'Hey, what's going on here with free speech? Why is the Left trying to get people kicked off Twitter? Why are they calling everybody racist and a bigot?' And I kept saying, especially at the beginning, 'Guys we got to look at ourselves. Let's fix this thing.' Now, I don't consider myself part of the Left anymore. And I don't think that the left vs. right-wing divide has that much value anymore, because I think it's really authoritarian versus libertarian. This gave me a special space to be in, because then when I started interviewing people, I was starting to get all the disaffected Left. And there's an awful lot of disaffected lefties. I would say it's probably the number one growing segment in the political spectrum, old-school liberals who obviously are not OK and want nothing to do with the modern Democratic Party. But they don't necessarily want to call themselves conservatives yet. I think that that's the challenge for all of us, is that it's basically 'woke' versus conservative now."*[285]

I have followed Dave for years, and he is not someone who shies away from tough conversations. He has a political irreverence to him that is refreshing and attracts people to him. I asked him how he views his brand:

> *"The real truth is I never put that much thought into it as if I was creating a brand or if I was supposed to*

285 Interview with Dave Rubin, February 24, 2021, via phone.

> *be a 'thing' or something like that. I felt I could sit down with people, some whom I agree with and some whom I disagreed with, and get their opinions in a respectful way. Vine videos, Snapchat was just starting, obviously Twitter existed and Facebook. And I felt it was making us dumber. And I felt like it was making us all angrier at each other. And I thought, let's go back to, like, some old school talk.... I think treating people respectfully shouldn't be that great of a leap. And yet, it bizarrely is. And that's all I've really tried to do. It's a little more difficult in the last couple of years, the general tenor of our politics has gotten kind of crazy."*[286]

I couldn't agree more, watching the tune of politics be either Harry Potter or Hitler, I have seen how silly our political debates can be. But Dave faces real pushback that when he has these conversations, he is platforming "bad" people, "literally Hitler." I ask him for a rebuttal to these lunatics:

> *"I think it's up to me to decide who I want to talk to. And the idea that there should be a blanket rule that these are the acceptable people to talk to and these are the unacceptable people to talk to, I think is a really dangerous thing. And by the way, that's why it's great that we have meritocracy in podcasting and everything else, at least for now. You could decide what you want to do on your show. That's a beautiful thing about independence. But I would say more broadly, the funny thing about that argument is that's one of the things that only people on the right have to put up with. It's only the people on the right that have to police who they're going to talk to. And by the way, they'll say, 'OK, well, you can't talk to Milo.'*

---

286 Interview with Dave Rubin, February 24, 2021, via phone.

> *You end up with a lot of people very upset that I had him on. And when I had Milo on at the beginning especially, he was just this weird person that seemed sort of interesting. So I said let me talk to him. And then he became this whole other thing. And I interviewed him a couple of times throughout that. But it's not that they're afraid of Milo Yiannopoulos. Look what happened when **Politico** had Shapiro put an article in. The whole political staff had enough...and said he should not be allowed to be platformed. And yet on the left, there's nothing too left for these people. There are genuine anti-Semites in Congress. But on the right, you always have to police things."*[287]

Dave has had some really great takes about the coronavirus and how that's exposed some of our political leaders and elites as wildly extreme. As we enter into a new age of political life, I was curious about his thoughts on where we go from here:

> *"There's an awful lot of people that want to control us. And if you're a progressive, you find an authoritarian under the skin pretty quickly. It's not a coincidence that the red states are doing pretty well, and the blue states are doing terribly. Florida is the second-oldest population in the United States. They've done an incredible job of vaccinating their elderly population. They stayed open. Ron DeSantis decided not to destroy the lives of the Floridians, the people that he served. And it was wonderful there. And I was at a restaurant indoors. And guess what? There were ninety-year-old people there, having dinner. And it was up to them to decide what to do. Some people didn't wear masks.... [Gavin Newsom] doesn't live by his*

287 Interview with Dave Rubin, February 24, 2021, via phone.

> *own rules...decided basically to destroy the middle class. And I think [their response is] consistent with people who think the government is everything. They think the government is God. And there's simply no science or evidence that the lockdowns have worked anywhere. And at this point, the only reason that any of them are still going on is because it was too obvious that it had more to do with destroying Trump than keeping us safe."*[288]

Sebastian Gorka

(1 MILLION TWITTER FOLLOWERS)

Sebastian Gorka, former Fox News contributor and Deputy Assistant to President Donald Trump, emailed me his concerns with the current political climate and how he develops his "influencer" role.

I asked him about his brand and how mindful he is about managing his image:

> *"I don't think in terms of 'brand.' I'm not a bar of soap or chocolate bar. This isn't some Bernays-inspired exercise in 'demo' or 'reach.' What we do with my radio show,* ***AMERICA First****, my TV appearances, and on our social media platforms is mission orientated. We want to speak the Truth in the interests of making the MAGA platform as vibrant and successful as possible so we can bring America back to the founding principles it was founded on and attain once more its rightful place as the 'shining city on the hill.'"*[289]

---

288 Interview with Dave Rubin, February 24, 2021, via phone.

289 Interview with Sebastian Gorka, February 17, 2021, via email.

Gorka is nothing if not authentic. We moved on to discussing what have been his most successful moments on social media:

> *"Depends who you ask. Based upon audience feedback, it's clear the most popular moments are the ones that are a public excoriation of the hypocrisy and mendacity of the Left, such as my interviews with CNN's Anderson Cooper when I was in the White House, or the moment in the Rose Garden when I called out 'journalist' Brian Karem for the fraud that he is after he insulted the President and all his assembled guests. Otherwise, in terms of deeper impact, I find the stories about my family suffering under both Fascism and then Communism really hit hard, as do the stories I tell about how the FakeNews media went after not only me during my time in the Trump Administration, but their attacks on my wife and our children. That's when people truly understand the diabolical nature of today's radicalized Democrat party."* [290]

In the fight and when combating fake news, there is a vital battle for young conservatives to get in the fight and be effective. Since Gorka's fan base has lots of younger conservatives, I asked how he would recommend them getting involved and curating a following; Gorka took a more wholistic approach in answering me:

> *"Not sure I would. That's the wrong metric. Cretins like the Kardashians or Lady Gaga have massive followings and they're still imbecilic. My advice is always the same. Get smart. Put the bloody phone down for 90 minutes a day and read a real book. Ideally an old one. Then on Social Media, and more importantly,*

290 Interview with Sebastian Gorka, February 17, 2021, via email.

> ***around yourself in real life, speak the Truth. The rest will follow."*** [291]

And finally, since there seems to be some debate from liberals on this point, I asked him if cancel culture is real. He replied, "Ask Gina Carano. Ask Mike Lindell. Of course it's real, and it is just a polite phrase for fascistic censorship and deplatforming, and as such it is in direct contravention with everything that America stands for." [292]

Camryn Kinsey

(112K TWITTER FOLLOWERS)

One America News Network White House Correspondent Camryn Kinsey is as in tune with how to grow on social media as she is with the real crises facing America. The former External Relations Director at the Presidential Personnel Office for President Donald Trump is no stranger to the inner workings of government and translating those machinations into tweets, views, and content. Now working for a news organization, Camryn has grown to over 112,000 followers on Twitter and over 157,000 followers on Instagram. Her coverage is watched by politicians, the punditry class, and the American people.

We spoke to her for this book, and she provided her insights on how to combat the radical Left and grow online.

As someone who has worked in the White House and now in the media, I asked Camryn how has misinformation plagued our public discourse:

> ***"Left wing media outlets bombarded the American public with misinformation in order to influence the 2020 presidential election and divide this country***

291 Interview with Sebastian Gorka, February 17, 2021, via email.

292 Interview with Sebastian Gorka, February 17, 2021, via email.

further. Throughout the entirety of the four years Trump was in office, the lamestream media did everything they could to demonize the Commander In Chief. The media's abnormal labels of Trump versus his actual policy prescriptions were extraordinarily contrasting.

They declared Donald Trump is a racist when he brought record low unemployment rates for black Americans, criminal justice reform and shifted millions of dollars to HBCUs. They declared Trump is a misogynist when he had more women working in White House than Obama, Clinton and Bush. These various narratives are engraved in radical leftists' minds and it caused individuals to vote because of their hatred for Donald Trump rather than their love and support for Joe Biden. The media proved to be less reliable by the day and I became a journalist to relay factual and reliable news to the American people, because sadly, it is hard to come by." [293]

Working in the Trump White House and now a media organization, Camryn is keenly aware of censorship that plagues conservatives:

"Free flow of information has been completely obliterated by big tech oligarchs. This can be seen when conservative posts are flagged, suspending conservative pages or shadowbanning people with alternative views. This is dangerous. America is the land of the free! Big tech oligarchs should never be allowed to dictate our constitutional right to free speech. Ever.

293 Interview with Camryn Kinsey, September 2, 2021, via email.

> *Twitter gives leading members of the Taliban a platform to disseminate their messages—the same Taliban who have beheaded, slaughtered and enacted an actual insurrection against a U.S.-installed government, but President Donald J. Trump, the leader of the free world, was deplatformed.*
>
> *A mother of one of the brave Marines killed in Afghanistan under Biden's poor leadership was **suspended** after portraying her son's death was because of Biden's ineptness to lead the United States.*
>
> *Are you paying attention yet?"*[294]

Despite these challenges to information and access, Camryn is hopeful about the future battle against Big Tech, misinformation, and the radical Left:

> *"I am very hopeful. Thankfully, the Biden/Harris administration is terrible at lying and the American people are reading right through their lies. It's also getting harder and harder for left wing media outlets to cover for them. So, not only are more conservatives moving to the front lines of the social media war we are facing, but Biden voters are getting redpilled. Newsom voters are signing the recall. Parents are joining their kids' school boards. The red wave is going to be bigger and stronger than it's ever been come midterm elections and 2024."*[295]

Turning to social media growth, I asked Camryn what attributes contribute to her success at increasing her follower count so significantly in such a short time:

294 Interview with Camryn Kinsey, September 2, 2021, via email.

295 Interview with Camryn Kinsey, September 2, 2021, via email.

"My Faith, Authenticity, and being unapologetic for speaking my beliefs. I would not be where I am today without being bound with my faith in the Lord. Every blessing in my career and life I attribute to God because of the road he paved for me. Of course, that doesn't come without hard work, dedication and a strong sense of self to navigate the goal ahead.

The American people want authentic individuals standing in the front lines of the conservative movement. They want someone who understands their struggles and tribulations. I understand a single mother trying to raise her kids to be independent thinkers because my mom was one till I was 11 years old and she remarried. I understand why a father is practicing his 2nd Amendment right to protect his family, because my dad is one. I stand for our brave law enforcement officers because my uncle is one. I stand for the national anthem because many members of my family fought overseas for years to give us the freedoms we possess. I understand someone who works for everything and sometimes it still falls short, because I've hit that low. I am someone who doesn't want my nine-year-old sister hyperventilating from a mask for eight hours straight during a school day. I understand someone who wants to turn on the TV and not be bombarded with blatant lies from corporate media, because that was me coming home from a fourteen hour day at the White House when President Trump signed a historic Middle East peace agreement, only to turn on the TV and look at Twitter to see how the Trump Administration was putting international relations at risk (insane).

I am not afraid to speak my mind and I will never bow to the rage mob when facing scrutiny. And I will always advocate for the wise words President Donald Trump once said, 'believe in God, not Government.'"[296]

Camryn said it well, authenticity is rocket fuel for social media growth.

Ryan Fournier

(944.2K TWITTER FOLLOWERS)

Ryan Fournier can be credited in part with getting up the hype about President Trump as the founder of Students for Trump, a grassroots social media campaign to elevate Donald Trump to the White House.

I met Ryan online, and we have developed a friendship that has helped both of our careers immensely. As an expert on ginning up a social media following both for himself and for President Trump, I had to pick his brain on keys to his success. We have focused on narrative in this book, and Ryan constructed entire narratives online in Students for Trump to help President Trump get elected:

"It's a narrative game. And the Left is so good at the carrot stick approach narrative. And this is an umbrella narrative. This is where they'll go onto a college campus and apply straight to the face of the student. They'll say, you know what, we want to eliminate your college loan debt. Who doesn't want to go to college for free? Right, right. If someone came up to you and you knew no better, you're going to say, wow, I love that, I'm voting for you. But really, at the end of the day, you know that that's

296 Interview with Camryn Kinsey, September 2, 2021, via email.

> *nothing more than putting the debt on the American taxpayer, taking it off the back of the student. Same thing with Medicare for all or health care for all. A very cool plan on paper. But when you inject it into the real world, it's the bankrupting option. It's not feasible.... The left has the emotional, the empathy kind of side that they try to play all the time using logical fallacies, red herring, all this. They play with the heartstrings, and there's a lot of young people who are more compassionate. And I'm not saying Republicans aren't compassionate. Democrats just know how to play that card very well...but we fought back, there's a lot of winning issues for Trump. I think the violence happening in these cities, the narrative that is being played for the Right, and I wouldn't even call it a narrative because it's what's happening."*[297]

I asked Ryan how he thinks Republicans can get better at this and beat the Left at their own game:

> *"What it comes down to is showing results, showing what the Democrats have failed to do...help Hispanics, help African Americans, help Asian Americans, women, whatever the case may be, it falls into place already because these are things that they promised and promised and promised and have never been able to deliver. Trump delivers on it. You take it to the bank and people know. They see that. They see that there's actually deliverables. It's not just campaign promises that were never fulfilled."*[298]

Showing results on social media is the name of the game, and Ryan is a pro at using social media to play back against

297 Interview with Ryan Fournier, October 27, 2020, via phone.

298 Interview with Ryan Fournier, October 27, 2020, via phone.

the Left. I asked him what he thinks is the most effective way that conservative young people can use social media in order to effect change:

> *"The meme stuff, that's all good and dandy. But I think that there's this perception out there that these pages and these groups can win the hearts and minds of people. Yes, they're funny. Do they necessarily convince people? That's where the debate is. Social media plays a big part because, yes, that younger block needs social media more than they look at traditional news, cable news. People, whether they use social media, you have to make it where the president is doing things, the presidency and talk. You have to know your facts and be confident and knowledgeable and doing your civic duty, understanding the candidates, understanding who you're voting for and just being out there in that fight. You have to find what is creative for you. You have to be able to make it your own. And maybe this is a way for influencers, by making it creative and making it fun and entertaining."*[299]

As both an influencer in his own right and running a major grassroots organization to elect a president, Ryan knows the hard work it takes to get movements, organization, and excitement among young people to gain any momentum:

> *"It really comes down to grassroots activism, trained activists who understand what the president has accomplished, what the president has done. You can't rely on the media...sixty percent of millennials eighteen to thirty-five use social media to get their news. We have to target social media. Students for Trump had over three hundred and fifty chapters across*

299 Interview with Ryan Fournier, October 27, 2020, via phone.

college campuses across the country. Thousands of young people motivated, energized, trained field reps, train track leaders talking about what this president is doing. And that is key. That has to be done. It can't just be done by us to be done by other groups and to be done by party. But at the end of the day, we can't leave it up to the media. We can't leave it up to that traditional source that would go on the five o'clock news…we can't leave it up to them anymore. To do that, it has to be a party, a united effort going out there, not just convincing Republicans, also convincing Democrats, you have to have this conversation with the people that may question you, criticize you, and make you feel a little uncomfortable."[300]

CJ Pearson

(344.8K TWITTER FOLLOWERS)

CJ Pearson, now the campaign manager for Vernon Jones who is running for governor of Georgia, sat down with me to talk about being an influencer and a young activist.

CJ was an outspoken supporter of President Trump early on, and I asked why he supported the president so early in light of all the backlash that it was likely to bring on:

"I think more than anything what President Trump did was be of conviction. He wasn't the type of conservative that looked for validation or approval from the Left, but he was a conservative in that he didn't need it at all because he had the support and backing of the American people.… He cares about what the seventy plus million people who elected him think. They care about him in terms of nominating the most conserva-

300 Interview with Ryan Fournier, October 27, 2020, via phone.

> *tive judicial branch that we've seen in modern history. They care about him in terms of the strongest economy as far as people can remember."*[301]

I asked him about his reach and how he went about gaining followers:

> *"I started making contact with people and making connections. I would look at the landscape of their commenting. Look at what other players are pushing, and after a while I said, I can do this better. I can speak to issues that they maybe aren't speaking to or what is an issue that I feel like a lot of people want to hear about. And no one else is talking about what I would also say. With any post, it's got to be relevant. You're not going to change the news cycle, so talk about what people are talking about. Sometimes you might go viral, and going viral often definitely gains followers."*[302]

In our interview, CJ was a big proponent of networking and attributed a lot of his success to the people he has been able to meet online:

> *"Networking is probably the most ubiquitous, applicable thing to any industry. It will never do you bad or never do you harm…people that I meet I would always share their stuff, and I would recommend that everybody who is getting in the fight, we're here against anyone not in the movement, but we are not competing against inside the context of the conservative movement. We're all fighting for a better America, an America made best by freedom and liberty. And so definitely don't be afraid to talk to other creators*

301 Interview with CJ Pearson, December 15, 2020, via phone.

302 Interview with CJ Pearson, December 15, 2020, via phone.

> *and collaborate and do things like that.... When you compete against everyone else, nobody wants to help you. When you compete against yourself, everyone wants to help you. The bigger influencers all say network, network, network. And obviously, that is key."*[303]

I followed up with a question about what CJ perceives to be his brand, which is in large part what he attributes to his success:

> *"For me and what I've always tried to bring to the table is authenticity. And I think that America has had more than enough political correctness that people who feel the need to beat around the bush on critical and important issues. And there is a thirst for people to just be real, be honest, unfiltered in their truth, and after that, seek to bring to the table every single day in my commentary to my activism is just to tell the damn truth. And I think the American people are fed up with being coddled, fed up with being manipulated. Clarity and honesty. That's what I try to do every single day. Speak about the issues in a way that is true to myself, true to how I feel, and true to the moral compass of the country."*[304]

CJ is a college student and a proud Black American, so I asked him if he believes there is a hope for Black Americans to be attracted to conservatism:

> *"Minority voters are tired of being used by the Democratic Party. They're tired of a party promising them so much and delivering so little cycle after cycle. I think a lot of people have been awoken to the fact*

303 Interview with CJ Pearson, December 15, 2020, via phone.

304 Interview with CJ Pearson, December 15, 2020, via phone.

that it seems to only matter during election years. You know since the election, I haven't heard the phrase Black Lives Matter outside of badgering about it. I haven't said it. I haven't heard it said by Congress. I think that people are really starting to wake up and say, damn it, people actually don't really care about us at all. And so, I think that we're going to see more of that. If people are tired of being lied to all the time, and they're tired of being, like I said, used to be used. And they're looking for alternatives. They're looking for people to fix their issues, to speak to the concerns of the community, Black voters in particular. They're tired of living in unsafe neighborhoods and tired of being told that economic poverty that they should just get used to, and they should be made more comfortable and not something that they should be given the tools that they need to escape, because that's what liberalism is: making poverty comfortable...I think as conservatives to simply continue to go to communities that we previously didn't go into before, share with them our message of opportunity and economic prosperity."[305]

Ryan Girdusky

(85.1K TWITTER FOLLOWERS)

I spoke with the talented and straight talker, Ryan James Girdusky, author of *They're Not Listening: How the Elites Created the National Populist Revolution.*

We're seeing a rise in populist movements worldwide, and social media has fueled a lot of these movements into world-changing events: the election of Donald Trump, to name one.

305 Interview with CJ Pearson, December 15, 2020, via phone.

Ryan has studied these movements and come to the conclusion that our elites still don't care. And since we are trying to champion the common man in this book and building movements through social media, we had to speak to Ryan, who is quickly becoming the expert on modern populism.

Ryan told me how necessary social media is to a movement. "If you look at all great populist leaders, they all use social media to get the job. [These leaders] use social media to get around the mainstream narrative because we have a liberal media that has the same message over and over and over again," he told me.[306] "The only way to get around them is to be the creator of your own narrative, because the Establishment media truly hates some of these populist causes."[307]

I asked if he thought social media has allowed people to see the growing disparity between how the elites operate and how the elites live their lives out versus how they tell all of the little people to live their lives out:

> ***"The biggest thing social media can do is expose the hypocrisy of the Establishment, traditional media. You saw the writing in 2016 saying that riots need to be violent. And then those same people demand on January 6, 2021, that all those who participated should go to jail.... You have an author in 2004 saying that it's absolutely necessary to challenge an election and the same author in 2021 saying, 'Gosh, this is a fucking democracy.' ...These people are hypocrites, and they live in glass houses. And if it wasn't for social media being able to show that inconsistency, I think a lot of people would believe what the media says at face value."***[308]

306 Interview with Ryan Girdusky, January 12, 2021, via phone.
307 Interview with Ryan Girdusky, January 12, 2021, via phone.
308 Interview with Ryan Girdusky, January 12, 2021, via phone.

I had to ask Ryan, whom I respect as a strategist, what are some techniques that we need to do as conservatives to push back against these liberal narratives that are just nonsensical:

> *"The most important thing is to be smart about this, but I think using their sources of information is extremely important. I think by using their own words and their own institutions against them, it makes it much harder for them to ignore you or lower your credibility. I think it's an immensely effective tool if you can also make it funny. The Right has become very good at this recently. Everything from Babylon Bee is incredibly effective because it's how we communicate."*[309]

Ryan has his fingers firmly on the pulse of conservative politics, so I asked him which areas he believes we are losing on right now:

> *"Lots of conservatives just want to be popular. So they go along with narratives pushed by Black Lives Matter and others that we know from experience are just false.... The Left is pushing the certain narratives that don't work for society. We're not conservative because we want our team to win. We're conservative because we believe that conservative ideas are good for people and benefit them. I think we must continue attacking the leftist narratives and continue to see the forest rather than the trees."*[310]

309 Interview with Ryan Girdusky, January 12, 2021, via phone.

310 Interview with Ryan Girdusky, January 12, 2021, via phone.

Andrea Catsimatidis

(39.8K TWITTER FOLLOWERS)

Any discussion of influencers wouldn't be complete without speaking with the head of the Manhattan GOP.[311], [312] "We work with candidates, tap into the business community, provide networking to bring more people into our party because it's going to help the business community. We are business-minded, both with our candidates and our events," she said.[313]

Having been profiled in a number of publications, Andrea is not a stranger to having the spotlight on her and her ambitions in a New York hostile to conservatives. I asked her about strategies she's used to build her brand and raise her profile, and if she had a message for young conservatives looking to emulate her trajectory:

> ***"My main message would be to be yourself, and people will respond authentically. I am unapologetically myself. And luckily for me, I'm the kind of person that has the confidence and the security to be able to be myself. And a lot of people would probably feel uncomfortable putting themselves out there. And the other thing is because of the rise of President Trump, who was definitely not afraid to be unapologetically himself, and as a result accomplished so many things because he wouldn't back down from his principles. It has given way for a lot of people to feel comfortable***

311 Olivia Nuzzi, "A Lobster Dinner with Andrea Catsimatidis Manhattan's Republican Party Chair Is a Self-Described 'Billionaire Heiress' and 'Business Bombshell,'" *New York Magazine* (July 23, 2019), https://nymag.com/intelligencer/2019/07/andrea-catsimatidis-manhattan-republican-party-chair.html.

312 Taylor Nicole Rogers, "Meet the Self-Proclaimed 'Billionaire Heiress,' Bikini Enthusiast, and GOP Crusader Whose Dad Spied on Her Date Using a Controversial Facial-Recognition App," *Business Insider* (March 5, 2020), https://www.businessinsider.com/grocery-heiress-andrea-catsimatidis-leader-of-manhattan-republican-party-2019-7.

313 Interview with Andrea Catsimatidis, January 12, 2021, via phone.

> *to be themselves.... Our party is all about freedom and opportunity for all. We're lucky that we live in the greatest country in the world, where we can express ourselves and be who we are. I can celebrate my femininity in a way that I want to celebrate it. I want to show more examples of empowering young women that can also be fun and successful and other things within the party. And I thought that was an important thing to share with people."*[314]

Given that she is a Republican in New York (having visited often for work, I can attest to its bizarre politics), I asked her how she goes about defending herself in a city hostile to her ideas:

> *"The truth is I was very surprised that I didn't have more negativity towards me. It's been overwhelmingly positive. Part of that comes from the fact it's like the rise of many of the new influencers within the Republican Party have been those like big-tent Republicans and more accepting of people and bringing people into the party. So I think that's helpful. And part of the reason why people have been so accepting of me and because I'm such an empowered and accepting woman. I've actually received a lot of love from people on the left that normally don't like conservative figures. And I actually do have people that will listen to me, even though they don't necessarily agree with my politics. So that's been interesting. But that being said, the Left has this crazy ability to cancel people. And unfortunately, I have no idea what to do to stop it because, if they can cancel the president of the United States and just wipe him off the face of the social media earth, I don't know what I personally can do about it."*[315]

314 Interview with Andrea Catsimatidis, January 12, 2021, via phone.

315 Interview with Andrea Catsimatidis, January 12, 2021, via phone.

Relatedly, I asked her how New York has taken an economic body blow during coronavirus:

> *"I unfortunately think the Left is creating conditions for that to happen, and people are really getting to that point now. And I was talking about it a little bit on Twitter because obviously Twitter's market cap has taken a huge hit. I was saying that I probably thought that this was going to happen because you don't have to invest in Twitter. They're going to lose a ton of revenue. We may not have free speech anymore, but we still have free markets and hit where it hurts, hit them in the market cap.... My family is such a New York family and very committed to New York and helping New York. And even we are considering moving to Florida. If these policies continue, people are just going to pick up and move their jobs, move their tax dollars elsewhere. It's going to be a huge problem for liberal places and liberal companies, especially because these liberal companies are starting to shut people down. And it's not like it's a small minority of people. They're literally alienating seventy-five million people in the country."*[316]

Very concerned about how influencers craft narratives online, I asked Andrea for an example of how she sees narratives play out online:

> *"During the defunding the police narrative the Left pushed, I started framing the narrative about how it was hurting minority and poor communities, because wealthy people are just hiring private security. And that really resonated with liberal people. Security shouldn't be just for the wealthy people. Everyone should have the right to safety."*[317]

---

316 Interview with Andrea Catsimatidis, January 12, 2021, via phone.
317 Interview with Andrea Catsimatidis, January 12, 2021, via phone.

Since she comes from a wealthy family, I asked if she was recruiting wealthy donors to combat the Bloombergs of the world:

> *"We really need to do that. We've seen that not only with like donor-type people, but also political people, the Left plays this game of psychological warfare where they try to make you think that you should feel bad about your position. And then as a result, we retreat further and further left because we think that we're going to appease the virtue signaling and maybe look good for doing it when, in fact, we should not be apologizing for our values. By doing so, we're ceding this moral high ground and admitting that we were wrong. President Trump was amazing at this. He didn't fall into the psychological trap. We need to figure out how to combat that better. We need more unity of people that won't give in. And I think that would be helpful in that respect, especially to put money behind that view."*[318]

318 Interview with Andrea Catsimatidis, January 12, 2021, via phone.

Chapter 7:
THE MEDIA

"Lot of dumb people in the media, I think all the smart ones went into finance or something. It's kind of the slow second son goes over to work at NBC. It's kind of sad since we kind of need a strong competent media."[319]

- Tucker Carlson, *Fox News*

"I think the whole use of the term media bias is completely obsolete. They're no longer the media. It's not a matter of bias anymore. They are an organ of the ruling class. And it's not even coherent anymore.... *They're creating the news to serve them to serve partisan purposes."*[320]

- Ron Coleman

319 Tucker Carlson, "Tucker Carlson Tonight," Fox News (January 20, 2021), https://www.foxnews.com/shows/tucker-carlson-tonight.

320 Interview with Ron Coleman, December 22, 2020, via phone.

"Conservative media doesn't understand social media. And this is why the Left wins. As if these outlets don't know how social media works and what it does for their company, they tend to not care, and we lose."

- Will Ricciardella, *Fox News*[321]

DEMOCRACY DIES WITH A dishonest media. There has never been a more dangerous time for conservatives fighting for this country than now. A perverse feedback loop exists between an already behemoth media and a social media construct that mirrors, rewards, and facilitates their dominance of the news that we see. We live in a time where almost daily the media will tell the American people the sky is purple, get proven demonstrably wrong days later, and cannibalize those who refuse to trust or question their credibility the next week. Some have even called this the era of "post-journalism," where journalists' intent is "never to represent reality or inform the public but to arouse enough political fervor."[322]

I could cite dozens of examples every day where the media lies to us. In my own life, I have had to fight the media's lies about me. My hometown paper, the *Ripon Commonwealth Press*, decided to publish falsehoods about me, trying to tie me to the events of January 6, 2021, at the Capitol. And like I want you to do, I pushed back. I sent a cease and desist letter and threatened litigation. And recognizing their wrongdoing, they were forced to apologize in their paper. We won because we called out the lies. *Reason* reported a pretty clear and blatant example: right after the inauguration of President Biden and Vice President Kamala Harris, "*The Washington Post* published

321 Interview with Will Ricciardella, December 17, 2020, via phone.

322 Martin Gurri, "Slouching Toward Post-Journalism: The New York Times and Other Elite Media Outlets Have Openly Embraced Advocacy over Reporting," *The City Journal* (Winter 2021), https://www.city-journal.org/journalism-advocacy-over-reporting#.YBoZ8rO8YXM.twitter.

a 2019 campaign trail feature...[with] an extremely cringe-worthy moment, even by the high standards set by Harris' failed presidential campaign. But now that Harris is vice president, that awful moment has seemingly vanished from the *Post*'s website after the paper 'updated' the piece earlier this month.... At a time when legacy publications are increasingly seen as playing for one political 'team' or the other, this type of editorial decision will not do anything to fix that perception.... Intentional or not, the memory-holing of the older version of the piece sends a message that the *Post* is willing to pave over its own good journalism to protect a powerful politician from her own words. Luckily, nothing is ever really gone on the internet."[323] By the time you're reading this, the media will have retconned, memory-holed, gaslit, and lied to the American people so many times, it will take six to eight editions of this book just to account for the first half of 2021.

And with proper competition, the media's lies might not have been a major issue. After all, local papers were a robust institution to preserve at least the vestige of journalism as a profession. The issue has become that the American people, or half of them at least, find themselves being told consistent, well-dressed lies and simultaneously told that our views are abhorrent and deserve ridicule and silence from the public conversation.

Pre-Big Tech, this wasn't a major issue. Most people probably laughed at the village scold—the rabble-rouser who wanted people tossed from the community with views they deemed abhorrent. We all have that neighbor or relative who's hyper-partisan or went down too dark of a rabbit hole on the internet. Most people are respectful of others' views and certainly are respectful when those views conflict with their own. But what happens when you amplify the

---

323 Eric Boehm, "The Washington Post Memory-Holed Kamala Harris' Bad Joke About Inmates Begging for Food and Water," *Reason* (January 22, 2021), https://reason.com/2021/01/22/the-washington-post-memory-holed-kamala-harris-bad-joke-about-inmates-begging-for-food-and-water/.

town loon, give it a microphone and editorial discretion over the community paper and, at the same time, access to the personal information of everyone in the town, and sole discretion over who can live in the community. That's the situation we find ourselves in.

Breitbart's editor in chief, Alex Marlow, notes how insular the relationship and messaging between the traditional news media and social media have become. "Twitter is really the assignment editor in most newsrooms. Most newsrooms are reacting to what people on Twitter are saying, which is a relatively small percentage of Americans are talking about and engaging with on. And the amount of people that read Twitter is pretty small. And the number of people who actually tweet is super small. And a handful of people are making up the vast majority of tweets," he said.[324] "You can't help but notice a huge pattern between what is popular on Twitter and what you see in the newspapers and on cable news, local news."[325]

Other than making reporters dumber and giving them credence and the platform to divide us with rhetoric tooled to be divisive, the media/social media apparatus has done little for us and drives narratives contrary to the aspirations of a freedom-loving people. Alex Marlow argues that the "Left [in the media] wants to destroy. They don't want to have dialogue. And this is a theme I'm becoming obsessed with. The era where we just want to hear each other out and let the best ideas win in our free marketplace of ideas, if it was ever here, is long gone. We are now at a spot where the goal is not to debate, not to be challenged. It is to stay in your bubble. And this is incredibly dangerous for society. Dialogue is far preferential to no dialogue."[326]

324 Interview with Alex Marlow, January 27, 2021, via phone.
325 Interview with Alex Marlow, January 27, 2021, via phone.
326 Interview with Alex Marlow, January 27, 2021, via phone.

In fact, the media has become so interested in shutting out and shouting down all opposition that it has single-handedly, as an institution protected by the First Amendment, become the single most ardent opponent to the precepts of the First Amendment. Be mindful that intolerance is ubiquitous on the left and in the newsroom. In reaction to Ben Shapiro editing *Politico*'s Playbook, "More than 100 Politico staffers signed onto a letter sent to publisher Robert Allbritton, expressing disgust with allowing right-wing firebrand Ben Shapiro to guest-author one day's edition of the Playbook, and with the outlet's subsequent handling of the fallout."[327] Senator Ted Cruz was on point when he tweeted in response to the *Daily Beast* report of the controversy: "We are the Borg. There is only one view. Any contrary view does not exist, or must be assimilated. Journalism does not exist. Only orthodoxy. And conformity."[328] Rupert Murdoch, CEO of News Corp and Chairman of Fox Corporation, spoke out against how totalitarian the media has become. "For those of us in media, there's a real challenge to confront a wave of censorship that seeks to silence conversations, to stifle debate and ultimately stop individuals and societies from realizing their potential.... This rigidly enforced conformity, aided and abetted by so-called social media, is a straitjacket on sensibilities. Too many people have fought too hard in too many places for freedom of speech to be suppressed by this awful woke orthodoxy."[329]

Writing almost a decade ago, Andrew Breitbart's message is just as relevant now: "The left does not win its battles in

327 Maxwell Tani, "100+ Politico Staffers Send Letter to Publisher Railing Against Publishing Ben Shapiro: The Signees Called Out Their Top Editor's Response to Internal Critics, and Reiterated that a Firebrand Like Shapiro Does Nothing to Advance Politico's Editorial Values," (January 25, 2021), https://www.thedailybeast.com/more-than-100-politico-staffers-send-letter-to-ceo-railing-against-publishing-ben-shapiro.

328 Ted Cruz (@tedcruz), Twitter, Jan. 25, 2021, 7:25 p.m., https://twitter.com/tedcruz/status/13539-06855882457096?s=20.

329 Cynthia Littleton, "Rupert Murdoch Slams 'Woke Orthodoxy' and Social Media's 'Rigidly Enforced Conformity,'" *Variety* (January 25, 2021), https://variety.com/2021/tv/news/rupert-murdoch-woke-orthodoxy-social-media-fox-news-1234891679/.

debate. It doesn't have to. In the twenty-first century, media is everything. The left wins because it controls the narrative. The narrative is controlled by the media. The left is the media. Narrative is everything. I call it the Democrat-Media Complex—and I am at war to gain back control of the American narrative."[330]

And that is what I am writing for you, how we work through the media outlets we do have to reclaim the narrative.

"Narrative is the way people relate to the news."

In an almost historically unifying moment in writing this book as I reference the words of the great Andrew Breitbart, it's almost poetic that I was able to speak to Alex Marlow, editor in chief of *Breitbart News*. Alex, who has appeared on *Real Time with Bill Maher* among other programs, is no stranger to a hostile media environment. Like Breitbart used to harp on, I asked Alex about the significance of narrative and the media:

> *"The narrative is the way that people relate to the news. People don't necessarily see individual headlines out of the context of the narrative and really get the full picture. It is the narrative that is the connective tissue from story to story. One headline at a time. And at Breitbart, we do it with factual stories and stories where we keep in mind a right of center audience.... Narrative is what is discussed in every newsroom in America more than what is the most interesting story of the day or what is the most even essential story of the day. What they're talking about at this point in time is they're talking about*

330 Larry Solov, "Andrew: One Year Later," *Breitbart* (February 28, 2013), https://www.breitbart.com/the-media/2013/02/28/andrew-one-year-later/.

> *what is the grander societal or geopolitical context to the story, that narrative. And so, when watching CNN, you notice that it's very similar stories about the exact same stories covered every single hour. Why is that? Because there's only one story or two stories or three stories. Any given day? No, because the objective is to push a narrative, to set an agenda, to push an agenda and to get you so familiar with certain concepts that you think that what you're hearing is for sure true…the whole trick that newsrooms use to manipulate people. And Andrew understood that. He understood what the media was doing in this regard. So he always talked about the narrative in the sense that that was how it was the packaging of the stories of the day.… He identified how the media was doing what they were doing in order to change people's political opinions and cultural opinions.… That's the nature of human beings—you forget details, but you remember bigger picture ideas and concepts."*[331]

Jack Posobiec, a senior editor for *Human Events* and former correspondent for One America News Network (OANN),[332] knows all too well the importance of narrative and the way the Left manipulates certain stories for their benefit. "Combating it is not necessarily the right mindset. The mindset should be that you need to tell a better story. Your narrative needs to be stronger than theirs.… You're always looking for a visual.… So the way to combat the narrative of climate change, for example, you turn it around and say, 'You guys want to cut off fossil fuels, are going to cut off fracking. That's going to kill these families. It's going to kill these towns.…' This is

331 Interview with Alex Marlow, January 27, 2021, via phone.

332 Brent Hamachek, "Thought Leader Jack Posobiec Joins Human Events Team as Senior Editor," *Human Events* (May 20, 2021), https://humanevents.com/2021/05/20/thought-leader-jack-posobiec-joins-human-events-team-as-senior-editor/.

something the media has done forever, something that Hollywood completely understands. Every Hollywood trailer does that. It's designed to grab your attention. Conservatives need to think a little bit like Hollywood and ask how do you get people's attention and then what do you do with it?"[333]

David Spady, president of Salem Media, echoes Jack by pointing out how interconnected Hollywood and traditional media apparatus are. "We are losing the cultural war and the cultural values where we've been losing for a long time. Politics certainly plays a role in all that, but I think politics is downstream from the broader cultural dynamics of the entertainment world. And so, what Hollywood has done to advance their cause, to change the narrative and really change people's values and how they view things is probably the most powerful and influential component of that."[334]

Jim Hoft, editor in chief of Gateway Pundit, points to the fact that leftist media views controlling narratives through the lens of power. "It's all about power. It's not about the people. It's not about the country. It's not about their ideas. It's just about power."[335]

This perceived gap is noticed by many of the writers and thinkers I interviewed for this book. For many, it is a troubling reality, especially those in the media. Jack Posobiec had this to say about what he calls the "balkanization" of our media:

> ***"I do believe that American media has become balkanized, and I think that is starting to drive more of a fracture between not only the states, but between individuals, between individuals and their neighbors. I don't think it's geographic."[336] This cuts along lines in which the media chooses to cover stories. Jack points out that regarding the Hunter Biden story, on the left, "nobody broke ranks.***

333 Interview with Jack Posobiec, December 10, 2020, via phone.
334 Interview with David Spady, December 7, 2020, via phone.
335 Interview with Jim Hoft, January 12, 2021, via phone.
336 Interview with Jack Posobiec, December 10, 2020, via phone.

> *And so, you had this interesting situation where the story exploded in 'conservative media' and was all over the place, the point where the numbers were actually higher than WikiLeaks in terms of Google trends for Google searches. However, people who were on the other side of the aisle, their media organizations or media's preferred outlets like CNN and MSNBC,* ***New York Times*** *refused to touch it and none of them broke ranks.... And so even saw a whole media research center did a poll after the election.... Forty-six percent of Joe Biden voters were not even aware that there was a Hunter Biden scandal."*[337]

And it's not just the Hunter Biden story. Growing research shows that Americans live in political silos, where, depending on the media that they consume, they receive vastly different information than their liberal or conservative neighbors. This daylight between perceptions from average Americans has produced radicalism on both the left and the right and led to massive distrust between Americans. This in part is due to competing narratives that rather than being opposite sides of the same coin are different coins in completely separate purses (if you will permit me to extend the metaphor).

While on the right and considering right-wing narratives more in line with my worldview, this is a very real problem that if too far attenuated could have devastating consequences for our great nation.

It's a Training Problem...

The crisis of how left of center our media has become is even more alarming by just how often the media gets stories wrong and has to issue major retractions, sometimes even gutting entire stories. In a digital age where there is a knee-jerk re-

337 Interview with Jack Posobiec, December 10, 2020, via phone.

action to print breaking news as quickly as possible, this can have dire consequences for the private lives of our people and instill deep, long-lasting distrust of the media. Many of the people I spoke to in conservative media point out that many outlets fail to properly train their reporters and that leads, at least in part, to many of the issues we see today.

Many of the people I spoke with stressed the importance of proper training and developing fundamentals for reporting. Others expressed that the desire to make the news fit a narrative is far less preferable than making a narrative fit the news. I don't bring this to you as a slam dunk on media reporters, many of whom are trying hard to deliver the news to the American people, but rather to teach from those in positions of leadership what skills those in media need to develop to be effective.

The tendency to make the news fit a narrative is a character flaw of the modern media. *Breitbart*'s Alex Marlow notes that the approach to stories is often the "opposite of the scientific method, where in the scientific method, you start with a hypothesis and then you test the hypothesis, and you get results, and then you draw your conclusion. In the CNN and *The New York Times* newsrooms, you get your conclusion. And that conclusion is Trump is bad, borders are bad, China is fine, for example. And you start with that premise, and then you go back and find data that confirms that premise.... It's the opposite of what critical thinking is supposed to be all about. And now what happens when you actually do critical thinking and you might come up with, regardless of your political worldview, a conclusion that differed from your hypothesis. Now, you either ignore it, or you just lie about it. And that's why you're seeing the cancel culture extend to people who are open-minded thinkers on the left side of the aisle."[338]

Amber Athey, the Washington editor for *The Spectator US*, told me that the way they run their outlet requires a balance

338 Interview with Alex Marlow, January 27, 2021, via phone.

between commentary and reporting, but that can still be an effective form of news media:

> *"**The Spectator** has always had a bit more of a British angle gonzo approach to journalism. So our writers are pretty open about their viewpoints. And a lot of our content is commentary mixed with reporting, which sounds novel when you look at the way the United States had their news outlets operating for the past thirty, forty years, where they disguised as objective, and everyone was supposed to be unbiased. We've never really been that way. And that's something that I think is more honest for readers, especially when they're so used to these news outlets like CNN and MSNBC, who claim to be nonpartisan and that obviously their reporting is very biased, and the individuals who work for those outlets on their social media, presenting their opinions and then trying to act on air and in their writing as if they're not. So I feel like it's a lot easier and more fair to readers to be open about where you stand politically or about what your opinion on a certain topic is."*[339]

Guys like Will Ricciardella say that conservative journalists need to arm themselves with the facts, "be prepared," and curate "more knowledgeable arguments."[340] He went on, "You have to know your arguments very well, know the facts. Because, look, the Left never has the facts. They never have the truth on their side. It's all very flimsy, so take it head on and fight back."[341]

And no matter the training for conservative reporters, the stakes are higher because the scrutiny is significantly more attuned. At *Breitbart*, Alex Marlow conveyed his publication

339 Interview with Amber Athey, January 13, 2021, via phone.

340 Interview with Will Ricciardella, December 17, 2020, via phone.

341 Interview with Will Ricciardella, December 17, 2020, via phone.

is always "looking for people who are able to write. There is a premium on speed, and there's always a premium on accuracy, particularly at *Breitbart*. They're constantly trying to throw *Breitbart* off the internet. Well, we were the original subject of cancel culture. We were just smart enough and strong enough to survive it. For the most part, though, a couple of us did get canceled over time. But it is the pieces; you're constantly trying to come up with an excuse to get us thrown off the internet. So we had to be extra careful on that stuff. We have to be accurate because they're constantly fact checking us. Any little detail that is out of place becomes a fact check, but we're harassed by the media hall monitors that exist either from Facebook or some sort of other outlet that polices conservative content. People who are upset because we create a ton of content. I appreciate, though, we don't have any political orthodoxy. I always appreciate people who understand the sort of populist nationalist wing of the conservative movement, don't have to agree with all the tenets, but I think at least understanding it is crucial and knowing where people like where Donald Trump and Mitch McConnell differ, what types of issues do they differ on? ...to understand that sort of political dichotomy is not really a binary anymore. It's not just left versus right that both of the groups are fracturing in a certain way. So I need people to understand that, to understand that the Left now is comprised of the sort of activist Democrat Establishment, corporate status quo supporting Left that you'll get on CNN or on MSNBC or at the *New York Times*. And then there are others who are more independent-minded that are liberals, but they're more sort of classical liberals and more supportive of the individual versus the collective. So that's a big deal. And then the Right is not just simple conservatives. It's just way too simplistic of a definition."[342] And with the

342 Interview with Alex Marlow, January 27, 2021, via phone.

changing of the rules, motivations, and roles in media, the necessity of conservative journalists is essential in remaining objective and mindful of the facts at all times because the stakes are very high.

"I don't readily say that Facebook did this on purpose, but Facebook did this on purpose."

"If Silicon Valley can eliminate the president of the United States, they certainly don't have a problem eliminating Gateway Pundit."

- Jim Hoft, Gateway Pundit[343]

With the market shift to politics reacting to social media rather than vice versa, the corporate media environment has been forced to alter how they cover and anticipate political shifts and candidates. Entire books have been written on the fact that but for the traditional media covering Donald Trump, he would not have been elected president, and one reason they covered him so pervasively was due to his outsized influence on social media. The landscape has changed forever as a result, and this chapter takes an in-depth look at how.

But Donald Trump won and served as the forty-fifth president of the United States. And as I discussed earlier in this book, the media, facing an unprecedented situation in an American electorate that they don't understand, went into freak-out mode. Silicon Valley, not far behind, immediately put in place tripwire and open pitfalls to prevent the president from being elected again. I will talk more about this in Chapters 9 and 10, but the impact on conservative media is

343 Interview with Jim Hoft, January 12, 2021, via phone.

a noticeable one. What's worse is that there is a perception among conservative journalists that "the DC media crowd don't care about America. They talk down to them. They hate them. And some people in conservative media have this pressure to be accepted."[344]

And much to the benefit of the media elites who aim to destroy their conservative competitors, they have significant help from Big Tech who specifically target conservative outlets. Several editors spoke to me on the record about the targeted attacks they have experienced. David Spady, president of Salem Media, shared with me that "there's probably no bigger threat to democracy, to our interests and worldview, advancing our issues and values. When you think about these Big Tech companies, they are trying to manipulate information and expose people to certain things in order to sell products."[345]

For even with the proper training and solid content, conservative sites noticed precipitous drops in traffic and bizarre behavior leading into the 2020 election. Jim Hoft, editor in chief of Gateway Pundit,[346] notes, "There were some huge websites in 2016 that are no longer here because Facebook shut them down, they shut down traffic to their websites.... [Many pages] were getting an immense amount of traffic.... They changed the algorithm, stopped traffic going to these websites, and they put a lot of them out of business. So, it's really tragic.... And what's interesting, too, is we're seeing these different tactics: how [the tech giants] collude together, how they make sure you don't have like email service or cloud service or any of these things if you're a threat to them.... Some of our stories, reporting Trump's message for example was having a more difficult time going through to suburban mothers, they eliminated it off of Facebook.... They weren't getting those articles anymore because Facebook eliminated it. So Facebook has been electioneering

344 Interview with Will Ricciardella, December 17, 2020, via phone.

345 Interview with David Spady, December 7, 2020, via phone.

346 Interview with Jim Hoft, January 12, 2021, via phone.

for several years now. It was very effective in 2018. It was certainly effective in 2020."[347]

And while many outlets openly dismiss Gateway Pundit's work, the reduction in traffic was shared almost universally by conservative publications. Hoft adamantly told me, "Gateway Pundit went from being the fourth most prominent conservative website [in traffic] and since then, our traffic and most conservative outlets have lost traffic.... I've been doing this for twenty years.... I know the climate. I know who's come and gone.... Our traffic this year, despite actually growing in traffic over the four years of the Trump presidency, like a lot of conservative sites, lost their traffic due to Facebook this past year."[348]

Amber Athey shared that *The Spectator US* took a similar hit following the Capitol riot:

> *"We did notice subscriptions dropped on the day of the Capitol riots, although it's not really clear if it's censorship or if people were just divided by the event. But I have noticed on my personal social media, as well as on* ***The Spectator*** *social media, that our follows on our accounts have dropped significantly, especially on Twitter. I lost about, I would say, twelve to thirteen thousand followers in the course of just a week, which is more than ten percent of my overall follower count. And when you look at Twitter, an explanation for why so many people were being removed from the platform, it doesn't really make sense with the numbers because initially they claimed it was just their standard routine, calling up accounts that did not have proper verification or didn't have an email address attached to them. But anyone who has been on Twitter for multiple years knows that they do this pretty routinely, and it's never*

347 Interview with Jim Hoft, January 12, 2021, via phone.
348 Interview with Jim Hoft, January 12, 2021, via phone.

> ***caused more than a few hundred followers to drop from any one person's account. It doesn't explain tens of thousands of followers. So then they actually came out with a second statement, which was a tacit admission that they had lied in their first statement, saying that the real reason for the follower drops was because they had gotten rid of seventy thousand accounts that were associated with QAnon and conspiracy theories. But that still doesn't explain the actual follower drop, because when you look at accounts that have more than one hundred thousand followers, for example, you'll see some of them actually lost more than seventy thousand followers.... So it seems much more likely to me that Twitter is making up an excuse to try to get rid of as many Trump supporters, conservatives, Republicans as possible, and just using the Capitol riot and the QAnon conspiracy theory as their excuse on the* Spectator *account."[349]***

Will Ricciardella, formerly of the *Washington Examiner* and now Fox News, echoes a similar phenomenon.[350], [351] "I'm watching the traffic. I've been on Facebook for ten years now. I watch it all day. I watch engagement. I look at the analytics with every other page. And yes, I had a discussion with them on the phone, and they implicitly admitted to restricting certain pages.... It did occur in October. They were running more erroneous fact checks, limiting the press pages, and suppressing content. *I don't readily say that Facebook is doing this on purpose, but they did this on purpose.*[352] They'll actually target *Washington Examiner* links all over Facebook, not just the page. That's typically what they do.

349 Interview with Amber Athey, January 13, 2021, via phone.

350 Will Ricciardella, *Washington Examiner*, https://www.washingtonexaminer.com/author/will-ricciardella.

351 Interview with Will Ricciardella, December 17, 2020, via phone.

352 Interview with Will Ricciardella, December 17, 2020, via phone.

You'll report someone saying something and then they say, 'factually false.' They give you a false rating. So then they target your page and then target your URL.... In August, we had our best month ever in social media. I couldn't lose interest.... It was a hard demarcation between August and September, down fifty percent, our traffic from Facebook and Twitter as well, and Twitter admitted it, at least restricting. *They're still targeting it now. They're not allowing it to grow. They won't allow this to go viral.*"[353]

Some conservative sites were able to stave off some censorship and attacks by unique clicks and searches. Alex Marlow says, "Thankfully, we have a built-in safety net, which is that we get the majority of our traffic from our front page. That's something that insulates us because if Facebook plays with the algorithm that day, and if they're not allowing certain stories to catch fire, for example, it was really hard to get any stories on the Georgia runoff race to gain traction on Facebook. Great stories. For whatever reason, Facebook was controlling their algorithm. It was very hard to get those stories a lot of promotion. They would tell you it's because they want to shut down election misinformation. But we know what it really is.... They didn't want the story to get out because they thought it would help Republicans. But stuff like that happens; the good news for us is it doesn't destroy our business because we put our stories on the front page, and we share it on our other platforms. But for other businesses that don't have a front page that people visit on a regular basis, it's pretty devastating because there's a lot of these upstart conservative outlets that really do exist just in social media. And if social media decides we're not going to promote your story, what other mechanisms do they have to promote it? I mean, maybe they got an email list, but what else?"[354]

353 Interview with Will Ricciardella, December 17, 2020, via phone.

354 Interview with Alex Marlow, January 27, 2021, via phone.

But as we've learned and continued to learn, some conservative pages weren't so lucky. With the crackdown that occurred in January 2020 and the reality that a change to the algorithm of Facebook and Twitter can completely alter the business model of a publication, there are serious threats to conservative journalism. And that's just the passive updates made at the whim of Big Tech, with the active approach to censorship and anointing themselves the arbiters of truth and information, conservative publications face significant obstacles.

With a Pen and a Journal, Facing Down the World

I asked the media figures I interviewed what are the important techniques that conservative media needs to understand and implement in order for conservative journalism to survive the obstacles in our paths.

Alex Marlow told me about the process he implements for his reporters at *Breitbart*:

> *"A few of the key tenets of what we do: The first one is to be accurate because anything that is slightly inaccurate, we get bombarded with fact checks. There's a much higher premium on accuracy; any mistake we make is going to be highly publicized. And there's always a running tab going like three years and ninety days or something. And they just throw you off of Facebook, for example. But we have to be extremely mindful of what narratives there is.... And once they start fact checking truthful stories, it shuts down the initial velocity that it's going to have."*[355]

355 Interview with Alex Marlow, January 27, 2021, via phone.

I asked Will Ricciardella the necessary investment conservatives should be making:

> *"I get young, idealistic writers in the office, and they'll write copy. And I look at it and I see click-bait nonsense. I ask, are you Charles Krauthammer? Unless you're Krauthammer, I don't ever want your opinion in a headline.... That's my job as a journalist is not to make value judgments. It's just to report it, and it doesn't get done anymore. You have journalists coming in, and I don't think people are telling it straight.... They look just exactly like they are propagandists, conspiracy theorists, and jokes. Clowns and clown people."*[356]

Will stresses the importance of investment in social media and personnel. "And that means in personnel and dollars, that means training people how to properly use Facebook. And again, that's the remnants of the old media that don't understand the tip of the spear of their entire news network. If you don't put your best foot forward on social media, if you're just going to lose people. Once you work that, then the other thing is content. Content is king. I've seen [the talent hemorrhage] over the years.... And if conservatives want competitive [human] capital, I mean, you've got to compete. You've got to pay. And that's something that conservative media hasn't really been able to do or want to invest in."[357]

Perhaps it makes sense for conservative outlets to engage more deeply in the culture, to take a different tone, as Amber Athey suggests. "We just try not to take ourselves too seriously. It's a bit more of an irreverent tone. And I feel that reality is so strange most of the time that it really helps with your sanity and also just with digesting what's going on if you're able to have a sense of humor about everything. And that's

356 Interview with Will Ricciardella, December 17, 2020, via phone.

357 Interview with Will Ricciardella, December 17, 2020, via phone.

kind of how we approach it. And certainly, politicians and some of the elites in this country deserve to be mocked in these photos because they're fundamentally ridiculous people, and they mock and make fun of the rest of America. So why shouldn't they get a taste of their own medicine?"[358] David Spady echoes this sentiment, especially for young people "who form their opinions based a lot more on emotional context and who are not as tuned into your daily news and what's going on around them. They get their information, maybe in the news context from *The Daily Show* or something else that's in the entertainment context more than a purposeful news program. So, from a cultural impact standpoint, I think Hollywood is probably the biggest influence on that."[359] David mentioned that for many of his programs they have had to adjust towards entertainment to attract new listeners from traditional talk radio. In our interview, he says, "So that's a dynamic that is almost impossible to take on from a direct engagement with the current world, I would say of Hollywood. But I think with the increasing sort of buffet of choices that people have for their entertainment from Netflix world, Amazon Prime, all these other sources of entertainment that are coming online, that there will be some space there for conservatives. When it comes to elections and the dynamics of dealing with democracy and needing fifty-one percent of people to agree with you to be elected or whatever, we have to win over converts. And so how do we go into that space, not just preaching to the choir.... So I think there is a whole digital revolution, I think, is going to allow us more opportunity because we're not going to go head to head with studios, going to be able to do things on our own. We're not going to have to rely on the old distribution channels of theaters to get our products out. We'll be able to go directly to the consumer in a digital environment."[360]

358 Interview with Amber Athey, January 13, 2021, via phone.
359 Interview with David Spady, December 7, 2020, via phone.
360 Interview with David Spady, December 7, 2020, via phone.

He goes on, "We have to be entertainers. They have to be entertainers first and then talk show hosts and philosophers or whatever else they are. Second most important thing, are you going to lose your audience or not have an audience? Is being good at entertaining. And I think we have to develop more and younger. It can be an older entertainer, but they have to be able to connect with that younger audience. And a lot of times that is better done with a peer-to-peer situation. But I think Charlie Kirk has tapped into a lot of that. And they do use a lot of humorous things that are part of the videos they put out. I think the university has done a great deal to deal with this new dynamic. We have a short attention span, you're going to have more impact probably with a five-minute video than you would with a thirty-page book with helping shape people's world views about ideas in this new digital age. And I think we have to become skillful in every one of these ways that are used to reach that younger, impressionable group in this country."[361]

And still further, Will Ricciardella stresses the importance of connecting with the Main Street American. "[The average American] just wants fair coverage. They want a fair shake. But *The New York Times* writes for the intelligentsia. So does *The Washington Post*. These intellectuals and the coastal elites, they neglect their readers. They write for overseas or intellectuals and leftists. [They] neglect an entire segment of the population."[362] This disconnect continues to grow from right to left.

Breitbart's Alex Marlow spelled out where we are heading if we don't bridge our media gap and resume talking to one another. "It is a threat not just to America, but to all of Western civilization. That there's just the alternative is so much worse. And yet that is increasingly what's happening in the Establishment Left. There's a few notable exceptions of people who

361 Interview with David Spady, December 7, 2020, via phone.

362 Interview with Will Ricciardella, December 17, 2020, via phone.

will dialogue and do so in, you can do it in a combative way, but not an unfairly negative way. Bill Maher is one of those people. Everyone who is a conservative consumer of news content loves to see their favorite person spar with the Left because our ideas are much better, and they are rooted in logic and reason, and their main goals are rooted in either the theoretical or delegitimizing, and delegitimizing the other side of the issue and stopping the debate there. Like Andrew would talk at length about how the most powerful tool the Left has is to call someone a racist. Because once you're called a racist, which is the worst thing you can get called in America, then you are delegitimized. And thus, people feel like they don't have to engage with your ideas because you're an irrational bigot. So how could you have a rational argument? And even if you did, it's not necessary to deal with them. That's been their trick, and they've just ramped up that tactic. That's incredibly frustrating."[363]

We all hope that everyone ramps down the rhetoric and we can come together. In the meantime, it's valuable and necessary we arm ourselves with the proper knowledge and facts, remember it's vital to speak to one another, and find common ground with the American people.

363 Interview with Alex Marlow, January 27, 2021, via phone.

Chapter 8:

THE ART OF THE MEME

Meme[364], noun:

1: an idea, behavior, style, or usage that spreads from person to person within a culture

2: an amusing or interesting item (such as a captioned picture or video) or genre of items that is spread widely online especially through social media

"[A Meme] is the cultural equivalent of a gene. So anything that gets passed from brain to brain, like an accent, or a basic word, or a tune. It's anything that you can say spreads through the population in a cultural way, like an epidemic. So a craze at a school, a clothes fashion, a fashion for a particular way of speaking, all these things are memes. Anything that could be the basis for an evolutionary process is a meme, simply by becoming more frequent in the population,

364 *Merriam-Webster.com Dictionary*, s.v. "meme," https://www.merriam-webster.com/dictionary/meme.

in the meme pool, in the same way the gene becomes more frequent in the gene pool."

- Richard Dawkins[365]

"Political cartoons are one of the oldest forms of memes. Memes today are just modern political cartoons, and it's something that develops organically. Frankly, it's something really only the Right can do."

- Rogan O'Handley, @dc_draino

"The Left can't meme and the Right can."

- Benny Johnson, Turning Point USA

"Never been on social media before. I didn't know anything about Twitter. I didn't know how to post. This is September [2019]. I didn't even know how to make a meme or anything. I'm fifty-six years old now, and so I just was flipping through pictures. I saw that cat with the glasses on somebody's head on Twitter. It's like a gif or something. It was a one minute decision. I never thought it would turn into a Homer Simpson character...it's beyond me. It's crazy. Crazy."[366]

- Catturd™

365 Mahmood Fazal, "Richard Dawkins Told Us What He Thinks about Memes, and then It Got Weird," *Vice* (May 8, 2018), https://www.vice.com/en/article/d35ana/richard-dawkins-told-us-what-he-thinks-about-memes.

366 Interview with Catturd™ (@catturd2) Twitter, February 20, 2021, via phone.

INTERNET CULTURE IS ALWAYS evolving through humor and trolling. One such evolution has been the creation of the "meme"—a photo or series of photos captioned in clever ways, often with political messaging. In recent years, memes have become a tool of political warfare, with some being tweeted by even the president of the United States (President Trump that is, little evidence exists at this stage that President Biden knows how to use Twitter).

While I don't hold myself out as a prolific meme-ster, I have had a meme of mine retweeted by Donald Trump Jr., which threw the leftist media into hysterics. Who knew SpongeBob could make the punditry class lose their bikini bottoms? The meme was of Patrick, a character on the popular cartoon *SpongeBob SquarePants*, attempting to open a jar captioned, "Obama is like a guy who couldn't open a jar for 8 years, and then @realDonaldTrump opens it and Obama says 'I loosened it for you.'"[367] Donald Trump Jr. retweeted it, and the meme went viral. While it might seem trivial, memes have the capacity to capture a relatively complex idea, the notion that former Obama officials over the four-year Trump administration took credit for all successes of the Trump administration without any evidence that they laid any groundwork to assist the administration during their tenure under Obama, into a simple snapshot. While our media class likes to regurgitate this narrative, the American people, not as stiff and stifling as the mainstream press, see and know the difference, and something as simple as a meme captures their feelings exactly—in the case of my *SpongeBob* meme, in a viral way.

And that's the way memes have gone. The Right drops a new meme format that people respond to, and the Left attacks the creators. Which is sad, frankly.

---

367 Tanya Edwards, "Donald Trump Jr. Shares a 'SpongeBob' Meme Bashing Barack Obama," *Yahoo News* (September 22, 2018), https://www.yahoo.com/lifestyle/donald-trump-jr-shared-spongebob-meme-bashing-barack-obama-162033854.html.

Memes are a lot of fun. Back in 2016, memes were the Wild West. A lot of the great Facebook pages of the 2016 campaign were run by random people across the country. (Facebook took action against "disinformation," and some of these pages were purged or censored, more on that later.) Many of these Facebook pages garnered millions of followers, "Hillary for prison" and "Trump train," to name a few. They were phenomenal.

The Right dominates at memes because the Left isn't funny and is offended by everything. It's so boring. Cancel culture and woke politics have really sucked the creativity out of their online behavior, which is strange since they run Hollywood.

Memes almost have a counterculture, revolutionary air to them. Charlie Kirk often says that when you have the mainstream media, Washington Establishment, news corporations, Hollywood, and the entertainment industry on your side, you are not part of the resistance or the rebellion. You are the system. And I think impolite memes are part of a culture downstream from rock-and-roll culture, resistance culture. The Democrats now often assume the hoity-toity, better than thou approach to politics, and they fail when they can't handle a joke. As *Mother Jones* puts it, "Conservative groups seem to be incorporating memes into their training arsenal for grassroots activists in a way that has no parallel on the left. In fact, 'the left can't meme' is itself a subgenre of memes, reflecting an idea accepted on both ends of the political spectrum that progressive activists are really bad at this form of political warfare."[368] Though, in their defense of why they can't meme, they concede the hilarity of their ineptitude. "Media Matters' Carusone says people on the left are more concerned with nuanced facts and gray areas that can't always

368 Stephanie Mencimer, video by Mark Helenowski, "'The Left Can't Meme': How Right-Wing Groups Are Training the Next Generation of Social Media Warriors, Memes Helped Elect Donald Trump. Now Well-Funded Conservative Groups Are Using Them to Proselytize," *Mother Jones* (April 2, 2019), https://www.motherjones.com/politics/2019/04/right-wing-groups-are-training-young-conservatives-to-win-the-next-meme-war/.

be boiled down accurately into a photo with a caption. On the left, he says, 'every meme has to have a million qualifiers, so that it's no longer a meme. It's a Medium post.'"[369]

Memes, now a tool of the internet and political warfare, are an important part of your tool kit to be effective online.

Rogan O'Handley manages the @dc_draino Instagram handle, a meme account boasting over 2.1 million followers. He has an interesting story, one empowering for anyone looking to create a conservative account with incredible influence. "I was a Hollywood entertainment lawyer for multiple years and became very frustrated once President Trump was elected that I could not openly support him despite the entire Hollywood machinery openly supporting President Obama," he told me, "I realized that just posting on Facebook to my friends only caused division between family and friends and myself." During the 2016 election, Rogan came across memes and thought that "most viral memes are the things that dictate what is trendy, cool, funny. I like these political memes, but I think I can do them better," he thought, "I can really tap into their power of transforming American culture. And so that's what I started doing."[370] He made an account the next day as a way to "provide others with strength and encouragement, to stand up for their beliefs when it seems like the whole world is fighting back against them."[371]

Benny Johnson, chief creative officer at Turning Point USA and master of the meme, took a break from being a content machine to speak with me. We discussed how conservatives are really winning the culture war from a mechanical perspective but lack in the dissemination.

---

369 Stephanie Mencimer, video by Mark Helenowski, "'The Left Can't Meme': How Right-Wing Groups Are Training the Next Generation of Social Media Warriors, Memes Helped Elect Donald Trump. Now Well-Funded Conservative Groups Are Using Them to Proselytize," *Mother Jones* (April 2, 2019), https://www.motherjones.com/politics/2019/04/right-wing-groups-are-training-young-conservatives-to-win-the-next-meme-war/.

370 Interview with Rogan O'Handley, May 21, 2021, via phone.

371 Interview with Rogan O'Handley, May 21, 2021, via phone.

I asked some of our interviewees about the methodology behind the creation of the perfect meme and how conservatives can build from meme templates in the culture. Benny Johnson told me his solution. "The Left can't meme and the Right can. So it's one of the very rare pieces of the cultural tool kit that the Right has and the Left doesn't. The Left clearly has a stranglehold, a death grip, on Hollywood, the entertainment industry, the media, cultural apparatus of social media, traditional media, corporate media, and they own scary amounts of our culture. I guess a good thought experiment would be does the Right own any institutions of culture? I guess for the last four years you could say the presidency, and that is no longer, the Senate, no longer. So we're entering a very scary moment for conservatives in telling our own stories and in being able to have someone look into the scope of media that they see and consume every day and see their opinion validated. Because you're not alone. That is why meaning, culture, and content for conservatives is so important. And obviously it's why they're trying to shut it down right now. That's why they're attempting to make memes illegal content, illegal for conservatives on the internet, because the internet is one of the last bastions we have.... And conservatives need to realize that we need our own steady white noise, drumbeat of our views and opinions. I believe that there needs to be more conservative creators, and we need to continue the drumbeat so that people can see that their world views of wanting their civil liberties defended, wanting their borders defended, and wanting for people to have a stable and steady economy are reflected."[372] The white noise he mentions is the idea that if something is constantly visible in a culture, even at its periphery, those words and ideas become part of the zeitgeist in a way that, in politics, can have real-world consequences.

---

372 Interview with Benny Johnson, January 12, 2021, via phone.

It's a common refrain online that the Left can't meme and frankly, from my own observation, the Left's political satire attempts online are cringey at best, or what I imagine would elicit no more than a polite chuckle at an Upper East Side cocktail party or perhaps an automated laugh track on the set of Saturday Night Live during a cold open. So I had to ask Benny, why can't the Left meme? "The Left can't meme because they have no humor, and they have no values. The most powerful memes are really quick, really punchy, and have a speck of humor to them. They've given up on their values, truth, and humor. And that makes a good, neat dash of truth and some humor for spice, a little bit of spice. That's how you make a good meme. And the Left can't do any of those things. Try explaining critical race theory to me. Go take all the storytelling geniuses you've got from Harvey Weinstein's old office and all the purveyors of culture and the social media companies and all of the cultural influencers that you have and try to explain critical race theory to me. You can't. Because there's no real truth to it, and it's a vicious and vindictive lie that you wouldn't even want to. They start shivering, too, because it's so you can't do it."[373]

I pushed him a bit since the Left dominates late-night shows, and it seems like a natural extension of the mediums they already control. "It's a very simple answer. The Left can't meme because they gave up humor and comedy a long time ago. Memes tend to be funny and reflect some type of truth. [The Left] also gave up moral truth a long time ago. So the Left is clearly [beholden to] whatever outrageous humor and whatever cultural norms are the flavor of the day ... vacuous, utterly devoid of principle. And so, memes are short and sweet and funny. They speak to a quick truth. And if you're a leftist, you have to have the entire 1619 Project to explain your next craziest harebrained theory about some dumb cultural mechanism. You can't explain it in a meme. And if you watch late-

373 Interview with Benny Johnson, January 12, 2021, via phone.

night television, you'll see that the Left is utterly giving up [traditional] comedy as well. And so I think that now is the long answer. But I think now is the time for the Right to grasp onto the truths that we know that are unmoving and the humor and the ridicule. And I'll end with this. The worst thing that can happen to an authoritarian is ridicule. They hate being made fun of. They cannot stand free speech. They don't like being made fun of, being made a laughingstock. And so, it is so important for us to make them a laughingstock, to ridicule them and make fun of them. And that's why memes are important."[374]

And I agree. As I have said time and again in this book, I want to give you a tool kit and inspire you to make your voice heard. While punditry might not be for you or TV or running for office or even Twitter, memes are a lower-cost threshold to joining the conversation.

So what have I seen work online? Let me give you a few quick tips for meme success.

Know Your Audience

Like any type of political messaging, you have to know your audience. That's number one. I see this on the campaign trail, I see this on Twitter, I see this on Instagram. Many people have unfocused or non-targeted approaches to their social media. While it seems obvious or unimportant, it's a failing of a lot of accounts.

For one, the attention span online is extremely small, the barriers to entry are incredibly low, and the battle for people's attention is so high. So to make your voice one worth listening to, you have to be very focused. For example, I know many friends who want to break into conservative Instagram and build a following, yet they will post pictures from

374 Interview with Benny Johnson, January 12, 2021, via phone.

a fishing trip or their cooking hobby. That's wonderful. I am happy they are able to get out on the boat or take up their culinary dream. But for people first seeing their account or maybe considering becoming a follower or being a fan, this is confusing and unfocused. I have both a public and private Instagram for this very reason. My friends want to know what I did last weekend; my political followers don't necessarily care. I am building a following for my political message, not one of where to go to dinner in West Palm Beach.

You also need to realize that a lot of the conservative audience is still a little bit older. So, the humor requires an understanding of how to connect with older generations while bringing in new followers. Over my political career, I have test-driven a number of strategies and jokes. There is a lot of content out there, and it's easy to go out and see what works and what doesn't. A meme with tons of language that looks clunky and confusing isn't going to play as well as a meme that is clear and funny on its face without tons of analysis. It's the poignant simplicity. Over time, after meeting with thousands of voters, I have figured out what a lot of people would laugh at.

As key as knowing your audience is knowing what your audience is talking about. As Catturd puts it, "I get on my home page and see what's crackin'. And then I make fun of everybody. I see an opportunity for some humor to take the stress off, and I make a meme out of it."[375]

Be timely. While it's important to be an early mover, being at least part of an organic, ongoing conversation is preferable to going off on tangents and having a conversation alone. (Please don't knock off other people's memes or ideas. We're a big tent and we can elevate everyone without poaching content for our own benefit. Be a person who is original, not someone who farms content.) What do I mean? Social media companies reward content that meshes with the conversation of the day. If everyone is talking about Ron DeSantis, and

375 Interview with Catturd™ (@catturd2), Twitter, February 20, 2021, via phone.

you're posting about an obscure gun law in Idaho, odds are your content won't be seen and has zero potential of reaching the effect you want. That's not to say, don't post your political interests. But, when people are talking COVID-19 and Florida, a meme mocking the Cuomo brothers is going to play better than a meme about solar panels and clean energy in California.

Another key component: every platform is different. What works on Twitter doesn't always work on Instagram and vice versa. Facebook is an entirely different platform and requires different messaging than the other two. The audiences are different, and what you might find to (at least initially) be your audience might not be the same across all platforms. The way I use Instagram is different than the way I use Facebook or Twitter. The formats work differently, the aesthetics are different, and the tone is different. So get a feel early on for what resonates with your audience and learn from that. It's going to take some trial and error, but with enough content, you'll have run solid case studies for yourself and have a good sense of how to manage your audience.

Conservatism is about Mutual Support

Go viral! Just go viral! I know what you're thinking, "Yeah, I know Alex, I've been on social media for years, and it's hard to go viral." You're correct. It is difficult. But one thing that can help is building a strong network for your meme work.

As Rogan O'Handley puts it, the best way to build an account is obviously to "go viral often, which is kind of the holy grail of being big on social media is to constantly be putting out content that goes viral. The second is to simply have your material showcase on larger platforms. So it's effectively like putting a billboard out for your business on a highway that says, 'Hey, come to my steakhouse, exit 17.' Whatever you think is the most effective marketing tool to showcase your business. It's a very similar concept. It's marketing. You're marketing your own team and on other accounts. That's a quick way to grow because Big Tech has censored conservative accounts so much that we don't show up in the regular algorithms. We have to get creative in how we grow our accounts in a world where Big Tech hates us and wants to censor us as much as possible."[376] He's right. As I wrote in Chapter 2, networking in conservative spaces is key to growth.

I would be nowhere without building out a strong support system. Early on in my career, I focused on building strong relationships where I build offline relationships with people. It took time and effort and commitment to relationships over establishing simple, cheap acquaintances, but it has served me well in my career. When I put out content now, I have many people who are friends, support my work, not necessarily because they love it 100 percent or believe in it entirely, but because they want to support me. Having a pool of people who continually support your memes is going to lay, at least initially, a strong foundation.

After this initial base, you have to build relationships with people with bigger platforms. If you have a particularly strong meme or piece of content, send it to them and see if you can be featured on their page. You'd be surprised the willingness of some of these bigger meme pages to feature content by small creators. Don't be shy in this space; the unasked question will never get answered.

And lastly, once you've developed a following, always remember to extend a hand downwards to lift up others as you were lifted up. The goal here is to spread our values and message. It's going to take a ton of people to make change, and we can't rest on our laurels for even a moment.

---

376 Interview with Rogan O'Handley, May 21, 2021, via phone.

If You're Not Laughing, You're Not Meme-ing

I like to laugh, and in the hard-pressed world of politics, it's nice to laugh a lot. The meme format lends itself to mocking the political landscape better than a tweet and more simply than, say, a YouTube video. Rogan O'Handley agrees with me that the "true power of memes is in telling the truth and a good joke; it's distilling complex, complex policies into simpler understandings. The media, Democrat leaders, and Hollywood will spin things, but a meme is a quick, incisive way to tell the basic truth about what's going on. And people like visual education."[377] He's right about the staying power of a meme versus a tweet. "If you showed me a tweet I wrote from six months ago, there's a good chance I won't remember writing it at all, but if you show me a meme from fifteen years ago, I'll know it's an old meme instantly. And not because it looks outdated, but because the visual recall in your brain for information is stronger and quicker, and so, memes are a great way to not only tell the truth in a clever or comical way but to educate people on how best to debate a certain point."[378] I can confirm; I write hundreds of tweets per week, and I remember way more of the most viral memes than any of my viral tweets.

Other users we spoke to confirm their personal joy contributes to their success. About the origins of Catturd, "I wanted to do a page where you can escape from the seriousness of the day and just kind of have fun."[379] He told me, "The first thing about the meme is that it's got to be funny, and it can't take itself too seriously. Through humor, it will get across way more than the average tweet. It will show the hypocrisy of the Left. But that's the best meme when you

377 Interview with Rogan O'Handley, May 21, 2021, via phone.

378 Interview with Rogan O'Handley, May 21, 2021, via phone.

379 Interview with Catturd™ (@catturd2) Twitter, February 20, 2021, via phone.

can select like a love movie or something and then make it show the hypocrisy of the Left."[380]

Grant Godwin is the operator of the "leading right-wing political meme page on Instagram, @the_typical_liberal," which, as of this writing, has over two million followers.[381] He weighed in on what makes a good meme: "Truth, humor, or anger. But there's got to be truth to it. That's the main part of how you get it to stick.... And have some value to it."[382]

He expanded: "It was good timing because it was getting towards the end of Obama. But that's not the main reason I'm so effective. The timing was good. But I realized quickly, how do you get somebody to remember something? You make somebody remember something, either through humor or anger. And when it's anger, they're pissed off about it, they're going to remember it that way. When it's comedy, it's something that gives them a laugh.... And it just puts a little imprint in your mind. If I can make these political memes funny and then put in information that people will remember and retain, then that information will stick in their head. And that's what I've done is just given a lot of these young Americans, who I target primarily."[383]

And these jokes can be powerful and make a big difference. I literally had a meme of mine get a member of Congress kicked off of her committees. A member of the House Democrats brought a little graphic design that X Strategies put together onto the House floor. It was a meme of Congresswoman Marjorie Taylor Greene holding an AR-15. I remember that photo shoot. Pardon my language, but it was a badass photo shoot. That meme went viral, and it said Marjorie Taylor Greene is the squad's worst nightmare. The House Democrats freaked out over that graphic. They said that is an explicit expulsionable offense. This little graphic that I storyboarded in my head was on the House floor of

380 Interview with Catturd™ (@catturd2) Twitter, February 20, 2021, via phone.

381 https://www.instagram.com/the_typical_liberal/.

382 Interview with Grant Godwin, November 30, 2020, via phone.

383 Interview with Grant Godwin, November 30, 2020, via phone.

the United States Congress, and the Democrats were trying to get her suspended. And the thing was it was not a threatening graphic at all. It was saying, come and take our Second Amendment rights, but apparently, that was too much. And so, she got censored for that. It took guts, but it exposed the reality: the Democrats are obsessed with taking away our Second Amendment rights and are willing to conflate issues and lie about members of Congress to do so.

Another one of my memes (more of a video, but memes can be videos too) was when Marjorie Taylor Greene was holding an AR-15 on her porch and this little five-foot three blonde woman says, "I have a message for the Anifa terrorists: stay the hell out of northwest Georgia." Very, very short. She puts it up, and of course, it goes viral: 2.5 million views on Twitter in twenty-four hours to 2.5 million views on Facebook in twenty-four hours. It was taken down because she was allegedly calling for violence. Congresswoman Greene gets the art of the meme. She gets the art of pissing people off online to expose the radical Left. And people try to replicate her, but they don't have much success. So there's been many instances that we've put up a meme that has triggered some of those, pissed someone off that has made the news.

Grant actually has monetized his memes through his Instagram account but has noticed a massive downturn in economizing his account. He recounted over the past year, "So it's impacting my business. In a huge way. I went from one hundred thousand to one hundred and fifty thousand likes on average to very few likes on a post and half a million plus views on videos to down to ten, fifteen, twenty thousand likes on every posting. It won't go higher than that is a clear sign of it. I have a Facebook rep that I met back in 2018. She was great. Warned me how to avoid getting a knock on my page, a strike on my page. I always played by the rules. I always removed it to play by Facebook's rules and community guidelines. So I was like, look, what's going on with this? Why is my page so limited? And they literally said, the reason that you lost your engagement is because you were posting false information. I said, OK, well, what was the false information? It turned out it was a quote. I posted a word-for-word quote of President Trump, that an 'independent' fact checker rated as false. And I posted it.... And it's been since October 3rd of just this absolute low engagement, because I posted a quote, a direct quote of the president of the United States."[384] And so, the limitations have real impact on the way he can monetize his page. He laments that the "six years of hard work that I built, these millions of followers, I should be able to talk to them. There should be no hold back. There should be no Big Brother, no ministry of truth telling you what I can and can't say to my followers, because that's deemed as 'false' by independent fact checkers that aren't independent in the slightest."[385]

The internet and meme culture has been the great equalizer in many ways. Entire industries have been built out of the meme, and in conservative spaces, the ability to change careers and make yourself online is a notable one. Twitter accounts like Catturd™ told me that pseudo-fame online has been fulfilling and encouraging. "It's weird, because I'm just, I've always been a political junkie, and I was a musician most of my life and a professional musician. I start getting arthritis in my hands from playing guitar on stage a lot of my life. So Twitter gives me an artistic outlet."[386] For Catturd and others, the meme moved from a creative outlet to a career.

But since we are effective, and the Left can't mount a counteroffensive in the meme world, the Left has used the main tool in their arsenal: censorship. Grant notes that Big Tech censorship can only worsen predictability in business and especially when Big Tech, never the one who should be judging humor, can now deny entry to the medium by which conservatives can spread lighthearted memes that carry actually conservative vision. "Big Tech targets me and has clearly

384 Interview with Grant Godwin, November 30, 2020, via phone.

385 Interview with Grant Godwin, November 30, 2020, via phone.

386 Interview with Catturd™ (@catturd2) Twitter, February 20, 2021, via phone.

shadowbanned me for over three months now. The reason they target me is because I'm effective. There is no humor. That's illegal in their book because of political correctness. And being effective with this makes us a target. One hundred percent, not just me, but anybody else in this room that's effective."[387] It's striking that conservatism has almost become the counterculture.

We will talk more about Big Tech and its chilling effect on speech in the next two chapters. Just imagine a meme where Big Tech is shooting "speech" and asking in the third frame why would conservatives do this?

Always remember: as Benny Johnson aptly notes, we are not without hope. "If you go back historically and look through what all tyrannical, evil dictatorships have done, speech is the first to go. And that is precisely what's happening right now with the fusion of corporate social media and our soon-to-be Democrat administration. It is a very scary time; however, I'm very much an optimist at heart. I believe in America. I believe that these values have overcome some major evils and threats over the course of history. And that revolution, civil war, two world wars, and very evil institutions and bad laws and bad decisions by our elected officials have been righted as we bend ever more towards the vision of our Founders. So now it is time to course-correct again."[388] He's right. With the tools in this book, we can fight back and bring some truth (and humor) to the conversation.

At the end of the day, the simplicity of memes mirrors the simplicity by which guys like Grant, Catturd, Rogan, and Benny view the realities of our country's aims and goals. "I don't care if you're red, green, blue, or yellow, but at the end of the day, your colors should be red, white, and blue. And that's it."[389]

Distracted boyfriend meme—on from Memes to Big Tech!

387 Interview with Grant Godwin, November 30, 2020, via phone.

388 Interview with Benny Johnson, January 12, 2021, via phone.

389 Interview with Grant Godwin, November 30, 2020, via phone.

Chapter 9:

CANCEL CULTURE

"Power is not a means; it is an end. One does not establish a dictatorship in order to safeguard a revolution; one makes the revolution in order to establish the dictatorship."

- George Orwell, *1984*[390]

"Cancel culture is probably one of the most disgusting and hateful aspects of current American culture."[391]

- Jack Posobiec

"I don't know if they're winning the culture war, but I do know they have the loudest voices in the culture war, and they're first to shame anybody or call them a heretic or burn them at the stake who step out of line. But I don't think most Americans think that way."

- Will Ricciardella[392]

390 George Orwell, *Nineteen Eighty-Four* (United States: Houghton Mifflin Harcourt, 1983).

391 Interview with Jack Posobiec, December 10, 2020, via phone.

392 Interview with Will Ricciardella, December 17, 2020, via phone.

ALMOST LIKE AN EPISODE of *Black Mirror*, the Left has adopted a social apparatus that permits them to effectively eliminate people from social life. It's called "cancel culture." You've heard of it before and maybe have experienced different aspects of it in your own life. More and more people are becoming familiar with it through their own experience or curbing their own behavior to accommodate or avoid its effects.

Cancel culture is a weapon in modern society where the mob, perceiving a slight against the culture or modern groupthink, seeks to embarrass, harass, dox, and ultimately punish (and possibly remove) an individual from polite society. Oftentimes this canceling occurs when an individual commits some "sin" against the modern liberal orthodoxy. Other recent cancel culture flashpoints were the #MeToo movement and, most recently, canceling ex-President Trump staffers seeking gainful employment after Trump's presidency.[393]

It's appropriately looked at as something out of sci-fi, with individuals living their life one day as normal as anyone else and the next finding themselves fired from jobs, deleted from social media, unable to access their website or bank account, and unable to engage in free speech at the level of any other American.

This isn't far-fetched or sci-fi unfortunately. Following the riot that invaded the US Capitol, social media companies banded together and canceled the president of the United States. Twitter permanently suspended the president's account on January 8, 2021.[394] Reddit banned one of the largest Trump

393 Claire Atkinson and Sean Czarnecki, "Trump Administration Staffers Are Getting Snubbed While Hunting for Jobs," *Business Insider* (Jan. 27, 2021), https://www.businessinsider.com/will-anyone-hire-white-house-comms-staff-2021-1.

394 Twitter, Inc., "Permanent suspension of @realDonaldTrump," (January 8, 2021), "After close review of recent Tweets from the @realDonaldTrump account and the context around them–specifically how they are being received and interpreted on and off Twitter–we have permanently suspended the account due to the risk of further incitement of violence."; https://blog.twitter.com/en_us/topics/company/2020/suspension.html.

communities by banning subreddit group "r/DonaldTrump."[395] Twitch "disabled Trump's channel." Shopify eliminated "two online stores affiliated with Trump—his organization and his campaign's merchandise sites—for violating its policies on supporting violence." Google, Amazon, and Apple "pulled Parler" from their respective app stores. YouTube has been cracking down on voter information and election information and removed at least one video from Donald Trump's channel. Facebook and Instagram "banned Donald Trump from posting on his Facebook accounts for at least the next two weeks until the transition of power to President-elect Joe Biden is complete." And Snapchat "disabled Trump's Snapchat account."[396] Overnight, Silicon Valley had coalesced to cancel the president of the United States from any real participation in online expression.

And while the president of the United States will survive—Donald Trump isn't going to go hungry or be unable to find a TV camera to express his opinions—average Americans don't have the same luxury. More and more often, the modern Left has shown a willingness to cancel individuals, destroy lives, and alienate people from work and society for expressing or failing to express anything short of the modern leftist ideology in public.

The Lincoln Project, a useful idiot of the Left (and political tool of MSNBC and now under investigation as the Pedophile Project (what I like to call them) by the FBI[397]) disguised as a right-wing organization, has expressed its intention to create a "database of Trump officials & staff that will detail their roles in the Trump administration &

395 Sara Fischer and Ashley Gold, "All the Platforms that Have Banned or Restricted Trump So Far," *Axios* (January 11, 2021), https://www.axios.com/platforms-social-media-ban-restrict-trump-d9e44f3c-8366-4ba9-a8a1-7f3114f920f1.html.

396 Sara Fischer and Ashley Gold, "All the Platforms that Have Banned or Restricted Trump So Far," *Axios* (January 11, 2021), https://www.axios.com/platforms-social-media-ban-restrict-trump-d9e44f3c-8366-4ba9-a8a1-7f3114f920f1.html.

397 The Associated Press, "FBI Reportedly Investigating Lincoln Project Co-Founder," *The Atlanta Journal-Constitution* (February 12, 2021), https://www.ajc.com/news/fbi-reportedly-investigating-lincoln-project-co-founder/XYLAJO2YTVGH7LEDC7D2BCKMZY/.

track where they are now."[398] Many low-level staffers have expressed difficulty getting employment following their work in the White House and Trump administration.[399] (By contrast, both the Obama and now the Biden administrations notably served as a revolving door between the White House and Silicon Valley and vice versa—it's no coincidence there remains a concerted interest between the Democrats and those of authoritarian Big Tech.)[400]

The corporatism of woke politics and adherence to the mob makes Republican politics and conservative ideals even more at peril in an administration friendly to the mobsters. As Ben Shapiro wrote in *Politico*'s Playbook (receiving insane backlash from the Left afterward for the record): "GoDaddy kicked AR15.com, the biggest gun forum in the world, offline.... Corporations ranging from AT&T to Marriott, from Dow to Airbnb, announced they would cut off all political giving to Republicans who had challenged electors. No such consequences ever attended Democrats who winked and nodded—and sometimes more—at civil unrest around the nation emerging from Black Lives Matter protests and antifa violence over the summer. Furthermore, many conservatives doubt that Democrats are applying any sort of neutral standard toward Trump in pursuing impeachment."[401] Read that closely, the Left, using the pretext of their extreme views, is willing to boot you off the internet and the corporations, no matter who you are, just by having an "R" by your name, and

---

398 The Editorial Board, "The Lincoln Blacklist: A Political Group Wants to Make It Easier to Cancel Trump Alumni," *The Wall Street Journal* (January 12, 2021), https://www.wsj.com/articles/the-lincoln-blacklist-11610494450?reflink=desktopwebshare_twitter.

399 https://www.pedestrian.tv/news/trump-white-house-staffers-jobs/.

400 Michael Scherer, Tom Hamburger, and Carol D. Leonnig, "'Old-School Revolving Door': Private-Sector Ties Complicate Biden's Efforts to Staff Incoming Administration," *Washington Post* (Dec. 4, 2020), https://www.washingtonpost.com/politics/biden-transition-ethics-conflicts/2020/12/04/a36d783a-34b1-11eb-a997-1f4c53d2a747_story.html; see also: Io Dodds, "Will Joe Biden Be Sucked into Big Tech's Lobbyist 'Revolving Door'?" *The Telegraph* (Dec. 26, 2020), https://www.telegraph.co.uk/technology/2020/12/26/will-joe-biden-sucked-big-techs-lobbyist-revolving-door/.

401 Ben Shapiro, "POLITICO Playbook: The Real Reason Most Republicans Opposed Impeachment," *Politico* (January 14, 2021), https://www.politico.com/newsletters/playbook/2021/01/14/the-real-reason-most-republicans-opposed-impeachment-491399.

standing up for election integrity will cut off the means for you to run for office.

And if that wasn't enough, the endless rage of the Left doesn't know any bounds, especially now that outrage can be perpetually liked and retweeted online, the fuel of the fanatics. And publications aren't immune to this frenzy. As former *New York Times* writer, Bari Weiss, put it, "Twitter is not on the masthead of *The New York Times*. But Twitter has become its ultimate editor."[402]

And speaking of the *New York Times*, the Left may argue that cancel culture works both ways. They point to former editor of the *New York Times*, Lauren Wolfe, for example. On January 19, 2021, Wolfe tweeted, "Biden landing at Joint Base Andrews now. I have chills," in anticipation of Inauguration Day of now-President Joe Biden. She also tweeted and later deleted, "The pettiness of the Trump admin not sending a military plane to bring him to D.C. as is tradition is mortifying. Childish."[403] Never mind the absurd hyperbole and the fact that, according to numerous reports, Biden chose to fly private to the inauguration.[404] Conservatives pounced, as the media likes to say, on her flagrantly biased approach to the new administration and for being just plain wrong. She was fired from her role.

And now she decries cancel culture as bills come due.

Welcome to life as a conservative, Lauren.

Don't ask me, use their logic against them. *TIME* used this same argument about comedian Shane Gillis who was fired from *Saturday Night Live* for "making racist jokes" in

402 Bari Weiss Resignation Letter from the New York Times (accessed January 15, 2021) https://www.bariweiss.com/resignation-letter; Bari Weiss (@bariweiss), "Twitter is not on the masthead of The New York Times. But Twitter has become its ultimate editor." Twitter, Jan. 24, 2021, 7:41 a.m., https://twitter.com/bariweiss/status/1353367300322316288?s=20.

403 Yashar Ali (@yashar), Twitter, Jan. 21, 2021, 8:22 p.m., https://twitter.com/yashar/status/1352471654425743361?s=20.

404 Krizzia Paolyn Reyes, "Biden Preferred to Fly to Washington DC Via Private Plane For Inauguration Day: White House," *Christianity Daily* (Jan. 20, 2021), http://www.christianitydaily.com/articles/10573/20210120/biden-preferred-to-fly-to-washington-dc-via-private-plane-for-inauguration-day-white-house.htm.

a deleted comedic video about Asians. Writer Sarah Hagi makes the argument that "having a job at SNL isn't a human right. And although Gillis' defenders have fretted about the sanctity of free speech in comedy, the audience of a comedic TV show should get to speak out about whether they want to watch someone who has espoused this type of humor. That's actually the marketplace at work. Why should Gillis be able to utter racist things but those affected by hate speech shut their mouths? Gillis is still a touring comedian. He will be fine."[405] He will be fine. Right. *Saturday Night Live*, the *New York Times* of comedy, found Gillis to be far afield from their acceptable comedic attempts (remember that he immediately apologized with a reasonable explanation: "I'm a comedian who pushes boundaries. I sometimes miss. If you go through my 10 years of comedy, most of it bad, you're going to find a lot of bad misses.... I'm happy to apologize to anyone who's actually offended by anything I've said"[406]). And to *TIME*'s Sarah Hagi, he'll be fine on touring comedy clubs rather than reaching the pinnacle of *SNL*. As if it's the same. Well, I hope Lauren Wolfe finds satisfaction writing for *Slate* or *Mother Jones*.

Let's not forget that as the massive leftist mob rushes to her defense and aid (no doubt she won't be out of work for long), another more compelling example of cancel culture existed at the same publication in June 2020, but the treatment is quite unequal and more flagrantly appalling. Remember that a sitting United States senator, Tom Cotton, penned an op-ed for the *New York Times*, "Send in the Troops,"[407] making the argument that troops should be deployed to curb rioting and violence that occurred following the death of George Floyd.

---

405 Sarah Hagi, "Cancel Culture Is Not Real–At Least Not in the Way People Think," *TIME* (November 21, 2019), https://time.com/5735403/cancel-culture-is-not-real/.

406 Sandra Gonzalez and Whitney Friedlander, "'SNL' Fires New Hire Shane Gillis," *CNN* (September 17, 2019), https://www.cnn.com/2019/09/16/entertainment/snl-shane-gillis/index.html.

407 Tom Cotton, "Send in the Troops," *The New York Times* (June 3, 2020), https://www.nytimes.com/2020/06/03/opinion/tom-cotton-protests-military.html.

The *New York Times* playground, I mean newsroom, revolted, leading to the opinion editor, James Bennet, resigning.

This is just a very public example. Thousands more are "canceled" every year—many without scrutiny from conservatives allowing any reasonable debate or airing of the issue such that the absurdity of what is being canceled can be properly exposed. For every Nick Sandmann, who was successful suing the media for falsehoods in an attempted canceling,[408] there is an unknown person who attended a Trump rally or made an ignorant post and lost their manufacturing job—a position wholly out of politics and public view.

The real issue and why conservatives ought to be fervently opposed to cancel culture is because the Overton window of acceptable opinions in the public square is ever moving to the left, and those opinions get you "canceled" at a rate unimaginable a decade ago. Don't believe me? Go to your corporate office space and offer up your hot takes on abortion at the water cooler (don't do this!). Which is more likely to get you a call from Human Resources that you are "sexist," "triggering," and "anti-woman"? What about wearing a Trump pin or a Biden button? You don't even have to think about it. You know the answer. The personal stories that I have heard of what is and isn't acceptable online and in the workplace (a place that ought to be apolitical) are worrisome for any conservative or libertarian who cares about freedom of expression and professional treatment at work.

It's also important to avoid allowing left-wing reporters to repackage the cancel culture argument as justified or eliminate it altogether. The Left wants to curb speech by making you think twice before you tweet. But not in the way that I argue to think before you tweet—please think before you tweet. Instead, they want conservatives to be wary of the mob.

---

408 WKRC/AP, "Washington Post Settles $250 Million Lawsuit Filed by Nick Sandmann," *Local12* (July 24, 2020), https://local12.com/news/local/washington-post-settles-250-million-lawsuit-filed-by-nick-sandmann.

They want to police and move conservatives off the forum of Twitter or Facebook. At that point, we can't contribute to the conversation, and they become the unencumbered disseminators of information. To them, there is no distinction between a corporate spokesperson for a major manufacturing firm or the guy who installs a bolt on the assembly line. If you have "bad opinions," under leftist mob rule, you deserve to be publicly shamed and fired. With any luck, you can resurface with time. It only depends on the mob's attention span.

Even in earnest debate, such as whether and to what extent transgender athletes can and should participate in sports, cancel culture can be so nasty that it prevents people from providing dissenting views such as "athletes [who] declined to speak on the record, fearing a public backlash against their points of view."[409]

Some journalists pretend that cancel culture doesn't exist. I would tell you that these faithless fools don't know how to use internet search engines, but it's worse. They don't view cancel culture as a phenomenon because they view publicly destroying people as something that has always happened and believe the public should be purging individuals from the conversation for bad opinions or "dangerous" ideas. They argue that because this either occurs in both directions or is amorphous, it doesn't exist. They are wrong.

Social media makes disseminating messages and assembling the mob easier than ever before. A flippant or ignorant comment can land you in a world of trouble online even if you are not a media personality or person of interest. In "How One Stupid Tweet Blew Up Justine Sacco's Life,"[410] the *New York Times* reports that Justine Sacco, with only 170 Twitter

---

409 Fred Dreier, "Commentary: The Complicated Case of Transgender Cyclist Dr. Rachel McKinnon. The Debate Over Cycling's First Transgender World Champion Can't Be Resolved, but It Can Be Better Understood," *VeloNews* (October 18, 2018), https://www.velonews.com/news/commentary-the-complicated-case-of-transgender-cyclist-dr-rachel-mckinnon/.

410 Jon Ronson, "How One Stupid Tweet Ruined Justine Sacco's Life," *The New York Times* (Feb. 15, 2015), https://www.nytimes.com/2015/02/15/magazine/how-one-stupid-tweet-ruined-justine-saccos-life.html.

followers at the time, posted a racist tweet about AIDS before taking off from London to South Africa. When she landed, internet fury was high, and she was fired.[411] A simple Google search of "people fired for tweets" produces a graveyard of professionals who made an error or errors of judgment online and lost their jobs for it.

Google search is law.

Fox News's Tomi Lahren tells me that cancel culture isn't necessarily a wave of momentum but rather platforming the loudest voice in the room (often the most obnoxious voices):

> ***"I think a lot of it has to do with the loudest voice in the room, not necessarily the majority. So if I have to imagine what goes on in corporate America or some big social media company or even Hollywood entertainment, sports, any of it, I would imagine that there is one leftist radical that is offended by everything who wants to silence everybody. And they are the ones who speak out. And there's a lot of silence by everybody else, whether they're on the left or the right or in between or don't care, they feel it necessary to accommodate that person, because they're afraid. They don't want to be labeled a racist or sexist or homophobic or phobic or anything else. And so that's when the radicals get the power, and they want to cancel other people and so everybody else will have to go along with it. I'm not sure that's what happened, but a lot of the companies over the summer that we saw with the BLM movement, which its full mission to defund the police enforcement operation. You saw something that was pop culture, everybody posting Black Lives Matter, posting BLM. I have to imagine***

411 Ed Pilkington, "Justine Sacco, PR Executive Fired over Racist Tweet, 'ashamed.'" *The Guardian* (December 22, 2013), "Justine Sacco, former IAC employee, issues apology to 'millions of people living with the virus' after social media erupted," https://www.theguardian.com/world/2013/dec/22/pr-exec-fired-racist-tweet-aids-africa-apology.

> ***that somewhat of what took place inside corporations is that you got that one voice. Everyone's afraid of that one voice because they don't want to be labeled. We need to be stronger and a little thicker-skinned and exercise a little bit more of a voice. Just to stop it. But we're going to have to come out in force as conservatives."***[412]

If you recall over the summer of 2020, the BLM riots led to posts of solidarity from corporations in support of communities of color. Some corporations and organizations were told that their response was insufficient (whether true or untrue), leading to resignations and dismissals even at hyper-liberal organizations and businesses.[413]

As Bill Burr tells it, it's only going to get worse as millennials take over the levers of power: "This is fucking Millennials! You're a bunch of rats, all of you!…None of them care! All they wanna do is get people in trouble!"[414] And if you think he's kidding, in January 2020, MyPillow CEO Mike Lindell came under fire for a meeting he had with President Trump in the Oval Office related to election fraud. Social media, the vehicle for being a tattletale, erupted with calls of major corporations to refuse to sell MyPillows. And the mob succeeded. And for any holdouts, "reporter" Seren Morris reported "MyPillow Products Are Still Being Sold by These Companies," as if to highlight for the mob which corporations had failed to adhere to the social media bullies.[415]

412 Interview with Tomi Lahren, December 29, 2020, via phone.

413 Jennifer Schuessler, "Poetry Foundation Leadership Resigns after Black Lives Matter Statement: The Departures Came in Response to an Open Letter Signed by More than 1,800 People Criticizing the Organization's Remarks and Calling on It to Dedicate More Funding to Antiracism Efforts," (June 9, 2020), *The New York Times*, https://www.nytimes.com/2020/06/09/books/poetry-foundation-black-lives-matter.html.

414 David Sims, "Bill Burr Knows Better," *The Atlantic* (September 24, 2019), https://www.theatlantic.com/entertainment/archive/2019/09/bill-burr-cancel-culture/598669/.

415 Seren Morris, "MyPillow Products Are Still Being Sold by These Companies," *Newsweek* (January 25, 2021), https://www.newsweek.com/mypillow-products-still-sold-these-companies-amazon-costco-1564093.

I'd list every example I can think of, but sadly, I am limited by word count and will use a few voices to speak for the countless people the Left has silenced or canceled for wrongthink or for mistakes in judgment or ignorance.

This chapter is difficult because I want to highlight examples of individuals the Left tried to cancel. And I also want to give them a forum where I listened and relayed their message, pain, and cancel culture's insane excesses. Finally, I want to highlight their dignity and the fact that while cancel culture may have won in the short term, it cannot win in the long term so long as conservatives band together (even with free speech-loving Democrats) to push back on a culture growing wholly opposed to grace, the reality of the human experience, and the recognition that there is a difference between the civilians outside the traditional space of politics and the fighters who willingly step into the fray.

* * * * *

The Trump administration was no stranger to attempted and executed cancellations by the rabid Left. Carl Higbie of Newsmax, a former Navy SEAL, told me about what happened with him during his tenure as chief of external affairs at the Corporation for National and Community Service (CNCS). Carl learned early on that the Swamp doesn't like when people come in and shake up the status quo:

> *"They started hunting in the media. And when I joined the White House, this is my biggest gripe.... I said some stuff coming back from war, going back six, seven, eight, nine years that could be a problem. I listed it. And that list exactly in order was almost what CNN published. So, that was rough. I came into an agency that was largely useless, and I started implementing what I thought the president's agenda*

> *would be, which is flushing useless spending. We were spending millions of dollars on contracts to make thirty-second videos for YouTube that weren't even good. I canceled those contracts. I tried to remove positions because it's hard to fire people. I tried to streamline the budget, and I cut tens of millions of dollars out of our budget within months of coming here. And that rattled people. And they didn't like that. And they went after me with everything they had."*[416]

Cutting budgets puts a target on your back quickly in Washington. Let's not forget that Washington, DC, has never seen a taxpayer dollar that they didn't know how to spend.

But let's not forget that Carl served this country as a Navy SEAL (training that would, within two minutes on Day 1, break every journalist in DC) and certainly wasn't going to let a few petty bureaucrats take him out or crush him.

> *"I moved on. I'm a pretty reasonable guy. I said, hey, look, some of the stuff I said, I know it's stupid. And it was just me being an asshole, trying to be a shock jock to get as much attention as possible. A lot of those things were said without sincerity, with the simple reason that I wanted to say something shocking. The apology just doesn't matter anymore unless you're a leftist. I apologized. I moved on. Then I go over to the Trump Super PAC. They said, 'We could really use you over here.' I was well-liked in the Trump world. I went over there. I worked really hard to get things implemented. And then CNN kept coming after me. The same guy was publishing new stories, but really it was the same story. And then they went after donors to the super PAC. And they said, 'We're going to publish a story against you that says you're racist if*

416 Interview with Carl Higbie, January 12, 2021, via phone.

> *you don't fire this guy.' It was no longer journalism at that point. It was vitriol and hatred and felt like you can't stick your head up any more ever again because these people said so, there's no redemption. It became almost like sport for them. Finally, I took some time off, and I started a podcast. And the whole point of the podcast was to find a middle ground."*[417]

It was during his podcast that Carl discovered that even making an attempt to meet in the middle and apply conformity isn't necessarily effective in an age where the internet is forever, and the trolls that enforce the modern woke orthodoxy never rest:

> *"People don't want bipartisanship. Even the people who say it like, 'Oh, we all just need to get along again.' But Ronald Reagan was right when he said, 'When you play the game of appeasement, you eventually have to compromise your own beliefs and you're always going to hit that critical mass.' And that's when it kind of dawned on me that these people aren't going to give up. They're not going to give an inch."*[418]

Carl is a prime example of someone made tougher by cancel culture (which is saying something since you know, he was already a Navy SEAL):

> *"Republicans, for so long, all we do is get into office and we bitch about stuff, but we don't actually do anything to swing the pendulum back over to the right. Anybody who does is considered an outcast and unelectable. The Republican Party wastes time. And this is what makes me so angry about the Republican Establishment. This is why we had Mitt Romney,*

417 Interview with Carl Higbie, January 12, 2021, via phone.

418 Interview with Carl Higbie, January 12, 2021, via phone.

because the Republican Party cares more about what centrist lefties think about our image than they do about our own base. And I told them about our own base: Who do you think puts out yard signs? Who do you think writes the checks? Who do you think goes door to door? It's not the centrists. It's the hardcore base. And if you forget about us, you're going to get screwed like we did in this election. They took the high road, and the high road, unfortunately, is not going to work with these liberal lunatics. We need to, and I'm not saying physically fight back, but metaphorically, we need to fight like hell."[419]

So how do we fight back? I asked a number of our interviewees how we push back on cancel culture that far too often targets conservatives.

I spoke with the dynamic duo and yin and yang of attacking cancel culture, Dana and Chris Loesch. We discussed how combating a rabid mob requires a balance between the Patrick Swayze *Road House* [420] technique and exhibiting grace.

Chris contends, "The temptation in the era of cancel culture is to fight fire with fire, but it's absolutely the wrong thing. When you're trying to counteract an environment of cancellation, and we're talking about canceling people's livelihoods, their lives, it's a dangerous fire to play with. You don't defeat that culture by becoming a part of their culture. I've always said, when you become a dragon to fight a dragon, all you've done is create another dragon, and now you have dragon proliferation and escalation of violence."[421]

Dana takes a different approach:

---

419 Interview with Carl Higbie, January 12, 2021, via phone.

420 *Road House*, directed by Rowdy Herrington (1989), https://www.imdb.com/title/tt0098206/.

421 Interview with Chris Loesch, December 10, 2020, via phone.

"If I was outraged by everything, then I would do something truly outrageous. But the problem of being like that is a bad tactic. And I think there is an oscillation between exhibiting grace and going scorched earth. I think that comes down to a judgment call. There have been times when I've been able to think strategically and judge what's going to get the ball down the field in the favor of the quickest solution. But that being said, I think that we've been able to develop some common ground, and that's one of the reasons we have the big tent in the Republican Party as it is right now. I mean, for crying out loud, we have a president that was able to peel off generationally Democratic voters because they were talking about pronouns, and he was talking about jobs. This created a lot of common ground. And that was incredibly frightening to the cultural Marxists, which is why all of the rhetoric just ratcheted up even more. But there are times when you have the fourth estate, our esteemed media, sit on news stories as to not negatively impact [Democrat] campaigns. That's a betrayal of the American people, and it is not the actions of a free press. And it deserves absolutely scorched earth outrage because this is a cornerstone of our republic. They are supposed to be the free press being an ally of a free people. And, instead of the so-called watchdog, it is mauling us. We have seen doxxing old ladies for running Trump's Facebook posts down in Florida. They go and find people that they can use as avatars of discipline. And they make everyone else too terrified to express dissent, either privately or publicly. And, honestly, that's a chilling effect on speech. Everybody's been walking on eggshells. Enough of it. I don't have the time when I think it's so egregiously awful that it does not merit grace."[422]

---

422 Interview with Dana Loesch, December 10, 2020, via phone.

And it's important to remember that cancel culture doesn't have any sort of age restriction. Conservative activist CJ Pearson knows this firsthand. "I started as a conservative commentator when I was twelve years old. And it's definitely a lot harder reading some of the lies, the brazen falsehoods that people would say about me on social media. But as you grow older, you realize that is just the nature of the business. The Left is...if you're effective, they're going to come for you. They're going to try to knock you off. They're going to try to take you out because they realize the threat that you pushed them on their agenda. And I've seen the people they've attacked, they attacked me.... I take it in stride. For me, I think that the fight that I've been called to is something that is bigger than myself. And so, it takes sacrifice and sometimes going through some things that I otherwise would not have to go through if I weren't really in this line of work, if I weren't as outspoken as I was. But I've got to tell you that I love this country so much. I believe it is a country to be thankful for and a country where I want to work to ensure that it remains the shining city on a hill and the beacon of freedom and liberty that it was intended to be. And I think that makes it a lot easier to undertake those attacks, because you realize that you have to do whatever you can to protect it."[423]

I don't have a complete answer for combating cancel culture. I wish I did. I do know that we have to stand together. Sometimes conservatives are so scared of being canceled themselves that they will steer clear of a canceled person. That's reprehensible. We have to stand together. Because you think it will never happen to you. It might—and not necessarily in the way that you thought. It could be a bad moment caught on camera, a text or tweet or interaction perceived incorrectly. That's all it takes.

423 Interview with CJ Pearson, December 15, 2020, via phone.

I wish our society was full of compassion and nuance and understanding. But it's not right now. And so long as it is not, we need to be vigilant to protect the innocent and those with our worldview who want this country to be great.

They want to pick us apart. They want to alienate us by ostracizing the extraordinary in hopes to curb the average American into their political worldview.

We cannot let them.

We will not be canceled. We will not let our friends, family, or peers be canceled.

We must fight back and stand for what made this nation the beacon on the hill for the rest of the world.

Chapter 10:
CENSORSHIP

"I feel a ban is a failure of ours ultimately to promote healthy conversation. And a time for us to reflect on our operations and the environment around us. Having to take these actions fragment the public conversation. They divide us. They limit the potential for clarification, redemption, and learning. And sets a precedent I feel is dangerous: the power an individual or corporation has over a part of the global public conversation."[424]

- Jack Dorsey, CEO, Twitter

"We now have these big social media companies that are more powerful than the president of the United States, and they're able to essentially decide in an election year if he does and who doesn't get access to social media accounts?"[425]

- Laura Loomer

424 Jack Dorsey (@jack) Twitter, January 13, 2021, 4:16 p.m., https://twitter.com/jack/status/1349510772871766020?s=20; see also Washington Examiner (@dcexaminer) Twitter, January 14, 2021, 8:18 a.m., https://twitter.com/dcexaminer/status/1349752813837037572.

425 Interview with Laura Loomer, December 1, 2020, via phone.

"If conservatives lose social media, we will lose every election."[426]

- Kyle Kashuv

TO WANT TO PARTICIPATE in the global marketplace of ideas is to be human; to be banned from that marketplace is to be conservative. Welcome to the day and age in America when political correctness on college campuses bled over into the mainstream, and it wasn't enough to police politeness, but rather it became a brutal, career-ending weapon utilized almost exclusively by a fire-breathing Left. George Orwell would blush at what has become of our public discourse and the lack of openness thereof. It's even more complicated when these rules are ever-changing, arbitrarily applied, and unevenly enforced.

During the coronavirus, the public square for debate went largely online. Conservatives didn't have to worry about being disinvited from college campuses. Instead, conservatives are policed on Facebook, Twitter, and Reddit. This has presented unique challenges and fresh calls for regulation from the Right. Any cursory glance of online representation reveals an uneven treatment by Big Tech of what is and is not acceptable online.

In this book, I have already covered the overt bias by the media and the narrative manipulation leveled against conservatives. But I want to present to you the more covert bias and mechanisms stacked against conservatives.

We truly live in an age where Silicon Valley has a dossier on every individual with internet access on the planet. What used to be a forum for freedom and ideas and connecting individuals—the World Wide Web—has become controlled by a few players who control the medium and the narrative that goes out over that medium. This presents untold long-

426 Interview with Kyle Kashuv, November 30, 2020, via phone.

term consequences for anyone who cuts against the whims of those in Big Tech who, as experience shows, are largely very left-wing progressives.

What follows in this chapter is a breakdown of how social media companies have situated themselves in the position of picking and choosing opinions appropriate for public discourse and the outcomes of this arbitration. I highlight how Big Tech has coordinated to "cancel" or censor individuals, including the president of the United States. And finally, I offer a few solutions from myself and other conservative thinkers on what can be done to reopen the internet for liberty.

My review of censorship comes from experience in the space both from myself and my clients. To the extent possible, I address alternative media outlets that have arisen as a result of perceived shadow bans or censorship, though I am not hopeful about the status of these alternatives going into a season particularly hostile to conservative ideas. In the writing of this book, several of our interviewees have been suspended or banned from Twitter or kicked off other social media outlets. Many have been harassed by the media for trumped-up allegations. Some have been doxxed. Many have faced or continue to face death threats. The uniting feature is that social media platforms serve as a forum for attacking conservatives as readily as they are willing to toss aside conservatives depending on the philosophical winds of the day.

This is only a chapter and deserves volumes of books to demonstrate the level of threat and what can be done to bring our online discourse back to the level. But I will try to be brief as Shakespeare.

(It almost feels naughty, a bit of subversion that I wrote much of this book in Google Docs—an almost polite revolutionary tract written with the tools of the Thought Police.)

Freedom of Thought, Ya Know, as a Treat

It started as a few nerds who dropped out of Harvard and MIT. But only decades later, with the full embrace of the American dream, these same entrepreneurs built massive companies that have quickly taken almost complete control of the way that business is done on a global scale. In an ideal world, the interconnectivity, the ability to find new customers, meet new people, and connect with fresh ideas would be a fantastic improvement on a world always desperate for innovation. However, all good intentions, especially when money gets involved, fall victim to abuse.

A robust, competitive Silicon Valley has made a profound impact on the way that we live in this country and are connected worldwide. But, quickly, much to the chagrin of conservatives, Silicon Valley quickly consolidated under a few companies. A handful of companies manage the way we do business, what we think, what we see, and what ideas go viral. It's easy to see how ownership of such power and control will only cut against ideas, businesses, and individuals at odds with the permitted worldview espoused by the tech giants.

Every single person I spoke with for this book bemoaned the fact that censorship is not only a real thing battled daily by conservatives but expressed concern that the encroachment into what is considered acceptable viewpoints is becoming further and further to the left at an increasingly fast pace.

Allum Bokhari, *Breitbart* senior tech correspondent and author of *#DELETED: Big Tech's Battle to Erase the Trump Movement and Steal the Election*,[427] spoke with me about the

427 Allum Bokhari, *#DELETED: Big Tech's Battle to Erase the Trump Movement and Steal the Election*, (September 22, 2020), https://www.amazon.com/DELETED-Techs-Battle-Movement-Election/dp/154605930X; see also Breitbart Tech, "#DELETED: 'Outspoken Trump Antagonists' Led Facebook 'Misinformation' Efforts," *Breitbart* (September 28, 2020), https://www.breitbart.com/tech/2020/09/28/deleted-outspoken-trump-antagonists-led-facebook-misinformation-efforts/.

perils of Big Tech and Silicon Valley.[428] "Big Tech picks winners and losers and, in terms of online media websites, even online businesses, and that's not a political issue," he told me. "They can remove anything from their platform that they consider objectionable or suppress it in their search rankings, make it impossible to find, and destroy people's livelihoods in the process. And there's no legal recourse, no due process available to the victims of that, regardless of their political affiliation. That would be what most people, including Democrats, find unacceptable for normal real-world tenants to be in that situation. But in the digital space, the equivalent of landlords. These big platforms have all the power, and the people who are dependent on the platforms for their livelihood, for their businesses, have no power at all."[429] And that's just the power they have in the free market. That's before the politics.

When politics becomes involved, the power of Big Tech becomes more blatant. "There's probably no equivalent in the course of human history to these tech companies in terms of their ability to manipulate people's political opinions, shape their political behavior, their voting behavior," Allum continued.[430] "A Facebook source told me for my book that around 2018, Facebook was looking at the whole issue of political polarization, and that Facebook was looking to build a model based on so-called members of political extremes, the Far Right who would move towards the center and to build a model based off of that by examining what sort of content, what sort of posts those users consumed as they made that journey from the so-called Far Right to the center," he said.[431] He described it as Facebook putting these people on essentially a content "diet" and learned "how they could deploy their technology, their ability to manipulate people combined

428 Interview with Allum Bokhari, December 10, 2020, via phone.
429 Interview with Allum Bokhari, December 10, 2020, via phone.
430 Interview with Allum Bokhari, December 10, 2020, via phone.
431 Interview with Allum Bokhari, December 10, 2020, via phone.

with their vast trove of data that they have on everyone to change political opinion, to change political behavior."[432]

At first, this might sound nice, maybe even life-saving—here comes along the very kindhearted Big Tech company to steer us towards our better angels.

But let's not forget that there is a dark side to these benevolent Silicon Valley saviors.

Publication heads like Jim Hoft (who has since been permanently suspended by Twitter) are all too familiar with the fact that social media companies can destroy entire media outlets, especially burgeoning ones, with a mere click of a button. "[Publications] are gone today because Facebook eliminated their content, and some of these other places were actually working with Facebook and patting them on the back and taking their money or whatever rewards they got. And I think it's disgusting."[433] At *Breitbart*, Allum Bokhari told me that it's not even as complicated as some nefarious strategy by Big Tech. "It's simpler than that; they simply delete a conservative media from such results. And that's what Google did quite recently to *Breitbart News* in the run-up to the 2020 election. Just completely eliminated search results for *Breitbart News*. Our search visibility actually from clicks and impressions to break the news from searches for Joe Biden went to zero after Google introduced an algorithm change and in the spring and late spring of 2020. And it stayed that way for six months, all the way up until the election. But they suddenly went to zero and stayed there. And we watched through the Google Analytics tool. So they weren't even trying to hide it. And this is sort of the trend we're seeing now. Big Tech is openly interfering in elections, are openly censoring politicians, censoring [President Trump], censoring mainstream news sources like the *New York Post*.... I think that's only going to escalate going forward."[434] Read that again: Big Tech openly works to

432 Interview with Allum Bokhari, December 10, 2020, via phone.

433 Interview with Jim Hoft, January 12, 2021, via phone.

434 Interview with Allum Bokhari, December 10, 2020, via phone.

shut down news stories they don't like, inhibit politicians they don't support, and bar conservative media from appearing in search results (thereby preventing them from monetizing their sites at maximum).

Surely, Washington, DC, is paying attention and is preparing to do something, right?

If you thought that, you'd be very wrong. For it's all a compounding problem for conservatives since there is virtually no difference between Silicon Valley and the Democrat Party at this point. A *WIRED* report in October 2020 entitled "Silicon Valley Opens Its Wallet for Joe Biden" found that: "A review of campaign finance data shows that contributions by employees at some of America's biggest tech companies are overwhelmingly going to his Democratic opponent, Joe Biden. *WIRED* found that employees at Alphabet, Amazon, Apple, Facebook, Microsoft, and Oracle have contributed nearly 20 times as much money to Biden as to Trump since the beginning of 2019. According to data released by the Federal Election Commission, which requires individuals who contribute $200 or more to a presidential campaign to report their employer, employees at these six companies have contributed $4,787,752 to Biden and just $239,527 to Trump."[435] It seems pretty clear who Silicon Valley wanted to win in 2020. Another way that the Swamp grows is through staffing the offices of newcomers. Many new members go to leadership and ask, "Who should I hire for this?" or "Who should I hire for that?" and the leadership puts in their personal loyalists. Personnel is policy.

The Democrats know that peddling in influence has made leaps and bounds changes over what they could otherwise achieve in Congress, yet the mere threat with teeth by Democrats is far more influential to Silicon Valley than Republicans

435 Daniel Oberhaus, "Silicon Valley Opens Its Wallet for Joe Biden: A WIRED Analysis Finds Roughly 95 Percent of Contributions by Employees of Six Big Tech Firms Have Gone to Trump's Democratic Challenger," *Wired* (October 6, 2020), https://www.wired.com/story/silicon-valley-opens-wallet-joe-biden/.

boohooing about censorship but showing no real inclination to regulate. "The fact that Democrats are far more willing to regulate corporations actually makes corporations more likely to do what Democrats tell them because they know there are consequences much more quickly because of Democrats. And it's precisely because Republicans don't impose any consequences on corporations, that corporations simply take their support for granted.... Biden is already selling his transition team with tech executives. The Obama administration had a revolving door of employees moving between the White House and Google,"[436] Allum told me. Their threats come with consequences both social and regulatory. Companies know not that soft conservatism often comes with all bark and no bite.

Which is alarming because of where we are going. New studies using facial recognition technology have found that "ubiquitous facial recognition technology can expose individuals' political orientation, as faces of liberals and conservatives consistently differ. A facial recognition algorithm was applied to naturalistic images of 1,085,795 individuals to predict their political orientation by comparing their similarity to faces of liberal and conservative others. Political orientation was correctly classified in 72% of liberal–conservative face pairs, remarkably better than chance (50%), human accuracy (55%), or one afforded by a 100-item personality questionnaire (66%)."[437] I am positive that Silicon Valley won't abuse this technology.

"It's only extreme opinions!" say the conservatives who are too puritan in their approaches to social media and free speech protections. Their view is that if the government gets involved calling balls and strikes, where will it end?

436 Interview with Allum Bokhari, December 10, 2020, via phone.

437 Michal Kosinski, "Facial Recognition Technology Can Expose Political Orientation from Naturalistic Facial Images," *Scientific Reports* (January 11, 2021), https://www.nature.com/articles/s41598-020-79310-1.

But it's not the extremes. It's any mainstream conservative depending on the viewpoint.

In *Politico*'s Playbook, the irony was that Ben Shapiro wrote that, "If you supported Trump in any way, you were at least partially culpable, the argument goes. It's not just Trump who deserves vitriol—it's all 74 million people who voted for him. And that claim, many conservatives believe, will serve as the basis for repression everywhere from social media to employment. Evidence to support that suspicion wasn't in short supply this week."[438] And he goes on to cite the laundry list of censorship that occurred in Big Tech in the middle of January 2020. True to form, Ben Shapiro faced another attempted canceling. The *Washington Post* ran a piece called "Politico brought Ben Shapiro on as a 'Playbook' guest author to bring balance. It brought a backlash instead."[439] and the Politico staff held a listening session because their feelings were hurt over Ben's column.

As Kyle Kashuv notes on censorship, "One thing that should be really alarm bells for conservatives is the fact that Twitter completely nuked the *New York Post* story. People posted the link and were banned or suspended." [440]

Kyle, of course, is referring to the *New York Post* story[441] which alleged that uncovered emails from a laptop seized by the FBI cast doubt on whether Joe Biden consulted with his son on his overseas businesses, many of which reek of corruption. The *Post* reports, "Less than eight months after

438 Ben Shapiro, "POLITICO Playbook: The Real Reason Most Republicans Opposed Impeachment," *Politico* (January 14, 2021), https://www.politico.com/newsletters/playbook/2021/01/14/the-real-reason-most-republicans-opposed-impeachment-491399.

439 Elahe Izadi, "Politico Brought Ben Shapiro on as a 'Playbook' Guest Author to Bring Balance. It Brought a Backlash Instead," *Washington Post*, (Jan. 14, 2021), https://www.washingtonpost.com/media/2021/01/14/playbook-ben-shapiro/.

440 Interview with Kyle Kashuv, November 30, 2020, via phone.

441 Emma-Jo Morris and Gabrielle Fonrouge, "Smoking-Gun Email Reveals How Hunter Biden Introduced Ukrainian Businessman to VP Dad," *New York Post* (October 14, 2020), https://nypost.com/2020/10/14/email-reveals-how-hunter-biden-introduced-ukrainian-biz-man-to-dad/; see also Peter Schweizer and Seamus Bruner, "Longstanding Claims of Biden Corruption All but Confirmed with Hunter's Emails," *New York Post* (October 24, 2020), https://nypost.com/2020/10/24/biden-corruption-claims-all-but-confirmed-with-hunter-emails/.

Pozharskyi thanked Hunter Biden for the introduction to his dad, the then-vice president admittedly pressured Ukrainian President Petro Poroshenko and Prime Minister Arseniy Yatsenyuk into getting rid of Prosecutor General Viktor Shokin by threatening to withhold a $1 billion US loan guarantee during a December 2015 trip to Kiev," thereby benefiting the younger Biden's company directly.[442] The *New York Post*'s Twitter account was locked on October 14, 2020, but Twitter "finally backed down Friday and unlocked the account after a two-week stalemate over the Hunter Biden exposé."[443] This is the *New York Post* being censored. "You couldn't click the link. You couldn't post a picture with the link. They did everything in their power to suppress this. That's insane. At a certain point, we are going to be past this line where there is no going back," [444] Kashuv argued. Kashuv didn't express hopefulness towards any real effort to push back against Big Tech: "I wanted to see which conservatives, elected officials would really do something beyond the generic, like writing a letter or dragging Jack Dorsey into a Senate hearing to ask me questions. Cause it's obvious at this point the silliness of the exercise—you ask a few questions. Now what? That's it. That's all that happened. It's just a performance. That's all it was. And that should have really been the point when conservatives woke up and thought, 'Wow, this is a real issue versus like the occasional individual gets banned on Twitter.' And this is so obvious because it is the *New York Post*. Like we're not dealing with a random non-reputable outlet; this has been around for hundreds of years. So it's definitely a different world, and makes you think—what are we not seeing when

442 Emma-Jo Morris and Gabrielle Fonrouge, "Smoking-Gun Email Reveals How Hunter Biden Introduced Ukrainian Businessman to VP Dad," *New York Post* (October 14, 2020), https://nypost.com/2020/10/14/email-reveals-how-hunter-biden-introduced-ukrainian-biz-man-to-dad/; see also Peter Schweizer and Seamus Bruner, "Longstanding Claims of Biden Corruption All but Confirmed with Hunter's Emails," *New York Post* (October 24, 2020), https://nypost.com/2020/10/24/biden-corruption-claims-all-but-confirmed-with-hunter-emails/.

443 Tamar Lapin, "The Post's Twitter Account Gained about 190,000 Followers During Blackout," *New York Post* (October 30, 2020), https://nypost.com/2020/10/30/the-posts-twitter-account-added-nearly-190k-followers-during-blackout/.

444 Interview with Kyle Kashuv, November 30, 2020, via phone.

we're not paying attention? Some of the other stuff like shadowbanning, etcetera, you can't really prove that, it's kind of iffy, maybe nobody sees your tweets, who knows? But this was something transparent and blatantly obvious." [445] And it's not just publications being censored.

Or what about Senator Tom Cotton, who wrote an opinion piece articulating a theory that the coronavirus originated in a Wuhan lab. Any mention of this theory pre-June 2021 was labeled a "conspiracy theory" by the Left, and social media companies purged content related to it. As of the first week of June, the *Washington Post* had to issue a correction. "Earlier versions of this story and its headline inaccurately characterized comments by Sen. Tom Cotton (R-Ark.) regarding the origins of the coronavirus. The term 'debunked' and The Post's use of 'conspiracy theory' have been removed because, then as now, there was no determination about the origins of the virus."[446] Keep in mind, these are examples from the past year.

These companies tell you what their truth is and craft entire narratives to support particular social agendas. They also shift the window of permitted discussion randomly and target people who miss the arbitrary shift. And as much as it pains me to sound like we are living in some dystopian world, it's becoming more true by the day. The fact that these companies have so much data as to manipulate people's behaviors and choose to do so is way more dangerous than the handful of Russians who created Facebook accounts to trick Americans into voting a certain way in 2020.

The thought police are out in full force, though it is almost laughable when some of these tech giants talk about freedom and liberty. It's a scary lack of self-awareness to be able to do so without some feeling of remorse.

---

445 Interview with Kyle Kashuv, November 30, 2020, via phone.

446 Olafimihan Oshin, "Washington Post Issues Correction on 2020 Report on Tom Cotton, Lab-Leak Theory," *The Hill* (Jun. 1, 2021), https://thehill.com/homenews/media/556418-washington-post-issues-correction-on-2020-report-on-tom-cotton-lab-leak-theory.

Persona Non Grata

Things were already dire for conservatives on social media. Then came January 6, 2021, where protestors broke through barricades and entered the US Capitol as Congress was set to certify the 2020 election results. Calls for censorship and bans sounded from the Left over President Trump's "incitement." Conservatives, as a group, and every Trump supporter, were deemed complicit in the event. The EU commissioner said of social media companies that "they can no longer hide their responsibility toward society by arguing that they merely provide hosting services,"[447] and that "the storming of the U.S. Capitol will herald an era of tougher social media regulation…comparing the violence with the attacks of Sept. 11, 2001, that led to a global crackdown on terrorism."[448] The events of January 6, 2021, are and will be used as a pretext to subvert liberty.

Mere days after Twitter banned President Trump and other corporations followed suit, Twitter, ever failing to look at itself in the mirror, pretended to be the moderator of a free internet in the case of the Uganda elections. The Twitter Public Policy (@Policy) account tweeted:

> ***"Ahead of the Ugandan election, we're hearing reports that Internet service providers are being ordered to block social media and messaging apps. We strongly condemn internet shutdowns – they are hugely harmful, violate basic human rights and the principles of the #OpenInternet."[449]***

447 Reuters Staff, "U.S. Capitol Siege Heralds Tougher Social Media Curbs, Says EU Commissioner," Reuters (January 11, 2021), https://www.reuters.com/article/us-usa-election-socialmedia-eu/us-capitol-siege-heralds-tougher-social-media-curbs-says-eu-commissioner-idUSKBN29G11S.

448 Reuters Staff, "U.S. Capitol Siege Heralds Tougher Social Media Curbs, Says EU Commissioner," Reuters (January 11, 2021), https://www.reuters.com/article/us-usa-election-socialmedia-eu/us-capitol-siege-heralds-tougher-social-media-curbs-says-eu-commissioner-idUSKBN29G11S.

449 Twitter Public Policy (@Policy), Twitter, Jan. 12, 2021, 10:22 a.m., https://twitter.com/Policy/status/1349059275461685250?s=20.

After all, they are committed to being the arbiters of free and fair elections. "Earlier this week, in close coordination with our peers, we suspended a number of accounts targeting the election in Uganda. If we can attribute any of this activity to state-backed actors, we will disclose to our archive of information operations."[450] The scope of the type of speech and speakers oscillated so quickly and the issues being so remote to the Western world, it's difficult to gauge during these events whether the undue influence is actually coming from social media companies themselves or actual bad actors. And in either instance, what is the real difference to Twitter or Facebook unless there are other motivations at play?

Take, for example, the elections currently underway as of this writing in Israel. With less than a week until the elections, Benjamin Netanyahu's son, Yair Netanyahu, was suspended from Twitter. As one of Netanyahu's fiercest defenders online, are we really to believe that Twitter is just protecting the purity of information online, or are there other forces at work? After all, Twitter has been a breeding ground of anti-Semitic content, from Richard Spencer to Congresswomen Ilhan Omar and Congresswoman Rashida Talib (or maybe they are the correct types of anti-Semitic and information sources per CNN?).[451]

"Access to information and freedom of expression, including the public conversation on Twitter, is never more important than during democratic processes, particularly elections. #UgandaDecides2021 #KeepItOn,"[452] Twitter says. The lack of self-awareness is shocking. It's like they were messing with the Ugandan people, only a week after banning the president of the Free World from their platform.

450 Twitter Public Policy (@Policy), Twitter, Jan. 12, 2021, 10:22 a.m., https://twitter.com/Policy/status/1349059276975857664?s=20.

451 We interviewed Yair Netanyahu for this book. As of this writing, we had not received those answers back.

452 Twitter Public Policy (@Policy), Twitter, Jan. 12, 2021, 10:22 a.m., https://twitter.com/Policy/status/1349059278917824512?s=20.

The coordinated effort is particularly scary across all of Silicon Valley. As mentioned earlier, overnight, the president of the United States was removed from every social platform (even Spotify, God forbid President Trump created a "CNN IS TOTAL GARBAGE" playlist—the horror!). "This is essentially totalitarian culture, which is the direction that we're heading, not a state director, just about every culture, but one that is quite attractive and which serves the state and people in power mostly," Ron Coleman told me.[453] After everything I told you already about the behind-the-scenes coordination and the overt coordination by different companies, people, and social media giants to make sure Donald Trump lost in 2020, this should be worrisome to any conservative, no matter how mainstream.

Congressional candidate Anna Paulina Luna spoke of her constant battle against social media companies in her last campaign censoring her and her campaign materials which she attributes to creating significant hurdles for her:

> ***"In my primary, the problem was that I was the only candidate that was censored on social media. But I still managed to make it through the primary being censored. Big Tech was preventing me from posting my fundraising links on different platforms. So first of all, like myself, the only way that I was able to get around that was by working harder."[454]***

The most banned woman on the planet, Laura Loomer, spoke with me for this book. No matter your opinion on her opinions and whether or not she should say the things she does—keep in mind that, as the interviews and views expressed this book confirm, mid-stream opinions from only a few years ago are now considered fringe viewpoints—truth and right is only what Twitter deems it to be, and that should scare you.

453 Interview with Ron Coleman, December 22, 2020, via phone.

454 Interview with Anna Paulina Luna, December 10, 2020, via phone.

And frankly, it's impossible to write a book about social media without including Laura Loomer. Laura was really a trailblazer to expose the clear bias in social media companies. Laura ran for Congress in 2020 in Florida's Twenty-First Congressional District. Loomer won in a crowded primary to fall short gaining 40 percent of the vote in the general election.[455] What was most surprising is that she won the primary without the use of her Twitter account. "I knew when I filed to run for Congress that I was going to face the handicap of being without a platform," she told me.[456] In running for Congress, Loomer expected to be treated like other candidates not only receiving her Twitter account back but receiving the coveted blue check mark. She received neither: "All of the social media companies changed their policies in reaction to me running for Congress. So the day that I filed to run in August, it became the number one trending story on Twitter. The very next day, Twitter changed their congressional policy. The policy prior to me running for office and announcing was that if you were to be a candidate, you would be given a verified account.... Twitter said, 'Our policy applies to everybody except for one individual.'"[457] Regardless of her politics, Loomer was singled out by a social media company and among those cut out from a company-wide policy meant to be politically neutral in its application.

Way more mainstream accounts also bear this out. Read this story from Rogan O'Handley, who was targeted and deleted by Twitter, he claims, at the direction of the State of California, and try not to deflect from the fact that conservatives have a real problem with social media giants:

"I got deleted and permanently suspended off at Twitter in March of [2021] for 'meddling with election integ-

455 Florida Department of State, Division of Elections, November 6, 2018, https://results.elections.myflorida.com/Index.asp?ElectionDate=11/6/2018&DATAMODE=.

456 Interview with Laura Loomer, December 1, 2020, via phone.

457 Interview with Laura Loomer, December 1, 2020, via phone.

rity.' And it didn't seem to fit. My tweets didn't seem to fit that reason because that was basically saying that you're suppressing people's ability to vote or misdirecting them. It was March. The elections had already happened. The tweets that they flagged were tweets where I was critical of election integrity from the 2020 election. I'm a licensed attorney. I look at evidence. I draw reasonable conclusions. And my reasonable conclusion was that there was a lot of election fraud, and I certainly was not afraid to call it out to come to find out that after my account was deleted, Judicial Watch had been requesting documents from the California Secretary of State office and found that I was actually put on a list by the California state government, one of thirty or so accounts that they wanted to have censored on social media. Because of my public criticism of California election policies, I wasn't racist, sexist, harassing anyone. I wasn't engaging in copyright violations. I am a licensed attorney in California that was criticizing election policy, things embedded in the Constitution. And they said it was 'misinformation' and wanted it censored. And then I was banned from Twitter soon thereafter. I have since hired lawyers and will be filing a lawsuit. And from what I've heard, this could be a very big case because this is one of the first times we have a smoking gun. Evidence of state actors suppressing free speech of American citizens on social media in this joint public-private partnership is extremely unconstitutional. And it'll take time for this to play out in court. But this is going to be a major push back and something I think, that is going to send shockwaves through the censorship world.... It's extremely alarming because they're effectively turning Twitter into government actors. There is legal precedent for treating private companies as state actors when they act in unison with the state. And it's a federal Civil Rights Act violation."[458]

458 Interview with Rogan O'Handley, May 21, 2021, via phone.

The Judicial Watch report he cites reported that "the Office of Election Cybersecurity in the California Secretary of State's office monitored and tracked social media posts, decided if they were misinformation, stored the posts in an internal database coded by threat level, and on 31 different occasions requested posts be removed. In 24 cases, the social media companies agreed and either took down the posts or flagged them as misinformation, according to Jenna Dresner, senior public information officer for the Office of Election Cybersecurity."[459] One of Rogan's tweets—"Audit every California ballot. Election fraud is rampant nationwide and we all know California is one of the culprits. Do it to protect the integrity of that state's elections"—is cited in the report.[460]

It may seem like a fringe idea, but the reality is that the bones are already in place for this to become a mainstream idea that people deemed "too radical," "conservative," or "Republican" become persona non grata, that is, people who are not welcome in the public space. European nations and definitely China already have these types of rules in place or on their way to enactment. In the US, between social media, Google, and Amazon, the entire success of your business can be dictated by the whims of four companies. Tack on the fact that our benevolent arbiters of truth also wanted to bake in the cake technology on our phones for a vaccine passport. It was reported "a coalition of health and technology organizations are working to develop a digital COVID-19 vaccination passport to allow businesses, airlines and countries to check if people have received the vaccine. The Vaccination Credential Initiative, announced on Thursday, is formulating technology to confirm vaccinations in the likelihood that some governments will mandate people provide proof of their shots in

---

459 Judicial Watch, "Judicial Watch: Documents Show CA State Officials Coordinated with Big Tech to Censor Americans' Election Posts," April 27, 2021, https://www.judicialwatch.org/press-releases/ca-state-officials-big-tech/.

460 Document archives, "CA SoS Big Tech Election Misinformation PRA FOIA 2021 prod 1," *Judicial Watch* (Mar, 31, 2021), https://www.judicialwatch.org/documents/ca-sos-big-tech-election-misinformation-pra-foia-2021/.

order to enter the nation."[461] Tech companies, therefore, want to use the assurance of COVID-19-free areas as a pretext for these same companies, who freely buy and sell our information and, as I have shared with you in this book, actively work to change your political opinions, to gain even greater access to our information. I also tend to shy away from slippery slope arguments. They tend to be a logical fallacy. However, looking at the trajectory of how social media has targeted liberty, conservatives, and leveraged current events for those aims, it's not difficult to predict where these attacks will land.

In Defense of Liberty

As you have seen throughout this book, and perhaps in your personal experience, there is a real concern that social media companies are too powerful, and conservative viewpoints are being silenced or altogether removed by social media companies. I have shown you that companies preach the freedom of expression and open marketplace of ideas, while simultaneously banning accounts, being the arbiters of truth in information, and punishing individuals who don't appropriately toe the line on particular issues—all of their behaviors undoubtedly have a chilling effect on speech. I then expressed how the targeting of individuals is widespread, and the scope and capabilities of these companies to target individuals with conservative viewpoints is growing. Which leads to the obvious, so what do we do about it?

I confess I am split on the issue, both professing a limited government approach but also recognizing the obvious reality that tech companies coordinate and consolidate at an alarming rate. I wanted to present for you a few options from my own views and others' that could be implemented to

---

461 Justine Coleman, "Tech Coalition Working to Create Digital COVID-19 Vaccination Passport," *The Hill* (Jan. 14, 2021), https://thehill.com/policy/technology/534228-tech-coalition-working-to-create-digital-covid-19-vaccination-passport.

protect conservatives. I'll leave it up to Washington and the candidates I help win to make it to Washington to decide how best to push back. But we have to push back.

Bari Weiss, a former *New York Times* writer, expressed skepticism about the reality of the free market and actual competition in social media: "Please spare me the impoverished argument about the free market and private companies not being bound by the constitution [*sic*]. Barring businesses from using online payment systems; removing companies from the App Store; banning people from social media—these are the equivalent of telling people they can't open a bank account or start a business or drive down a street."[462] Buck Sexton knows this fight is inevitable. "It's not a concern [about being canceled or disrupted by social media]. It's a certainty. I'm very much prepared for it. And I'm finally starting to see conservative media waking up to this reality and understanding that if we exist based on the goodwill and the good faith of our political opponents, whether it's on social media or on the actual hosting of websites, as we've all seen what happened recently with Parler and Amazon Web Services, if you exist at essentially the forbearance or rely on the forbearance of our leftist political opponents, we're not going to exist for very long at all."[463] The reality is a dire one because, for conservatives, we had always anticipated that the threat to our basic liberties would come directly from government. As attorney Ron Coleman notes, "The concept of free speech as a linchpin to that political health of our republic was always premised on the idea that if government doesn't suppress speech, then no one else will. And guess what? We're living in a world where someone else will. We said the Founders certainly didn't cognitively quite understand the possibility, but a nation of

462 Bari Weiss, "The Great Unraveling: The Old Order Is Dead. What Comes Next?" (January 12, 2021), https://bariweiss.substack.com/p/the-great-unraveling.

463 Interview with Buck Sexton, June 1, 2021, via phone.

private actors and a network of that would make it so difficult to overcome that kind of restriction of free expression."[464] It's hard not to see a future without conservative action, or conservative viewpoints will either be extinguished out of fear or banned by these companies more generally.

Platform access is a real concern. The reality of access is scary: "Conservatives need to be building. It's not a joke to say we need to build our own internet. Maybe we can't build an independent internet, but we do need platforms. We need organic growth. We need companies that are willing to be sponsors. We need to start having more control and advertising dollars and run advertising campaigns that are explicitly pro free speech and are comfortable with conservative messaging and ideology."[465] Though as many note, creating alternatives is no easy feat. "We've had two to three years of conservatives trying to compete with Twitter, Facebook, other social media on the ground, essentially on censorship access," Will Chamberlain told me. "We found that that hasn't been particularly effective. Even Parler, the most successful of the group, has had spurts of popularity. Why is that? Well, it's because Twitter has a competitive mode that's pretty much insurmountable given the fact that every journalist, political pundit, and celebrity uses the platform for public square social media and that network effect, that first mover advantage."[466] Realistically, creating an alternative is fraught with complications. The tightened market share allows social media companies to exert undue influence on competitors. "There'll be pressure on the financial companies, the banks, the credit card companies, the Apple payment processors like PayPal and Square to not allow these alternative platforms to process payments from their users...anything that becomes a serious threat to the mainstream social networks," predicts

464 Interview with Ron Coleman, December 22, 2020, via phone.

465 Interview with Buck Sexton, June 1, 2021, via phone.

466 Interview with Will Chamberlain, November 20, 2020, via phone.

Allum Bokhari.[467] The lack of platform and inability to realistically create an alternative is alarming.

So why not boycott? As Ron Coleman puts it, "Companies by and large are not sensitive to the boycott. Maybe if there is a will for a very well-executed boycott. But I think changing the nature of the cultural conversation is probably going to be more valuable."[468] I am deeply skeptical of the effectiveness of boycotts long-term as well.

If we can't battle with alternatives and extricating ourselves entirely isn't a practical reality, how should conservatives respond?

Some conservative organizations like TPUSA take a different approach and advise working within the system. COO Tyler Bowyer says that TPUSA takes the position not to openly attack social media companies:

> *"One thing that you'll notice is we never go out and blatantly attack any of the social media sites. We rarely do that. A lot of organizations that do, when they do it, look, I'm a big believer in Reagan's eleventh commandment, not just from the topic of Republicans and conservatives, but I think there's a deeper issue there, which is: you should exhaust every possible avenue with people that you have conflict with in order to really understand where they're coming from and try to resolve your issues before you go out and publicly attack. And, quite frankly, it's been kind of embarrassing at times because we've seen people attack the social media giants for something that they were possibly wrong about themselves, or they were just ill-equipped or ill-prepared to really take on the fight against a Goliath like Google or Facebook or others."*[469]

---

467 Interview with Allum Bokhari, December 10, 2020, via phone.

468 Interview with Ron Coleman, December 22, 2020, via phone.

469 Interview with Tyler Bowyer, December 28, 2020, via phone.

Other people we spoke with advocated different approaches. Will Chamberlain, the editor in chief and publisher of *Human Events*, expresses a more public square approach to social media companies:

> *"I would treat them the same way as public universities. A public university, even if it's not a for profit enterprise, tries to keep a bottom line together and tries to make sure that it is offering a good product. We say to the public university, because you're part of the government, you're constrained by the First Amendment, and your ability to prevent people from speaking out on campus [is, therefore, constrained as well]. And that's kind of the attitude I would have: yes, you are able to curate your product under the constraints that we impose on you by law. Under current law, you're not allowed to discriminate on the basis of race, for example.... These companies have to conform their corporate behavior and make a profit within the bounds of the law, so we're just creating one more type of restriction that we think serves a very, very important and beneficial purpose."*[470]

This did come up in another interview; Attorney Ron Coleman sees hurdles to any sort of regulation of Big Tech on the basis of viewpoint discrimination: "It seems increasingly clear that there are a couple of very big obstacles involving the legal system. One is legal, and I think a much more substantial, one cultural. And I think the cultural one is the tougher one because judges are social creatures like everybody else. And what we have seen, for example, in the election litigation they have once a judge in one case does something about, characterizes that case in a certain way, seems to be a very strong inclination among many judges to do the same thing unless they have some kind of signal that it's OK to do something different."[471]

---

470 Interview with Will Chamberlain, November 20, 2020, via phone.

471 Interview with Ron Coleman, December 22, 2020, via phone.

On Capitol Hill, there are calls by some to reform Section 230 of the Communications Decency Act. "Section 230 gives these Big Tech companies broad protection that other private businesses don't have...that puts them in the judgment seat, and they judge whose voice is allowed on their platform and whose voice is not allowed.... They judge what is deemed acceptable in society, acceptable speech and what is deemed unacceptable speech,"[472] says Congresswoman-elect Greene. Congressman Paul Gosar echoes Congresswoman Greene by saying that perhaps "we're not going to get Democrats to help us with Section 230, then maybe what we have to start looking at is anti-trust, because it's going to be very hard for them not to look at antitrust and the monopolies that share their values." [473] The actual efficacy of these policies is undetermined, but a future of protection from liberal abuse is a beautiful one.

Further away from Capitol Hill in the great state of Florida, Governor Ron DeSantis is a leader on fighting back against Big Tech. BBC describes the legislation as a "first-in-the-nation bill that can penalise tech companies for deplatforming politicians."[474] DeSantis says that "Big tech is beginning to look like 'big brother' with each passing day."[475] The bill prevents social media companies from banning accounts for more than fourteen days and fines companies for each day afterward.[476] Florida is leading on the issue and the rest of the nation should follow.

As Alex Marlow of *Breitbart* says, "We have to figure out a way to break up these tech companies so that they can't discriminate based on ideology. They're clearly discrimi-

---

472 Interview with Congresswoman-elect Marjorie Taylor Greene, December 10, 2020, via phone.

473 Interview with Congressman Paul Gosar, February 18, 2021, via phone.

474 Cody Godwin, "Florida Governor Signs Bill to Ban Big Tech 'Deplatforming,'" *BBC* (May 24, 2021), https://www.bbc.com/news/technology-56952435.

475 John Kennedy, "Gov. DeSantis Says 'Big Tech' Looks Like 'Big Brother,'" *Herald-Tribune* (Feb. 2, 2021), https://www.heraldtribune.com/story/news/politics/2021/02/02/ron-desantis-backing-effort-stop-tech-censorship/4352705001/.

476 Cody Godwin, "Florida Governor Signs Bill to Ban Big Tech 'Deplatforming,'" *BBC* (May 24, 2021), https://www.bbc.com/news/technology-56952435.

nating against conservatives. And the longer they're able to thrive like that, it's kind of like a shark. If they're not swimming, they're dying. So they're not going forward. They're not making progress. They're dying. And so, what's actually happening is these values that led to conservatives getting thrown off of these social media platforms and getting silenced on these platforms and getting demoted on these platforms is now taking over other corporations.... It's going to get to the point where we're going to be drinking from the proverbial separate drinking fountains just based off ideology. That's where we're headed at this point. And Big Tech is leading the way on that and then preventing the free flow of information and the equal opportunity for certain information to get out there makes them the de facto ministers of truth, the people who decide what's true and what's not."[477] Scott Parkinson of Club for Growth echoes this sentiment: "When you look at Big Tech and sort of the holds that Facebook or Google or Twitter have in their own respective markets, those aren't free markets, and they're not operating with competition.... Google is tied in to all these other companies. And then the way that they promote information through their search engine is also stifling information to other markets."[478]

What I do believe is that Allum Bokhari is exactly right in how we prevent the deeply encroached danger of free speech: "Conservatives have to retake the Republican Party primary. Voters have to rebuff any candidate that doesn't support the idea of maximum possible penalties on any company that doesn't respect constitutionally protected speech."[479] We lack a lot in the conservative movement. We lack the vision for a future where our ideas aren't purged from the public square.

477 Interview with Alex Marlow, January 27, 2021, via phone.

478 Interview with Scott Parkinson, November 24, 2020, via phone.

479 Interview with Allum Bokhari, December 10, 2020, via phone.

Never forget that Laura Loomer confronted the king of censorship in the people's hall: "I confronted Jack Dorsey in front of Congress, but people just decided to laugh at me, and it was much easier for members of Congress on the Republican side of the aisle to make a joke and try to auction me off. If you recall the video, a congressman tried to auction me off like I was cattle. As if free speech was for sale to the highest bidder on Capitol Hill."[480] And never forget that Laura Loomer said: "I still had my Twitter account at the time that I confronted Jack Dorsey and Twitter. If you remember that he had just gotten done lying to members of Congress and saying, 'Oh, yeah, we don't censor people, we don't censor conservatives. Yeah, we definitely don't do that on Twitter.' And then Infowars and Alex Jones were banned."[481]

Dealing with social media companies and Big Tech at least initially was confounding for conservatives, the intersection of free enterprise and censorship. We waited, hoping the market could respond with alternatives that met the needs of a wider group of people. However, this boom happened so quickly, and we were so nonchalant about its hostile intentions that we ceded the marketplace to monopolies. While I don't believe there is a silver bullet that protects conservatives online, what's clear is that the majority of Republicans in DC aren't immediately serious about the nefarious intent of Silicon Valley. While conservatives lose speech, businesses, we also lose ground in the accumulation of power by tech giants who are not our best advocates. Unfortunately, at least for now, we live in an age of censorship, of silent cowardice by some Republicans, and where conservatives have to hide in plain sight online. We have to fight back, we will make them listen, and we will reopen the marketplace.

480 Interview with Laura Loomer, December 1, 2020, via phone.

481 Interview with Laura Loomer, December 1, 2020, via phone.

Chapter 11:

THE FUTURE: WHERE DO WE GO FROM HERE?

I WISH I COULD TELL you that the road before us was an easy one. I wish that I could say to you that the America we know and love will continue on forever and ever. But all good things require good people to stand up and protect them.

Social media has created an entirely new battlefront for us. We might have been slow to the game at first. I think we had a tendency to trust the true nature of capitalism to make a competitive marketplace of ideas. Unfortunately, as we have covered in this book, that marketplace not only narrowed significantly but limited access or created artificial barriers to entry.

I worry for the immediate future. Turning Point USA's chief operating officer, Tyler Bowyer, told me that the future looks "extremely dark. It's going to be a dark age for conservatives on social media for the next couple of years, maybe the worst two years of our lives, where we're going to be impacted profoundly because we don't control anything."[482] The way that the Left has attacked the economic well-being of every American and fundamentally sought to alter the culture should alarm anyone. They are incredibly gifted at crafting

482 Interview with Tyler Bowyer, December 28, 2020, via phone.

favorable and manipulative narratives, but their underlying policies are wholly devoid of any helpful substance for the American people. It's narrative fairy dust but without the magic. As Mike Davis puts it, "Mantras have become their religion."[483] The narratives we are fed every day are as wrong as they are scary.

Meanwhile, I grow concerned that Establishment Republicans are more inclined to enjoy the trappings of Washington, DC, than to make actual change for their constituents. The *Washington Post* writes, "The American Right is a machine built not for governing but for opposition."[484] We have to send fighters to Washington. "Republicans, when you take off the gloves, put on the brass knuckles, and punch, you break the Left's glass jaw.... Bash them and point out their hypocrisy. You need crazy people like me who are willing to have very thick skins and are willing to fight," Mike Davis says.[485] My firm and friends—and hopefully you after reading this book—are and will make the concerted effort to elect Republicans willing to stand up for this country and against those forces that seek to silence conservatism.

In this book, I described some of the tools I use when working with clients, influencers, candidates, and politicians. I wanted to give you a road map so that we can raise each other up. I want thousands of conservatives coming together with a platform to speak for conservative principles. Start small, but start. Join this fight because the stakes are too high.

Writing this book for you has truly been a pleasure. I hope you have gleaned as much from my wisdom and insights as the views and tips I have pulled from those I have spoken to—true patriots who live out the messages and themes of this book every day.

483 Interview with Mike Davis, November 30, 2020, via phone.

484 Paul Waldman, "Why the Right's Machine of Opposition Is in for Some Tough Times," *The Washington Post* (January 21, 2021), https://www.washingtonpost.com/opinions/2021/01/21/why-rights-machine-opposition-is-some-tough-times/.

485 Interview with Mike Davis, November 30, 2020, via phone.

To win the social media war, it's going to take all of us getting involved, getting online, and battling back against the narratives that divide us, undermine our freedoms, and make us a weaker country. As the saying goes, freedom is but one generation from extinction; social media has accelerated that timeline, so let me rephrase: freedom is a few clicks away.

About the Author

Photo by Moshe Zusman, Headshot DC

ALEX BRUESEWITZ IS A top conservative political consultant. He advises members of Congress, the Senate, former White House political appointees, and other influential conservative leaders on their public policy and political strategy needs. Since the founding of his consulting firm X Strategies four years ago, he has consulted dozens of political campaigns with a high success rate.